FINDING ANGELS

PARIS CHRISTOFIDES

ISBN-13: 9798851644436
ISBN-10: 1477123456

Cover illustration by: Elizabeth Kirrane
Library of Congress Control Number: 2018675309
Printed in the United States of America

Dedicated to all that I found in my journey, those that walked with me, those that are around and those that flew away, all remembered.

Paris Christofides

DREAM

'There was dizziness, as if you are about to be sick, while you are going up and down, running to hide somewhere, as if someone is trying to get you. I am feeling hot and I am sweating. An arm is holding me tight, there is more running, I am trying to focus my vision on these colorful birds, and suddenly I see some monkeys hanging off the trees..., lots of flying birds...colourful! I am hungry, empty stomach pains. I look up to see the birds flying but my head turning made me feel dizzier.

The running stopped, a black face of a woman was looking at me tenderly, but uncertainty grew into a panicked expression. Another pair of long arms embraces all of us. There is a loving warmth... the arms are tied so hard around us, as if they don't want to let go.

There is a cry of pain as the hands let go of us and more cries of distress and such uncomfortable voices.... I am sitting on the ground, still feeling hot and the ground is dry. I have a pain in my stomach, I am hungry, but the dizziness is gone. I raised my hands to reach ...' I opened my eyes still feeling the loving warmth, spread from the strength of the arms around me.

THE GRAY YEARS

1990 was a bad year. I lost my father. An empty space in my life that can never be replaced. It will always be there in silence, but yet with so many voices in my head. It felt that nothing really mattered to me any more. Conversations became meaningless. The emphasis I used to give to details and the effort to make everyone happy started fading into this disappointment of losing a loved one, my reference to everything. Saying this and going back, we did not have a good relationship. Perhaps because I was like him. It took us years to become eventually good friends, after I became successful at my work. You see, he had all the pressure to run and provide, alongside my mother, for a family of five, and they were at the beginning of their lives too. He had no time for me, he had health problems and so many things to do. He was involved in many business ideas.

It was my mother who brought me up and kept me company. She gave me advice and direction but he was involved too, or at least interested. They were both conservative in showing their emotions with hugs and words. I got hugs and kisses only on special occasions. I grew up in an environment where hugs were not a form of expressing love; nor did I ever hear ‘I love you’. I felt a sense of loneliness and disconnection that I couldn't explain. I was never able to express my own emotions in the same way, and it was hard to feel truly connected to my family. In this lack of physical affection, I learned to express my love and appreciation through less verbal communication and more acts of kindness. I developed an understanding and acceptance for the non-physical forms of love.

It was my mother that explained to me, all the necessary growing up matters, from a child to a teenager, while dad saw that I needed no advice, as to how I developed from a teenager to a man! In contrast with my brother who was conservative, quieter and who needed to read a book titled 'When you become a man'. My sister was a beautiful blond, always caring about her looks and her youth, wanting so much to be married and wear that white dress, as most girls are programmed to do from birth! I was supportive of her single years, always waiting for her to come back and wake me up to relive the highlights of her night out, as with whom she danced and how everyone looked, what they wore, etc. All wonderful stuff adding to my romanticism and imagination. Never really understood my sister and her friends as to what they really expected from these men. They were so contradictive in their comments and I felt it was much simpler for the men.

My father's origin was from North Greece, from a region near the Dead Sea. My grandfather traveled to Cyprus on a gypsy caravan, going from place to place, scrubbing copper pots and utensils, for other people, to make a living. My father, Kypros, was born on a caravan in Cyprus in 1921, a generation that has seen a world war, diseases, economic and technological evolutions. Later in his life, there was a struggle for political stability, independence but yet again in 1974, a Turkish invasion and partly occupation of his country. Some 200,000 people became refugees. He studied at an English private school in Nicosia, the capital, and has received training as a hygiene inspector that gave him employment at the Municipality of Nicosia. He loved to hunt, and he kept many species of birds in huge cages in our garden. He had a passion for birds. He would whistle to them and expect a reply.

Nicosia was divided into a Turkish side and a Greek side. From his office, when I was visiting, I could see this town divided with minarets on one side and Greek Orthodox churches on our side. The Muslim call for prayers in contrast with the Orthodox Church bell ringing were a daily reminder of the town's division.

Once, I was in his office on the first floor, killing time with my toys, while I waited for him to take us home. A big lady, untidy and angry, stormed in shouting at him that he had to do something about her problem. She unbuttoned the front of her dress to him and exposed her huge breasts, showing a red rash all over her and claiming that it was from insect bites at the house she was living in. It was a disturbing sight to me as it looked like the rush was ready to burst with blood. Later on, in conversation with my father, he explained! He was also responsible for the hygiene levels of the brothels of a certain street, well known as the red light district, quite popular those days. Young men had to be tested for their sexuality and their orientation to be respected. Then the regulars at all ages had sexual needs, and to some extent, it was a must visit place in town, as relationships with women were on a different platform those days.

One story that is always with me, as it probably depicts all the genes and individual characters of my parents, is how they met. My mother was the daughter of a very successful merchant, in the aristocratic world of Nicosia, and in a different caste from my father, whose ancestors came as refugees on a caravan and definitely at a lower social caste in the eyes of the conservative society.

It was the norm for young men and ladies to be recommended for marriage. Many older ladies such as my aunt had this interest to recommend and suggest men and women to marriage. One day my father's sister, aunt Anastasia, escorted by her brother Kypros, visited Lady Emilia to suggest to her daughter Ero a certain noble doctor to engage in marriage. From the gate, as the young girl Ero passed through the lush gardens, she looked at this man escorting Anastasia to the house and smiled! It must have been that smile that intrigued whatever forces in my father's brain and body that he stopped the proposal and insisted to his sister Anastasia that he should be proposed instead. Anastasia had no faith in this happening, as she knew well the snobbery of the aristocrats in accepting an ordinary man struggling to survive with a civil servant's job, and having no answers as to how he would support her in the life she was used to enjoying.

Ero had a nanny and later on a lady maid, looking after her. She was one of five children, all having their own quarters in a mansion with lush gardens and fountains, personal maids, private lessons and lots of participation in aristocratic social and family events. They were taken by a private coach to school and their parents used to import Swiss chocolates for them to take to school – a real luxury just after the Second World War!

Kypro's pressure to be introduced to young Ero gave way to Anastasia's proposal, and Ero's parents gave her the choice to accept seeing him in the garden, with the presence of her personal maid, of course! This was the beginning of their journey. Through these brief meetings in the garden and the maid distancing as time went by, until the first hug and kiss. My father describes mum as very shy and naïve when it came to matters of men's natural behavior of body expressions during a kiss and a hug, expressions of passion or lust. It took him a long time to guide her and unfold her into this unknown new world for her. Dad always joked that mum got a fright on an occasion, as she thought that a mouse was moving in his pants!

Soon after these developments, because of Ero's father Cristoforo's weakness for gambling, his aristocratic fame started to fade, as money was lost which brought a lot of problems to the family and they had to sell even the mansion they were living in.

Kypros took this opportunity to ask for her hand, stating that he wants nothing from them, no dowry but just her. Although Christoforos objected to this, Kypros and Ero decided to leave together. This was an action that in those days, when a man went out of the house with a single woman, it was like they were 'stolen hearts ' for each other. Socially, there was no going back and the honor of this woman had to be saved. They married in church and lived with his family until it was time for them to build their own house nearby and start their lives. A few years later, Cristoforo's economic situation deteriorated so much that he, with his wife Emily, needed a home and found refuge with Kypros and Ero where they were looked after till their last days.

In all of these developments and through stories of relatives, but also through funny stories exchange between my parents, they came across as unique individuals, where they went through many problems and managed to set up a good family, giving all three children, Agatha, Achilles and Paris, myself, good principles and values for life. My mother was shy, even when well into their lives, and she always hid behind the cupboard door to get dressed. She was kind, gentle, polite, caring and loving. She always dressed well and wore dark red lipstick. She had the one and only master to look after. Her man was her pasha.

Dad got ill at 45 with heart problems, just as my mother was pregnant with me. In her worries that dad may not make it and she would have had to raise three children, she attempted to go for an abortion. She was then stopped by Agatha, my father's mother, who ran after her at the doctors and stopped her, saying that 'God will be angry and will take another one of your children away' should she proceed. Ero was concerned and respected her advice. Hence, I became a reality.

I was born just after midnight on the 16th of April 1958 in Nicosia, on the island of Cyprus. As I was a big baby and with demands for attention, I was causing a nuisance as I was crying all the time. My mother was trying to keep a tranquil environment for dad to cope with his illness so I was often shifted to a room away from them so as not to create a disturbance.

Whenever I travel back to my early years, images have no color, but are in black and white. I had no attention as a child, which made me stronger. I shifted into moods and created my own worlds. Worlds that I did not know they existed. I lived through images, I looked and became a warrior, or perhaps Mowgli from the Jugle book, or a Prince in that 18th century history book... I held the bagpipes wearing a kilt in endless green landscapes with rivers and was certainly an African warrior at one point. While being a child, I held in my mind the background conversations of the grown-ups around me, echoing concerns and rumors of war between the Turks and the Greeks. Confusing talks, about this one who died or there were rape stories in mixed villages or stories of the British torturing people in the struggle for Cyprus independence.

You see, Cyprus is an island in the East Mediterranean of strategic position, and throughout its existence whoever was stronger, invaded the island and left strong influential marks on the island's civilization; The Assyrians, Egyptians, Persians, Lusignans, Venetians, Alexander the Great, Ottomans and more. After the Ottoman Empire, in early 1923 Cyprus came under British rule. Its inhabitants were Greek Cypriots and a minority of Turkish Cypriots, mostly living separately. In 1955, a group of brave men started the struggle against the British regime. There were killings in ambushes, assassinations, hangings and tortures. Finally, in 1960 Cyprus gained its independence and democracy. The main guarantors of this independence deal were Britain, Turkey and Greece. However, peace and harmony were not successful, as there was trouble between the Greek Cypriots and Turkish Cypriots. Both ends did not really respect each other and there was rage and hating feelings between them. There was insecurity and danger.

My aunt Anastasia had a son called Vias, whom I remember always escorting her, in all her visits. She was a widow and quite large, needing a walking stick to walk. Vias would come in and sit alone, smoking one cigarette after the other. He was talking to himself, perhaps in a dialog too, with some imaginary people. He got angry with them too. Sometimes, Anastasia was sensing he was becoming hyper and called at him to stop talking and he was obedient. He asked me about my school and wanted to know of my lessons while he would pick a name that reminded him of something and would start a dialog building into a heated argument. I would try and interrupt him, offering him a soft drink, he would thank me, take a couple of sips and carry on the heated dialogue. He would build the argument ending to hit whoever was in front of him but thankfully his mother got control of his anger. He liked me, to sit and talk to him as he needed attention and company, or rather someone to listen. He was kind and told me many stories that made no sense to me or had no interest. He asked many questions, one after the other, and repeated to himself my answers.

I must have been ten years old when I was in a position to understand his story. It seems that when he was eighteen years old and at the Greek Gymnasium, where apparently, he was the best student, he was enthusiastic alongside the campaign against the British. In 1956 he was arrested by the British police, as they found on him some propaganda flyers. He was taken in for intense interrogation and eventually they electrocuted his brain, as it was a method used those days to punish someone or to deactivate the brain. He was sent to a sanatorium for therapy and then released on regulated medication, in the condition that I knew of him. I always looked at him and felt sorry. I tried to think of him strapped on a bed with wires on his head and many people around shouting at him. He was young, enthusiastic and brave to fight for his ideals and beliefs, but then a sad picture.

All these political stories and the unsafe atmosphere around these happenings on the island, were somehow confusing, disturbing and adding to unhappy emotions that I carried at that stage of my life.

Through my creativity and my imagination, I was escaping reality and started drawing anything that would look good. Big rolls of paper, colorful pencils and lots of patience. I needed to create and to come to a result. All this was accompanied by music. I was kept busy for days. Perhaps a dress of an aristocratic lady in the 1700s ornated with millions of tiny flowers in pencil, or an abstract face of an African warrior made of a million small squares, just anything that will last for a week's drawing to keep me going places and feel good.

I was quite happy being on my own for hours and traveling to unknown places with my music... such a drug! I loved all genres from a young age, classical, jazz quite a bit, ethnic sounds and definitely the blues and the shakes! They were my magic carpet to mental traveling. I had a few toys, mostly what was left from my older brother and sister, and have always buried them in the ground to find them later as a surprise. I needed that too.

Some friendships developed along the growing up to teenager years, playing football with other boys of the neighborhood but girls too! I loved girls and their way to get ready, always looking at my sister and friends gathering at ours, preparing for an outing. A bit of scenes and conversations from Sex in the City! The excitement and colors and how they wore their hair, especially in the 70s... the orange and greens, the blues and pinks and the large printed patterns and those pants! It did affect my taste on women that came to my path a few years later! I used to look after them and make them sandwiches and lemonade, while their music was in full blast and trying make-up and getting ready. The perfumes were interesting too, scents of femininity! It was all exciting to me.

Psychologists maintain that the first months of your childhood are critical in your character formation, but I would doubt that. I believe it is long before that all these is decided in you, as it probably comes through the genes of your parents. I grew up to be an average man! Everything about me was average: my size, my performance, my abilities. I was awarded a compliment by many that I had a nice smile. I wanted to be a gifted taller man, masculine with developed muscles, broad shoulders, lots of black hair and green eyes. Instead, I held on the myth, carried by my special name, Paris, also known as Alexander, the prince of Troy, a nobleman. Blessed by the goddess of beauty and love, Aphrodite, he stole Helen, the Queen of Sparta, the most beautiful woman in the world. I was in search of mine...

I see myself as shy, sensitive, proud, stubborn, a little snobbish too, but thoughtful as in considering others around me. I quite like to respect and appreciate good feelings and things in life, all from my mother. I also see myself as forever investing in people, caring and daring in life, loving adventures and taking risks, forever being disappointed with people but never giving up, like my father was. After all, I am the result of a gypsy man and an aristocratic lady, a contrast. I often feel confused about who I am, as one day I am eating delicious dirty street food with my hands in Bombay and another day having a formal gala dinner at a palace with royalties. I was quite happy to sleep on a beach under a palm tree, in Guadeloupe or anywhere in the world, but also lived an extravagant holiday on a private island, and in palaces. It was all enjoyed at the same level. In the process of enjoyment, there are other images blended in, from my fantasy world. A world that I needed to create and entertain myself.

It started during the gray years. I imagine people and create a plot when I see them. Perhaps before I even speak to them, I imagine, where they came from or perhaps when they have lived before. I actually see them in a scenario and in a film set, in another dimension or time. I see beautiful ladies walking and looking like real gigantic birds, with colorful feathers and chunky jewelry, in a magical background of lush palm trees, fringed with flowers that move and there are sounds of Tropical drums and happy people. This may occur on an airplane too where the passengers are all elephants, zebras and giraffes and the pilot is a lion as he howls through the speakers announcing where the next destination for a feast is going to be! I see a workman resembling the gelled hair man with high waisted pants of the 30s while in a gray film set in a New Orleans bar, as he enters the room. Perhaps I was there too. There is a man wearing a white wig with curls of the 1800s and is covered in white powder while he is drilling holes on the road and there is music too, Mozart's Magical flute. These images do not always stop, even when people speak to me about the reality of the moment, I can hold the image but yet respond to them as now. This is what the brain needs to do, fantasize and travel and I am having fun with it!

THE FIRST KISS

In my time, boys and girls at nurseries wore the same grayish checked dress, really ending in a skirt with pleats and for some reasons it was accepted as a common uniform. Only the hair styles made it possible to separate the gender. At the age of five or six I was drawn to Miranda, black hair, black eyes that looked deep into everything around and something inexplicable those days, about the lines forming her lips. We held hands at every break and felt nice, simply nice as innocent as it seemed from a distance. The other kids were making fun of us but mostly me, calling me 'a friend of women', insinuating that I was gay. Miranda waited for me at the gate of the school every morning, to see me and hold my hands before we enter the classroom together.

One happy day, full of flowers, butterflies and colors around us, as she was looking at me, in an inexplicable way to both of us, she forwarded her face towards me and she attached her lips on mine. I cannot recall the feeling, but the achievement, which was penalized by the rest of the children, ran straight to the teachers to declare 'the offense!' The incident became a tragedy when it was reported to our parents. My mother, bless her, tried to explain to me, on what she could base her conservatism, that this is not something that boys do to girls at that age, while my father has positioned himself looking at me with a thrilling smile!

Later on, at primary school, matters made more sense with the opposite gender. We were somehow aware of more interactional behaviors. There was a Marianna in my life, a girl with beautiful hair and round eyes, very properly presented with a white ribbon in her hair and looking clean and neat, as was important in those days. We were looking at each other, till I asked her to talk to her mother, should she be allowed to be driven by my mother to the movies! She came back the next day with the good news and the time to be picked up. The mothers met on the street and confirmed times and monies, as if there was a contract to be signed, and us committing to obey all the rules. We had money for the ticket and for a sandwich with a soft drink during the intermission of whatever film we chose.

After this procedure to go to the cinema there was a certain behavior. Me, being the little prince opening the heavy door for the little princess and always following what I have heard from the older men that your girl should be on your left side when walking on the pavement. So, I was trying to fit in all these little gestures while looking good in my short pants, shirt, socks to the knees that mum prepared for me. This cinema experiment was followed by small birthday party gatherings at other children's houses where I only had eyes for Marianna and she for me. We learned to dance the blues together and we adventured the shakes. 'I'm a believer' by The Monkees,'It's not unusual' by Tom Jones and 'Hippie Hippies Shake' by The Swinging Blue Jeans, were amongst my favorites, and God, we were shaking over and over to the same tracks!

The magical thing in these parties was the procedures as all the girls were sitting around the dance floor looking busy looking around, while the boys were piled up in another end of the room in waiting for a song to start and to choose a girl, they would ask to dance. This was happening in some parties where there were no outside grounds, in which case most of the boys would be running after a ball to kick it and have the pleasure of success! But my Marianna was very pleased with me, as I was holding her hand and was there to dance with her and eat together with her! That was all that could happen. I cannot remember at this age what we were talking about, but certainly it was not about technological advancements, but more on the romanticism of traveling to other countries, and our dreams, as her father was stationed at the Embassy of Paris and she planned to study there. As this innocent relationship carried on for a few years of primary school we did establish a kiss every now and then, at the end of parties when it was the blues time, prior to our mothers coming to pick us up!

Marianna left to go to a high school in Paris, and I went to a Greek Gymnasium in Nicosia, but we kept writing letters to each other about our news and what is happening in the little world at school. I used to write to her about my favorite songs and she was sending me cassettes of Jo Dassin, Mireille Matie, and of course Edith Piaf. The letters ended with an 'I miss you'. For a few following summers we got to see each other and go to the cinema, now holding hands and kissing much more and feeling strange, not knowing how to get to that something else around the corner. I started feeling something in my pants but was scared of the next move and never wanted to be seen disappointing to her. I wanted to suggest something, I was not sure of, but I preferred to stay shy. Perhaps, she would have been offended.

I was thinking of her, the warmth of kissing each other. One night in my sleep, I felt a pleasure, an unknown pleasure and then, an awkward feeling of having wet boxers! It was a good feeling, a guilty discovery. An imaginary journey through Playboy magazines distributed for money by the older students at school and thoughts followed. I was hiding away in the bathroom quite a lot!

THE SCOTTISH ACCENT

During primary school, and since it was planned by my parents that I would take my higher education in the UK, I started taking some private English lessons with Mrs. Houri, an old lady of a mixed heritage background.

Mrs. Houri was brought up in a Jewish settlement in Scotland. She carried the Scottish accent with her which I found interesting and amusing during her teaching. She was a big lady, living at the back of a house. To myself, her room was a film set at least a century in the past, with her frilly long flowery curtains and embroidered cushions on the bed, the China she was using, the wooden chairs and the dark green velvet sofa, all so a grandmother's lifestyle everywhere you looked. Old pictures of her family on the walls all with a story attached. She was witty, sharp and very serious during her teaching. I was drawn by the thick long dark red nails pointing out every syllabus and word in a sentence for me to read and correct my pronunciation! I loved her rrrs and her ooos and words singing in my ears till now! She was calling me what it sounded like Parrres and I loved her, as she always asked me,

- ' Have ye red youurr bouuk?'

She used to make fun of my walking as many other people commented that I walk like a ballerina, or rather a duck. She often addressed me a - 'Paris tha doouk!'

I remember these sessions so well, and I treasured the time with her.

She was not always clean. I had a developed sense of smell

and was indeed... sensitive to smells there! Every day, she had a slice of cake for me, at arrival, which was never fresh, but I always enjoyed it with a cup of tea served in the beautiful porcelain cup as it should be. Sometimes, when my mother was late to pick me up, she got into story telling about her time in Scotland, which made me add on to my travels as when alone at home I played a cassette with bagpipes that she gave me and my magic carpet took me to these mountains, rivers and lakes she described to me. I felt I was there in her stories. It felt familiar.

She married a geologist, a Scotsman, and ended up in Cyprus with him. He was carrying out some university studies on the formation of Cyprus, which was part of Africa at one point. He died in Cyprus some years later but she stayed on and started teaching private lessons to make a living for herself. My time with her was so precious, I loved her warmth and her wisdom, her space, her fatty legs, her dark red nails and I was not bothered by the old cakes and the smells in the room! She gave me a lot!

One day my mother stopped me from going to Mrs. Houri as she got sick. The next day, I left school and walked to hers. She was indeed in bed and poorly. I made her tea and cut a piece of the old cake for her and sat next to her bed saying nothing. She asked me to go home and ' rread me boouk'! Not more than a week later she passed away, which brought me great sadness. I drew many landscapes of what she described Scotland to be, thinking and missing her. My Scottish teacher, my friend was gone. My mother took me to her grave. I placed the drawings and a bunch of flowers that I picked from people's gardens in the neighborhood, and tied up with a tartan ribbon.

Perhaps, if I lived somewhere else in another life, Scotland may have been one of them as it exerts fascination to me till this date. I'm drawn to the singing of the language, if not to say, it is so sexy to me. I admire the landscapes yet to be discovered in full length, the strength in the characters of the people and I drink whiskey. It feels as if I was there!

Over some years, I made friends with a guest, back in

the early 90s, when I ran a French restaurant called 'Le Bistro d' hier' in an old simple farmhouse tucked away at a corner in Ayia Napa. This beautiful soul of a Scottish lady, Barbara, was running an old people's institution in Aberdeen, but sadly has been diagnosed with cancer. She has gently informed me that it would be the last year she sees me in Cyprus and at my restaurant. She invited me to visit her at Aberdeen a couple of months later and also attend the wedding of her daughter.

I wanted to create memories and share love, so I invited some very close friends and her at a dinner held privately at the garden of my restaurant where I cooked myself, served my best wine and we all enjoyed love and created memories to last a lifetime over that table. The hand sewn serviettes, the Christofle cutlery and the French porcelain laid the table. An antique gramophone player with a spring on the side gave power to spin a ceramic record, an old authentic song by Edith Piaf 'Non, je ne regrette rien' to which I asked her to dance with me gently and without talking as silence was enough to show the respect I felt towards her. Perhaps she is now watching over me!

The wedding of Barbara's daughter was in a grand place like a castle, in Aberdeen. I arrived a week in advance, stayed at her beautiful house of what looked in the middle of nowhere, to help with the preparations and also enjoy the long and cold walks in the pure Scottish nature. I walked around fields unfolding into hills and in different shades of greens. The views were magnificent and endless. It felt as if there was no one there and yet...it looked familiar and the ground had a certain smell I was acquainted with but I could not tell how.

The nights were spent over a bottle of whiskey by the fire and Scottish storytelling on traditions and clans and historical battles, exciting and fascinating. Memorable times but often admitting I was making an effort to understand all the words which they had to repeat!

The day of the wedding everything was beautiful and well organized from the ceremony to the end party at a local pub full of Scots and buzz. I was lost in the pleasure of listening to the

Scots singing their language.

The groom, after some drinks, paid me a compliment on my blue suit and I replied the same way that I loved his kilt. Little that we knew, ten minutes later, we did a clothes swap, in the men's toilets. The kilt was in blue and green tartan, and the shirt was white with a blue waistcoat. I had a belt with a buckle and a sporran. As per Scottish men, I wore nothing under the kilt and felt comfortable and free! I must have looked very convincing, as I made my way to the bar. I dared and asked for a round of drinks in my 'Grenglish' accent! A guy at the bar, who listened to my order, turned and said

- ' Jings, crivvens...wha tha hell happened to ye?'

I smiled and said,

- ' My name is Paris and I come from Cyprus!' He looked away and had a large sip of his whiskey.

The next day I returned the kilt and all the gear to the groom, but he kept my Armani suit being a real Scotsman! However, I still love Scotland.

MUMS

Thinking back, being the youngest of the three children I have been spending more time with my mother Ero, and because of my fathers' health situation, and his work, he had less time for me. I was taken everywhere with her, when visiting her friends and when she was going shopping. As there were no other children, I was bored.

No one described me as being an easy-going child until my first 10-12 years. I was always unhappy wanting more things to happen and attention. I do not think I knew what I wanted. It was a gray memory time in my life. I was happy when I was alone and dreaming in a corner mostly when listening to music.

My mother had a circle of lady friends, often playing cards around green tables and they had breaks to enjoy tea, cakes and sandwiches, a kind of high tea time. I must have been around six years of age. I loved preparing all that with her, when these afternoon parties were at ours. I enjoyed looking after all the ladies, taking them a glass of water or else, they asked for. These ladies were perhaps in their mid-forties. They often placed me on their knees and rubbed my back, which I loved, just like when you stroke a cat. They all wore nice shoes and had fat legs, suits and dresses with jackets and colorful shawls with broaches, formed hairstyles, lots of perfumes and powdered faces, simply mums!

I was reminded of this story. When I was seven or eight, as being bored, at one party like this, I got hold of the end of the long table cloth covering the table, loaded with the teas and cakes and all the goodies, and pulled it with me walking away while looking at them. Everything broke on the floor and I apparently had a lot of fun until my mother took me to a corner of a room to sit standing for an hour. Another day, I was playing on the floor, next to them, and went under their round green table and shouted to them 'you are all fat, with fat legs and your feet smell bad too!'

During my teens and further on, I was a complete rebel, as I had long fair hair and wore the same size pants with my sister a size 28, male colorful platform shoes and colorful tide shirts. That was the fashion. I liked to wear anything new and fashionable and I started being interested in Italian designer clothes, especially when I was listening to Italian romantic songs.

Meanwhile, I was a football fanatic, kicking the ball with other boys in the neighborhood, but I was kicking them too, when I was losing. I was a strong and insistent young boy, wanting to boss everyone as to their position in the game and wanted to have the best team and surely to always win. They all listened to me, being the organizer of the games. I created new games in the garage, when it was raining, perhaps I was the leader of the gang. Once we borrowed, or rather stole for a while, other children's bicycles in the neighborhood, to have racing competitions, to which I was always winning, for their sake, as I had stronger legs.

From my teenage years my mother was definitely treating me like another daughter of hers. Christmas and birthday presents, except socks and pajamas, were tablecloths and new bedsheets, as well as tea cups and plates. I began to have a greater interest in cooking. She showed me how to make cakes and bake them, butter cream and mayonnaise too. I was fascinated by the use of a hand-held mixer. She was forever telling me how to fold clothes and keep cupboards and drawers neat and tidy. When she was newly married, she lost her first baby daughter and perhaps she saw her in me.

Because of my mother I have developed a passion for crockery of different eras and collected many sets just like her. Glassware from grandmother came to my possession too. Crochet blankets and family handicrafts were given to me. I collected old cutlery from antique shops and with the years they were used at my first French restaurant. My mother was like that too, a collector of good quality crockery.

Her aristocratic approach to understanding quality, was the start to become aware of good manners around the table. I was eating properly and wiping my mouth with the napkin before and after sipping water or eating something during a meal. The signaling of cutlery on the plate, the wishing and the proper holding of a glass were part of her upbringing as an aristocrat which she passed on to me. I learned to be polite and gentle, to create a conversation and give everyone the right to talk around the table. She taught me to listen well and answer last. All these were useful when I found myself in formal parties and events as I was always comfortable and I felt I belonged there as my mother's proud prince.

I remember there was a time when we had at home a hi-fi record player. There was silence and we all looked at the vinyl spin and the needle moving towards the beginning of the record and there was sound, which we could even increase in volume. We danced to the music with my parents, and my sister would have joined in while my brother would watch. Sometimes, their friends were coming to have a little dance together and have a cold drink and go back to their homes just after that little session. Vinyls were a discovery; it was a big thing those days after the gramophone records. It was a novelty for a household to be able to afford a vinyl player and a black and white TV! Another reason for gatherings!

At twenty-seven, I was successful in my own business. I was finally accepted as a clever man by my father, with whom we became the best of friends. He got me to talk about girlfriends, he told me his stories when he was a bachelor, and more about my mum. Much more he prepared me for when he was going to pass away. He wanted me to look after his beloved wife. He said that she will have enough money to live well, and to make sure that she will keep buying nice clothes and to live her life well. I was listening to him in admiration and re- assured him that I would be there for her.

At one point, I bought for them a trip to the Greek island of Rhodes and gave them the tickets one day when they came to have dinner in my own restaurant. They were happy and holding hands as they walked away from the restaurant. There was an extraordinary emotional feeling in me and I was proud of them.

I loved traveling and it so happened that most times my father had a heart incident, and I was rushed back to be part of supporting each other in the family and mostly my mother. In December of 1990, I was off to France for Christmas with some friends, and I have sent my parents a bottle of Champagne and flowers for Christmas and a message of love that 'for every bubble in this bottle, a thank you for what you have done for us in life'. They were happy and my father proudly talked to all his friends about my message.

As I came back from a night out at the show of Moulin Rouge in Paris, on the 26th of December 1990, there was a call from my sister that our father is in intensive care in Nicosia and I should make my way back. I moved mountains to be on any flight as there was no last-minute availability and I was in despair. I flew from Paris to Athens and then to Cyprus. I managed to arrive the next day where I went straight to the hospital. He was there, not responding and no sign of life at all, looking like a factory with all the pipes and wires. I held his hand and said to my mother who was next to him,

- 'This is exactly how he did not want to go'.

His fingers moved, as I talked. His cardiogram showed an activity, and the nurses ran in. One nurse said to me, he knows you are here, usually they wait for the loved ones to come and say goodbye. A few hours later he passed away to another world and join his ancestors perhaps. But I know he is still around, sometimes!

From there on, my course caring after my mother, had begun. I made sure I spent all the time I could with her. I was busy with the restaurants but running a film production company, from above my mother's house where I set up a bedsitter and a little office, so that I would be close. My mother felt there was a female around me, as she could see from the way I was dressed to go out for the night, and that after shave filled the room, as I wished her goodnight.

Years went on and I loved to see her enjoying her friends and the card playing gatherings, still with all the fat ladies. She was always nicely dressed as my father wanted her to. She traveled a little with her friends. I took her on a trip to Athens for holidays and to theaters and shows, shopping trips and in restaurants too.

She was continuously kind and generous. She never placed herself as a priority, she never talked bad at all about anyone even to those that did things to hurt her. She cared about everyone and she also enjoyed her grandchildren now from my brother and sister. She always worried about me being single and wanted me at times to be with someone. She also, somehow agreed with me that, I was not going to ever get married as most of my close friends were in a second marriage with disastrous divorces. She could see that I was independent. I explained to her, I was happy being alone and not lonely, quite busy with work and enjoyed my travels. I think she knew I was seeing someone.

We used to spend hours over a coffee and around a table. I loved to ask her for stories of her past with my father, her pasha. Stories of love, stories of other friends they had at different stages. Mostly, I loved her stories, when she described her younger years at school, and about her brothers and sister, and her parents and how it was the political situation and their economic welfare. Life was so different then. I wanted to know how she learned to drive a car and how technology was coming in rapidly with fridges and vacuum cleaners, hairdryers and music systems.

One story that I treasure was about her pasha who was jealous. Ero being an aristocrat, she took on lessons in tennis. In those days the tennis skirts for the girls were longer and just up to the knee. At a game of tennis tournament, as Ero tried to reach the ball, her thighs probably showed to the audience. To her bad luck, some men expressed a liking seeing her legs. Pasha, my father, was there, and listened to them, so he has from there on, forbidden her to play tennis as he did not like his wife to be shared with the eyes of other men.

In 2014 she got weary and ill with different things of old age and one day she was rushed to the hospital. As I was in Ayia Napa at work, I heard the news and was followed up by my sister. As late as I finished, I felt I needed to be with her. I drove back to the hospital in Nicosia, and sat next to her, as she was asleep. She opened her eyes, she recognized me and said,

- 'Free me! Let me go!' looking at me in the eyes.

- 'What would you like me to do?' I asked, as I thought that she was uncomfortable in the bedsheets, but she did not reply.

The next morning, she opened her eyes, we had a little talk about me being there with her all night, and then she suddenly deteriorated not breathing well and it was dreadful to see her closing all taps and how the body reacts until you pass away. I was holding her hand until it let go of me and felt colder and colder! I cried and cried and there was nothing to hang on to. My sister and brother entered the room, there was silence!

'Oh, mum you were so important in my life and I could never understand how much was there connecting us until you were gone. I am part of you and you live inside me now, in my genes and in my mind and I am forever missing you and dad. I feel you are both around. I regret not introducing you to the woman I was spending time with, as you would have got on perfectly well, perhaps you were the same souls. I regret I did not spend more time with you, I regret I did not tell you I love you'.

FIRST TIME

At the gymnasium school and during the breaks, I was walking, embracing my mate Andreas, who was blind, very clever, a good student and with a great sense of humor. He was born blind and developed an intense sense of smelling. As the wrapping was coming off the sandwich, under the desk while expecting the bell to signal the break, I could see his nostrils behaving like an elephant tusk and recording 'salami, cucumber, cheese...' He would exchange my sandwich for his, as he would smell the salami or the bacon in mine.

I remember, when I asked my parents to be away from the house for a whole day, as I planned my birthday party, to which they agreed. It was then that I became a Hollywood producer, the biggest party organizer and the most hospitable host to at least fifty other teenagers. Some had duties to execute.

I organized my teams to dismantle all the beds from the three bedrooms and move all the furniture in the back garden. Others covered the rooms with rolls and rolls of black plastic bags where we stuck fluorescent cut outs of stars and planets. We placed a special light in all the rooms to make these cut outs to shine in order to create a dreamy atmosphere. Another unit of girls, some were in hair rolls, came earlier and had to prepare the sandwiches in platters and some others set up a bar with some palm tree branches hanging above it and featuring not just soft drinks but beer too! Some friends older than me brought a bottle of vodka and a bottle of whiskey which we all sampled and felt we were doing something adults do. Perhaps it made us feel a bit cocky at that age! The music was in full blast the party was on, there was dancing and some cigarette smoking in Humphrey Bogart style. There was kissing, stroking and bottom grabbing. At that age, everyone was someone else, older. There was dreaming and attempts of projecting a different persona than what we really were.

I found myself at a corner feeling a superstar producer staging such an event. I had no time to explore any possible relationship with the opposite sex, as the event was more of a dramatic happening in front of my eyes. I was so thrilled for the party to be going well and that was my only concern.

They all ended up in their parents' cars piled up outside the house, and some teams stayed behind to restore the house to its running form. At that point my parents returned and I vividly remember the look on their faces, as they saw the number of plastic bags coming off the walls and the whole house being in a state. I was hyper and could not stop moving fast to restore everything. I was talking about the success of the party for hours. I started trembling. My father had experienced me in this mode once before, and he gave me a valium tablet to calm me down. It seemed that as a young boy, I was very hyper in producing a scenario and to make everyone happy but in the process, I needed something to calm me down.

At school breaks there were a bunch of animated girls, always approaching us to joke with Andreas and myself. They had invited us to another birthday party to which I escorted him and made sure he ate enough sandwiches. There was this girl Dina, who had the growing advantage of age and formed her curves from all angles that attracted my interest as I looked at her. She responded in a more evident way by winking at me! I was a little intimidated at first, as I could feel she was coming forward and that scared me. I did not know what to do other than blushing! Such a feeling when your legs are suddenly feeling weak as your confidence is abandoning you. She came across and she asked me to dance to the blues to which she almost asphyxiated me into what seemed to me huge balloons. The exhilarating excitement increased my pulse to red high, as if my father was to give me another valium. I squeezed her in all parts my hands could reach, there was a response in my pants and then the song ended. She kissed me on the cheek and sat down.

What on earth has happened there! It is such a provocation to any male of whatever age when a female makes advances and seats back, as if she is saying 'now show me what you have got!' It bothered me as I was so scared to retaliate. Instead, I went and sat next to her and she grabbed my hand in silence while my brain was trying to find a solution. She turned her head and said to me in my ears,

- 'I like you' to which I smiled and didn't know what to say.

- ' I like your smile too,' she said'

Lost for words, the evening ended and she gave me a kiss on the cheek to say goodbye. But the terror did not end there, as the next day at school, she gave me a note saying, thank you for the good time at the party and would I like to spend Saturday night at her house, as her parents are going away? Rivers of warm and cold temperature started running in my body, I was so happy for such an experience and yet so afraid. I did not have a clue what to do and yet that sense of someone else directing every little muscle in your body or even thinking for you.

Saturday came, and I felt brave enough to enter her house. There was soft music of the Bee Gees and romantic light in an all beautiful and warm atmosphere. We had a soft drink and she showed me to her bedroom with the same atmosphere as the living room. There was a lampshade covered in light red fabric, a green bedspread, a homework desk and a large picture of David Bowie on the wall. We sat on the bed next to each other. I made the first move and put my hand over her shoulder and gave her a quick kiss on the cheek to which she pushed me on the bed and attached her lips on mine. It felt like I couldn't breathe. My pulse started racing so much I needed a Valium. My legs were cut off my body, while there was a feeling of lust but scared, so scared I could not feel any progression.

Our lips must have developed blisters from the kissing and our hands were burning from the rubbing on each other's clothes. She suggested we take our clothes off and get under the bedsheets and we did. I turned the other way and I took my clothes off as Bowie was looking at me. The kissing went on under the bedsheets and after an hour or so and with not any male body reaction she said:

- 'Can you not?' to which I replied the most stupid verse of an apology, as there was no other index
- 'My leg hurts!'

Humiliated and embarrassed, scared and lost in one million versions of miserable thoughts, I managed to sleep and in the morning I gave her a kiss and felt apologetic for disappointing her. I thought about the whole experience and tried to understand why I could not respond and overcome my inexperience and my fear as to what should have been happening in that room. I had images of those Playboy magazines in my mind and wanted to do the same. I definitely wanted the thrill of success! I felt that she had done this before and she was more ahead of me in expectations which probably held me down into that awful stage of despair. The whole day I had a hard-on thinking of the warmth of our bodies under the bedsheets and could not wait to go home and lock myself in the room to masturbate to these thoughts. Again, and again...

I did not lose my virginity till I was 17 years old. A charming, funny, sweet and chubby blond girl called Anna, a year younger than me, invited me to her birthday party. This was a big party of some fifty teenagers. Some were there with established relationships, hand in hand, some were speculating and some boys were playing football in the garden while the girls were talking about their hair and their clothes. Anna made me feel the important person at her party, always smiling at me, bringing me food and drink. We danced, and she held my hand all the time. We kissed and kissed and had her dad's whiskey with coke, as we felt we were older and mature enough. She had a cigarette on the balcony where more kissing took place. I felt very relaxed with her until she broke the news to me, whispering in my ears that she wanted me to stay the night as her parents will come back the day after the party! Terror again and uncertainty creped in but as she was so playful and smiley, I began to relax and fell for this adventure.

When they all left the party, we found ourselves developing blisters from the kissing. Clothes came off easier and cuddling began and I could feel the passion through my body as all weapons were ready to fire! It was dark in the room, which probably helped a lot, and I used my hands to explore her clitoris as in the magazines, from the hairy patch, with reference to pictures, downwards where it felt like a wet mouth and that was where I aimed to penetrate. At that point she said:
'Slow', with an edge of little pain and that it was when the dark room became warm, and fire was around as I moved in and out, feeling better and better at every move. She was smiling and breathing heavy in anticipation which did not last for long as it was that wet feeling, when stars shined all around me that came out of my body in what I could understand was the meaning of a fuck!
'Woah... what sort of chemistry is this?' I said with amazement.
We stayed embraced for a long time, till nothing could be held inside her. She dressed up before me and grabbed me tight saying:
- 'So now you are my boyfriend?' to which I had no time to process the thought and replied
- 'Of course, and I feel things for you!'
It was a lie typical of me being polite and not wanting to hurt her, instead of me saying, I had a thrill, great I overcame this and let's do it one million times more again and now!

We carried on these meetings for sex. It added to my confidence and sex education. It was time I had to enter the army after high school graduation which was compulsory to do for twenty-six months. Anna was a naughty girl when sex was on offer and she did not leave me in peace. It was quantity and not quality in those times. She was playful. Pinching and squeezing bottoms and tits was our game all the time.

I was stationed in a camp as a telephone operator and had a duty schedule together with another soldier. This allowed us to have a break for 20 minutes. Anna made sure she parked outside the camp in a discreet corner and had a kebab ready for me in exchange for a quick session of sex in the small car. Quite adventurous as she was, she was big but manageable.

One night, just as I had released my love juices and my bum was clearly showing off through the windscreen, a short gold swagger stick, recognizable as the Generals of the army, knocked on the car and a voice said, 'soldier back to your duty!' I thought that was my duty! I got dressed and flew to position by the telephones. He called and I picked up the phone only to find out that he wanted me in his office first thing!

I did not sleep all night thinking of the outcome as such a punishment could cause a destruction to my plans ;to go to the UK for my higher education. The next morning, I referred to him in full army severe expression. He took some time to think and gave me a speech on abandoning duty and its importance. He gave me a delay to my army dismissal for two more months which would have canceled my plans to begin my studies in September of that year. However, he left a window open that should I behave as a specimen of a good soldier for the rest of my time there, he himself will delete the extra time. He also had arranged to send me to another camp where I would be the assistant secretary to the General there. That was an upgrade in the army and inside me I wanted to upgrade in other fields too. I was beginning to explore and be explored and knew that there was more to this!

I informed Anna about my transfer and that I had to stop seeing her in the small car. We met a couple of times, building more sexual experience, when on leave from my army duty, as it was time for her to go abroad and study.

THE ENGINE ROOM

The new placement in the army was more demanding in skills as I had to handle a lot of correspondence with an old typewriter and keep archives, learn to bury army secrets coming to us in administration. I was lucky to be the assistant to a young General who was in the stage of falling in love with a woman. In private sessions with me he needed to talk about it. We formed an amicable relationship as General to an assistant and we talked about work, but every day about his outings and his gestures towards this woman that was a possibility of a life spouse. I became the contributor of romance in his relationship. I suggested flowers once a week and taught him mannerisms of good gentleman's behavior that I did not know I had gathered from my short life till then!

I taught him how to pull a chair in restaurants, open the car door for her, wait for her to start dinner first and eat slowly to match her tempo. I gave him examples of complimenting her on her clothes too. I had to choose ladies' perfumes and buy women's underwear in imaginative sizes, as I have never met his potential. I went clothes shopping with him and made him look like a new man. Nice grayish pants, dark blue shirt, camel leather jacket, Paul Newman style but without the looks. He really wanted to get married and I could not see the urge seeing everything through my lens of life. However, in return for my advice, he made me be on duty only during office hours which enabled me to work at nights as a DJ in various nightclubs, celebrating music as being so important to my life and my magic carpet to mental traveling .

When I was 20 I became a DJ. I wore tight blue jeans and an open front shirt, slim and fresh and always attracting all sorts of girls wanting attention and more. There was one version of a Maria, blond and older by 10 years, therefore, more upfront, and sexy ready. She looked undressed to me as she was talking and my mind was creating various scenarios. She was dressed in red leather underwear with red fur trimmings, devil's horns, red lipstick and red nails when she smiled at me. She was thirsty and I was a little scared of her, knowing all about sex. She waited for me on Sunday afternoons, where we staged matinee disco parties in one club called Paradise.

We had no private place of our own to go to. My cousin had a block of flats to which one day I showed at the top of the building, the engine room of the lift, to the maintenance man and so I knew where the key was. A blanket from home on the floor made the engine room softer and there we were. Every Sunday in the engine room I heard the wheels clicking and spinning the with the metal wires, to move up or down to a level, every time someone was in and out, and as I did.

Maria was beautifully crazy; she could not see anything else in me other than the ability to perform 5-6 times a session. She was hot and complaining to me that there is burning inside her all the time, she was in rhythm and singing 'ayi-ayi-ayi' like the red Indian dance around the fire. My imagination started growing, as I traveled to having sex with a red Indian woman with feathers on her hair and around the fire, a scenario that encouraged me to buy her necklaces with bones and stones to wear at our private sessions.

This routine carried on, we never went out to a restaurant or café, I knew nothing more about her except that she was totally mine and obsessed with me dare I look or speak to another girl at the club. I felt that she was going nuts over the idea that she could not possess me forever which eventually drove me away.

One afternoon, while at the club, one girl wearing a short tight dress came to ask for a certain song which I had with me. I said I will play it quite soon and I smiled at her.

Maria saw her talking to me and stormed in the DJ booth

yelling:

- 'Who was this girl? What did she say and why did you smile at her? I am going to kill you if you go with her'

- ' Look, she asked for a song and I will play it for her...what is your problem?' I replied quite upset.

- 'You are mine and no one else will have you' she declared, and I looked away.

I had to break free from this rope tidying around my neck. What can a man do when he is mentally gone but physically there while the woman is craving for togetherness? It was never on the cards; she could have known that from the beginning. Especially when your direction in life is towards other dreams that you cannot possibly share with the other party.

One day she was different. When we entered the engine room, the routine was not followed. She burst into tears and drove me crazy to get her to talk about it.

- ' Ok, come on tell me what is bothering you' I said.
- 'Promise that you will not be angry with me first,' she said and I looked worried to this.
- 'I am pregnant,' she said with her eyes full of tears '... I want to keep this baby of yours!'

There is me, an irresponsible young man of twenty years old, let loose, and there she was a thirty-year-old woman, who did not think for me not knowing stuff and considering how irresponsible young men are.

- 'Look at me,' I said. 'It is my fault for not asking you before, so that we are careful. I am on my way to study abroad for a few years and then I want to travel the world. A baby... I cannot be there... It would be unfair for the baby to bring it to this world and especially when I will not have any money to support you, can you not see this?' I explained feeling sad seeing her like that in a state.
- ' But I want to have it and to be thinking of you, until you come back from your studies,' she said, and made me feel frustrated for not understanding her.
- ' Ok then, let's leave it to this. I am not going to force you. I am

taking you home to think and we will talk about it tomorrow', I concluded and drove her home.

There was no way I wanted this to happen. I could not let her go, for what she wanted to do.

I was upset and worried for her to go for an abortion. The next day we spoke on the phone and she credited me for making sense to her. I borrowed money from work. We went through this very unpleasant and painful experience together. I was with her and followed with lots of phone calls. I did not feel good about it and had been sending her flowers.

I did not feel emotionally attached to Maria. She was an attractive lady, I gave her respect, and in return she gave me love and sexual experience, as weapons to move on. I was still a little reserved when it came to women and sex but slowly coming out of it. We both had fun exploring our feelings created by lust when we touched each other's bodies. After three weeks she was back at the matinee sessions and brought me a lemon cake as my favorite taste in sweets. I was happy to see her and sat her in the DJ box with me.

The meetings in the engine room continued with more protection now. She was the red Indian in voice but in spirit too. She was the high mountain and the white wolf to me...my mind was traveling. Sometimes I was the strong cowboy that forced her on the ground for sex!

It was time for me to start planning for my studies in the UK. I had to leave her behind and often suggested to her that she should find someone else to love, perhaps someone more established and closer to her age, to build her own dreams with him. It made her feel more for me that I was thinking like that! I felt inadequate not knowing how to stop her being unhappy.

She kept calling home to talk to me and crying, missing me and that she will forever wait for me. My mother, who ended up talking to her, to stop her crying, had some strong words about responsibility and advised me to explain to the girls calling that I have other plans, while my father made comments of men's experiences in the sense that I should learn from it and he looked at me in a funny way. I don't know if he was implying ' it served me right' or there was a bit of jealousy or there was a note of pride! Perhaps all three!

FIRST TIME ABROAD

After my army years, in 1978, I traveled, for the first time on an airplane, to Heathrow and first time on a train to Oxford, with my brother who was already a student there. I was to start my studies in hotel management. This idea came from a close family friend, Kypros, the father of Marios who became a good friend of mine and he was studying in London. Kypros gave me attention during family gatherings and parties and noticed my passion for music and looking after people. He thought I would be good in a profession offering services and entertainment to others. He was a successful director of an insurance company. He had a certain serious look, respectful and he would see clearly through situations. I always liked him and he was inspiring to me. I always wanted to please him and prove him right. I kept this as a sense of purpose while studying, to return to Cyprus a winner. I had to try very hard to do so. My English language knowledge, even with some Scottish words here and there, was not an advantage. One way to go ahead fast, was to meet people and try conversation.

The first day I arrived, nicely trimmed from the army, sun tanned, young and with a foreign accent, readily available for troubles of all sorts, I met a girl called Olivia. A local girl with a jumper and feeling cold, but with a packet of crisps and a cigarette on the other hand. She smiled at me as she walked near the front door of our apartment. My brother first said,

- 'Hello, do you live around here?'
- ' Yeah, I live a couple of blocks further down... where are you from?' She asked
- 'We are from Cyprus' I said.

- 'You both look so tanned... we are all white here, there is no sun,' she said while coughing,

We started talking as my brother went into the apartment. I had to ask a couple of times for everything to be repeated, while I tried to pronounce everything the correct way.

- 'France' she made fun of me,' you have a nice smile... but I think you are stupid that you came to the UK to study. It must be wonderful to live on an island in the sun. Do you not have universities there?'
- 'We do, but here they are better' I said, walking to reach a flyer that flew in the wind further down.
- ' Look...' she said. 'You look like this!' She tried to imitate how I walked and said laughing,
- 'You look like a duck coming out of a lake but with a nice smile!'

Olivia and I became friends and lovers. Meeting every Friday night while her folks were at the local pub. We had from eight till eleven to play games in bed. I was always out before eleven. The parents met me at other times, going to theirs for coffee and a chat with all of them. They knew that we were friends, going for walks and going to see the horses at some stables nearby. They liked me, as I was a good young lad, they said. One Friday night, her parents came back earlier than the schedule, while I was in bed with Olivia. Just like in films, I got into the cupboard while she handed me all my clothes. I was in there, hardly breathing, till her dad came into her bedroom to say goodnight, but my Scottish Tartan socks were right in front of him. He saw them and commented

- ' Scottish socks? Where did you get those, I haven't seen you wearing them!'
- ' I bought them last Christmas and started wearing them now when it is cold' she replied.
- ' You should find yourself a man to keep you warm instead. That Steve the plumber was at the pub tonight, he is a good

chap!' he said as he left the room.

When he was in his bedroom, I came out of the cupboard as quietly as I could, got dressed and opened the window of the first floor, some 5 meters high, to jump out as I could not use the old wooden staircase to go down and make a noise. I held onto the window sill and was ready to jump down when the neighbor's Doberman saw me and started barking! Not any 007 or even Tom Cruise could have imitated my jump, landing on a spiky bush at first and jumping over the fence for salvation. I ran as fast as a bullet, stormed into our apartment and my brother checked me out in disgrace saying, where are your socks? My heart was going to explode until I put my head on the pillow.

Olivia was a girl never sure of herself, always feeling less of what she was and I was forever trying to boost her self- confidence. She had green eyes; brown hair and she was chubby. She had unhealthy eating habits and was coughing from cigarettes. I was making her laugh as I always repeated a quote from the film' The main event' when Ryan O' Neal said to his coughing girlfriend ' you are a walking ashtray and you wear that rose perfume, sometimes I don't know if I should kiss you or water you'!

I loved her English humor, her support of my studying time, our walks and the teaching of the English expressions like ' I'm pulling your leg', 'it rings a bell' or ' they are like chalk and cheese'. She also made fun of my rare words in Scottish that I used sometimes, like 'Rocket' meaning crazy or ' You are crabbit' referring to bad temper.

Years later, I met Olivia when I went back to Oxford and almost created a mess in her life. As one does, while into his career, he goes back to where he had experiences and received his education at least to see the differences and changes and re-live the atmosphere, which, by the way, is never the same. I must have been 30 years old when I did that and walked the frequented places back as a student. It dawned on me to visit Olivia's house to see how she was doing and catch up. Indeed,

I met her alone at home, married now and with kids and she suggested to meet me later at our old pub for a drink.

Happy to see each other and wanting to know more we went to the pub where time stood still and had a few beers and shots of whiskey. But then we had more of them and more of them. We laughed about the past. She talked to me about her husband Steve, the plumber, and her two young kids and she sounded so happy throughout the conversation. She was proud of me having my own restaurant and moving on and while on the last embrace almost at the exit of the pub, I smiled and called her bony to make her laugh. A full kiss changed the whole atmosphere!

The alcohol overtook all the logic and gave way to lust as we felt to be lovers back in time. I looked at her in the eyes. I probably had an expression written on my face,' I want you now!' She grabbed my hand and led the way to the ladies' toilets where we did what we should have not done.

I felt awkward, an unnecessary situation that ruined all the previous conversations at the bar. Afterwards we felt cold about it and agreed that it should not have happened but all good on both sides at the end. Two months later she rang me to announce the news that she was expecting another baby and she was sure that was ours. We went through talks debating the truth on this, we talked angrily to each other, we felt so irresponsible and stupid blaming ourselves. I asked her for a little time to think and to call her back the day after.

- 'I have put all my thoughts in line with logic. I want to explain the situation to you.' I said in confidence and carried on.' I would never be responsible to ruin your life and your relationship with your loving husband and kids. The same way I would have not been there for the outcome anyway, living so far away and in a career developing situation.'

- 'Yes, I understand' she replied.

- ' I accept responsibility for the mistake and I apologize for what happened. I would like you to consider not to ever reveal this happening to anyone in our lives as it will cause unnecessary catastrophe.'

- 'Yes, I understand and it will be terrible news to many,' she said in an agreeing note.

Overall, my feelings and thoughts towards this decision have been a complex mix of emotions. While I felt a deep sense of guilt and shame for having caused such a situation and for having chosen to keep it hidden, I also knew that it was the best decision for all involved. By keeping the story hidden, I was able to protect all involved and to ensure that no further harm was done.

We placed the truth at a premium and we held our own pain without any 'medication'. Time proved us correct and mostly sensible. As a man I was proud of this decision. I felt that was the right thing to do. It was a big lesson of life. She called me months after when she must have had the baby, to ask how I was and we talked about nothing of importance. I did not ask any questions and she did not offer any information. I was very prompt in saying,

- 'I am proud of you and your family, and wish you to enjoy good times together and if you ever need something you know where to find me'.
- 'Thank you, good luck Paris' she replied.

I have been curious for years to see what this baby looked like, but I convinced myself to shake everything out of my head. Four years later, Olivia called to exchange Christmas wishes and said,

- ' How is your family... and your restaurant doing?'
- 'Yes.... Fine.... all good here...' I said, but dying to ask so many questions.
- ' I... It's difficult to say this,' she said sounding emotional and with a trembling voice ' I am sorry for this situation we caused... It was my fault'
- 'Olivia, please do not say this' I strongly said while I could hear her stumbling to say something and crying
- '... she walks like a duck,' she said laughing in her tears

It put a smile on my face.

Today, thanks to social media I have seen how our daughter looks, now married and has two of her own beautiful girls.

KAMA SUTRA

My friend Marios had a flat in Hampstead. I stayed at his, on a number of weekends, experiencing many London restaurants and nightclubs. One outing was at a party in an apartment of some of his friends near Baker Street. A beautiful Georgian apartment full of art on the walls, with wooden floors and high ceilings. The people there were in the film business and had some cousins and nieces from other areas. There I met Kate, a lovely chatty girl who took interest in where I was from and my story. We all had dinner and watched a film that one of the guys had produced. As we were leaving, Kate gave me her telephone number and said:

-' I enjoyed talking to you, call me one day when you come back from Oxford to hang out together and show you London'.

I was very thankful and did not know what to make out of this invite but for sure I wasn't going to miss this opportunity.

I knew nothing of this girl but she seemed to know a lot about everything around us and certainly a London girl knowing all that was happening and where to go. A week later I called her to see how she is and started the wrong way

- 'Hi Kate, remember me, Paris, the guy from Cyprus, we met....'

- 'Yes of course', she replied ' are you well, how is it going there in Oxford?'

We chatted for a while as I wanted to feel welcome and take on her invitation but she mentioned nothing of me going to see her. I could not get around the conversation. When we hung up, I felt so stupid and small not being able to say what I think. Five minutes later the phone rang and it was Kate asking me if I had any time free to visit her in London. It was obvious that she felt there was more to be said on the first call and she called back to correct it. She offered me accommodation and to go somewhere to eat.

A week later I called and made my way to hers. It was a little hard to find my way with trains and street addresses. Kate had an amazing apartment in Kensington, near Harrods. Beautifully furnished and very well put together. Leather chesterfields, wooden floors and Persian carpets, some mirrored walls and lots of abstract paintings. We had a drink and she suggested we walk together to a small restaurant nearby to grab something to eat. She went to get ready while the phone rang and she was brief and sharp in answering with small words. I felt that plans have changed. She explained that she had to go somewhere and that she would send me a takeaway. She made me feel comfortable, showed me the tv and her bed to sleep in when I would be tired and in case she would come back late. All agreed she took a bag of clothes with her, kissed me on the cheek, apologized and left me alone to explore her apartment.

I looked around and I was sure of a few things. There was no man in her life as there was only one toothbrush. There was a lot of money spent in this apartment. I had no clue as to what she does to earn all this wealth. I thought she may have been an actress, as her cousins were film producers but there was nothing in the apartment indicating that this avenue may have been right.

She returned the next morning at nine, with a bag of croissants and yoghurts and was wearing different clothes. She looked tired. She was interested to know what I did on my own in her apartment. She lied down on the sofa listening to me explaining the film I watched and she fell asleep. I covered her with a blanket and sat on an armchair opposite her. It was midday when she opened her eyes, apologizing to me for not being a good host and thanking me for covering her with a blanket. She said to me just out of the blue,

- ' I like you Paris, there is something calm about you. You make everything easy to be with. Your smile reveals your kind soul. I like that you are a little shy, I reckon, and careful in what you say, you are very gentle and not very many men are genuinely so!' I smiled in return and asked her

- ' Would you mind telling me what you do in life?' She stopped to think for a minute and said,
- 'What foreign person would word your question in such a polite manner? You are too young to be like this'.
- 'I am not young Kate... I lived other lives before' I said with wit and she laughed.

We sat on the rich blue Persian carpet and talked about our pasts. She was such a pretty woman with long straight chestnut hair, green eyes and a trained body. Her trimmed waist formed feminine curves on the hips and made her breast reveal their perfect shape. She was an orphan and was brought up by some other relatives. She studied art and dance and she found her way to express through dancing in London shows. She was kicked out of the group as she refused to obey the sexual demands of the choreographer in charge. Not finding a job she became a bunny girl in a nightclub for rich gentlemen. She had a deal with the management that she will not be 'hired' or exploited in any way. Someone, however, became very important to her. A sheikh from one Arabic country who fell in love with her and so did she. He bought her an apartment and a new Mini Cooper car to go with it. He supported her and only he can have priority in her life. She confusingly admitted to me that she had feelings for the Sheik and that it was him in town the night before that she went to see. Woah.... I am in London in front of a really pretty woman, my first months away from home and so close to such a strong story. Later that afternoon she drove me in her mini to catch my train back to Oxford and made me promise to return asap. The next weekend I went back from Friday night.

We walked to a Spanish restaurant that I could have never afforded and had a beef steak with grilled vegetables and some Spanish sounding sauce, salad and chorizo sausages, then to hers for a salted caramel cheesecake, shared on the rich carpet of hers. It could have been my magic carpet to take us somewhere but there was no music... Grace jones filled the room with her voice and a weird world became alive. Some small black tiger statuettes became bigger and walked in the room with diamond necklaces around their necks, a lion appeared almost real in front of my face! The parrots of the wallpaper started flying in the room too and there she was naked in this scenario, lying right in front of me on the rich Persian carpet. All my fantasies! She changed the music to background jazz and said,

- 'I have an idea! You may think it's crazy... but I will say it anyway... I want us... to have a bath together. Come with me, take your clothes off, don't worry I will not be looking! You go in first and then me. I will light the candles... we will have a glass of something and we can read to each other anything you like from my books.'

' I will not be looking ' was stuck in my mind. All sorts of thoughts started rolling as to this challenge to get into a bath with her and how it would be... and all sounding scary but an adventure.

Her bathroom walls were all shelved with books and objects of interest and a free-standing bath in the middle of the black and white granite floor stood in all grandeur. As it filled with water, a little shy me, a student from Cyprus with one foot in Oxford, a brother wondering where I was and my parents not having a clue of my experiences, I bravely took my clothes off and hid under the foamy water. She simply walked in, so cool about herself took her clothes off, black bras and brief, exposing everything in front of my eyes. She elegantly sat at the other side of the bath with our legs touching all the way. I did not feel sure about that but had no choice in this expedition. One thing I was sure of, I was beginning to get a hard on and I was feeling embarrassed in case it showed above water level. She gave me a book of Rumi poems on love and she said choose one poem and I will choose another.

So, I read the following which I found appropriate

'At night, I open the window and ask the moon to come and press its face against mine. Breathe into me. Close the language-door and open the love-window. The moon won't use the door, only the window.'

She replied with this one

'Your task is not to seek for love, but merely to seek and find all the barriers within yourself that you have built against it.'

Later on, while excited in exchange of Rumi's quotes on love we found ourselves on the rich carpet with towels around us and on our heads too as turbans. I asked her to play some mystical music to take us places and she followed. Her carpet and the music took me to a room that was very hot and steamy and there were beautiful fragrances that opened one's heart. There were pots of oil and they started gently to wrap these oils into each other's body. I described the whole scene as I was traveling through. There were movements and touching of each other's private parts, passion and lust, voices of pleasure and the bodies became one with hands all over and deep breathing from both.

Matthew from the bible… *'Enter by the narrow gate. For the gate is wide and the way is easy that leads to destruction, and those who enter by it are many. For the gate is narrow and the way is hard that leads to life, and those who find it are few.'*

The music penetrated every aspect of the experience, gave them rhythm, their bodies were rubbing together and the body heat made them sweat and the opulent spread of pleasure filled their bodies and the room.

- 'Can you see all that'? I asked her.

She came from behind me and placed her hands on my back and she rubbed some oil on me, handed me the oil and said you can now touch me too. We created our own hot room and fantasized together but she was the first to touch my cock and she was looking at me straight in the eyes to feel my pleasure from masturbating me. I did not want this travel to ever end. She explored my body and she clawed me on my back and whispered - ' I want to eat you..torture you, i'ts bizarre, it is an awakening to passion and challenge. It is like an authority an ownership over your body...a pleassure'

As she whispered and feeling her claws on my bag there were lions walking by us, it was hot and one of them came right to my face... there was a smell of a dry soil, we were lost in another dimension of the letting go, weak and with no self-control.. I touched her body with my oily hands and her firm breasts, her waist and then her clitoris. She was totally mine, in my hands this beautiful soul that has probably never felt loved for who she is and what's inside her. A beauty! We became one as I penetrated her vagina in a lustful rhythm giving us both a long lasting pleasure and a fulfilment expressed in exhales of orgasm. We felt romantic. We were tested for our warm touch and respect for each other. I covered her with a thick blanket and placed a cushion under her head while she slept in my arms on the carpet.

The next morning, she cried on me saying she did not want this to happen to us. She wanted a real friendship from me which is missing from her life but she found me charming, polite, gentle and shy that she has never felt this in a man before, and she fell for that.

Strange to me, most women I met in my life have been attracted by my shyness and my mannerism! This awareness made me think of what attracts women and what they are looking for in relationships. Kate was a kind, sexy, spirited, spontaneous and caring soul, a bonny lass. She added so much confidence to my manhood. Let there be light, experiences, travels and scenarios add to who you become. I am a lucky man!

'Ask, and it will be given to you; seek, and you will find; knock, and it will be opened to you.' Mathew from the Bible.

MAKING SALADS

During my studies and as a part of the course, I had to also work for six months and I moved to Manchester where I was employed as a young chef in the cold kitchen of a Carvery restaurant, in the Crown square. A place where it was busy with judges and businessmen during lunch and with an older crowd in the evenings as there were special offers with soups, salads and cuts of meat.

I lived in a bedsitter at Didsbury, an outskirt in Manchester, and took the bus to work in the mornings and back late at night. My job was to make salads and soups in a kitchen of ten other chefs where the Head Chef was from Scotland. I loved his accent and although he was in a top white chef's hat and Kitchen pants, I chose to see him wearing a kilt and a black chef's coat and have always seen him smarter looking in my eyes. Ian was very shroud and sharp towards me and I could hardly understand his accent but loved his singing to me and rewarded him with my answers with 'aye' and 'nye' and my rrrs and my ooous and he laughed back at me.

It was all going well, as he was giving me the ingredients and telling me what salads to do, which I was following until the English manager, Tony, a very womanizer kind of a person, told me that women need different salads and could I bring in some other ideas. So, I did. Being Mediterranean and creative I started mixing in different dressing featuring cumin and basil, I used fresh coriander and baked the tomatoes in the salad, I made tahini dips and hummus with pesto, used pulses and all was becoming a rhapsody of colors and tastes. Comments were coming in until the crucifixion of the young Cypriot chef. At a kitchen meeting Tony in front of Ian, my Scottish chef, said to all that Paris has upgraded the whole kitchen level with the salads and that I should be suggesting more ideas for the hot kitchen too. Ian, has then stopped talking to me in a nice way and I seemed to have been his enemy. He was asking me to do more and more things, he was not letting me have a break and I had to clean all the kitchen at the end of the shifts. I did everything he wanted; my Scottish kilt was showing his real colors.

One day he brought me some almost rotten apples to make a salad mixed with cheese. I did that but to take away the old parts, I caramelized them in small pieces in the oven and mixed them with gorgonzola bits of cheese, fresh sage leaves and chicory. He did not serve the salad as he said it was not an acceptable combination. The same night, as it was busy and the salad bar was replaced a few times, I served everything we had in the fridge as well as the apple salad. The following morning at the meeting Tony, amongst other things, he queried as to whose idea was, the apple salad on the salad bar the night before. The Scottish chef apologized to him and said it was the Greek that did it and disobeyed his order not to serve it and he wanted me fired, showing me a knife he had in his hand. At that point Tony made it worse saying he found the salad amazing and that he also wanted to try me serving tables which was my salvation from my chef as I was going to get killed in his kitchen.

The table service was such a fantastic experience, meeting all sorts of serious people during the day, all talking about laws and money, properties and plans while at night all the sweethearts were coming in groups to eat. Gladys was a lady perhaps just over 80 years old. Short and curly red hair, red lipstick and lots of powder on the face, a blouse, pearls and jacket with a matching skirt and short heel shoes. She smelled of perfume and had a leather handbag hanging off her chair where I always stumbled on, while collecting their plates. I think she was placing it there on purpose. After a few visits and leaving me increasingly more tips, she started taking an interest in me, together with her friend Patricia, another old lady a little quieter as she could not hear very well. We went through conversations about me and where I come from, my family and my studies, my friends back home and they felt sorry for me being far away from home. Some nights they stayed behind at the closing and waited for me in the car outside so that they could drive me home, not having to take the bus as it was a little dangerous. I loved them both but especially Glady's whose husband died in World War Two and she has been alone with the memory of him since. They had no children but now she had a Labrador waiting for her every night.

I became Glady's point of reference at least every week. She was coming in the evening with a group of friends or with Patricia. She was booking in advance and asking if she could have a table in my section. I started giving back some of the love she showed to me and had a rose for all the ladies at the table on their napkin. Sometimes a love heart chocolate. They often asked me if I had a girlfriend in Manchester and I said, no I have in Oxford and Indeed I was in touch with Olivia and she was planning to come by train and visit me. Gladys was on my mind more and more and I cared for her, not having anyone else in her life and what happens to these people when they get weary and sick!

I invited her to have a coffee and cake with me. One afternoon, during my break, we went to a nice café nearby. I wore a jacket and I noticed there was a greater effort in her clothes too. She wore a black cocktail dress and held gloves and another leather handbag, more evening wear. The lipstick was fresh on her and she smelled something of Elizabeth Arden, as a lot of women of that era were on. I opened the door for her and I got into a gentleman's role looking after my date. I pulled the chair and waited for her to sit. She looked as if she enjoyed the ceremonial procedure. I paid compliments on how wonderful she looked. She had a golden necklace that her husband bought for her at their engagement, she said. We had a whole leaf tea, served properly in silver pots and real porcelain. As the cake tray came by, she looked at me and said with such a little girl's smile on her face, lifting her shoulders,

- ' Ooh... shall we be naughty? '.
- 'Well, why not? Naughty is nice!' I said, smiling.
- 'Paris... you are gifted with a nice smile. It shows you have a big heart', she complimented me.
- ' Oh... thank you, Gladys', I said. 'But look who is talking... Gladys, you wait for me to finish work and drive me to where I live. Can you understand how it felt for me being a foreigner in a big city and being looked after by a lady? You are special to me; you have a bigger heart than everyone I met over here and thank you for being so nice to me'

We shared two cakes each, raspberry cheesecakes, a lemon meringue, a strawberry tart and a chocolate delice. At one point, I loaded on my spoon, a mouthful of cheesecake with a raspberry on the top and moved my hand towards her mouth. She held my hand and brought the cheesecake to her mouth, taking it in and looking like a little girl that tried an ice cream for the first time. She looked around if someone else was looking at us and if she wanted that.

We talked about my early years, she wanted to know how Cyprus was and what I wanted to become in the future. I spoke to her about Mrs. Houri teaching me English and that perhaps I lived in other countries in previous lives,

'It's good to dream like that, I do it all the time' she responded.

I could not tell her; I see things and I travel to different sets as she would have thought I was mad! I asked her how she spends all her time at home and about her hobbies and her friends. She told me stories of her dog Max getting lost in the area she lived. She named Max after her lost husband as she wanted to think that he is still with her.

Such a splendid afternoon dedicated to friendship, flirt and love. If only she could feel that I wanted to squeeze her in my arms and say to her how happy I was to meet such a lady and how sorry I was she missed her most of her life without her man or any other man to love!

When it was time for me to leave the city and continue my studies, Tony, with all the restaurant staff, gave a little drinks' gathering in the function room and Gladys was invited too, which made me happy. The manager gave a small speech about good staff leaving behind a higher lever and that everyone has to continuously raise standards. Gladys came up front and gave me a kiss on the cheek and a hug and had a little cry coming out of her eyes while saying to all,

- ' I would like to tell you all how happy Paris made me feel, through being a charming, kind and caring gentleman and I wish him all the best things to happen to him and to find a good lady to love.'

My Scottish hero, Ian came right at the front too, and struggled in singing Scottish

- ' On Behav of tha Kitchen we wesh Paris, all tha saccess en to becoma chef... as he'll be gooud at et'.

I had a whiskey thanking everyone of this milestone and said that I was very fortunate to meet all kind of souls and they all gave me a lot to take with me!

MY FIRST JOB

In 1982, having received a professional qualification in the hospitality industry, I was interviewed in my speedo by a reputable hotelier in Ayia Napa, an upcoming holiday resort in Cyprus. As I happened to be enjoying a swim with his daughter, an old acquaintance suggested I meet her father, a serious man with a white beard sitting behind a grand desk. I stood there dripping with sea water and making a mess on his carpet. He asked about my studies and where I was born and whether I wanted to work in the hotel. That was all!

It was exciting to start at a five-star hotel as an assistant to the General manager, my first job. There I was young and fresh in the profession, parading amongst the clients and associates in my new and modern Italian cut suits, looking increasingly tanned and fit from the water sports. The nights were beginning to be exciting at that time in Ayia Napa, not yet the commercial young people's hotspot that became in the late 90s. There were people still in suits and long dresses and all elements of having an elegant time out mattered. I got to meet many different nationalities from Scandinavians to the British, Swiss, Austrians and Germans, and learned their individual idiosyncrasies or behavioral mannerism, as in understanding their cultures.

Some tourist company representatives were a good flirt, as they were popping in and out the hotel to check upon their clients. One Austrian soul approached me with wit and provocative humor in my presentation, stating that she has been following how smart I dressed and how different I behaved to the norm. I have put her directly under my spectrum. Valentina was a rather short lady with short bleached blond hair and sunburned skin. She used to appear daily with colorful dresses and unmatching accessories, with impressive weaved ropes tied around her hands and different patterned scarfs on her head with various color highlights in her hair. She was quite 'hippyfied' and had a very pleasant behavioral flair around her. Smiling all the time with a note of 'I don't give a shit' and parallel through her strong effort to speak English in an Austrian accent. She was a flirt and did not take her long to ask me out for a drink to a local pub, where I discovered that everyone knew her well and of her fast driving from hotel to hotel, often causing accidents on the way. I was quiet at first, as those days the strong personalities had priority over me, and I tend to be a little reserved and sometimes blushing.

The second date was at her apartment which was an extension of her colorful personality, with emphasis on a very cozy bedroom, provoking me at first glance. She tried to pour a drink but I dragged her into my arms and kissed her warmly with closed eyes. She was like a fish trembling in the hands of a shark and was ready to be eaten alive. We lied on the bed kissing, when that little fish suddenly came to be an octopus on me and sucking my lips. She opened up my shirt and my pants and felt my private parts. I helped her take her clothes off and we sexually presented our experiences to each other with the common purpose of self-satisfaction and again and again! She was repeating 'ayei, ayei' which reminded me of the Scottish yes, 'aye', but when I asked her, she explained that she felt wonderful and hot and that was her Austrian expression.

Her skin was so soft and her body was warm. I had visions of this hippie lady resembling a peacock having sexual intercourse around the fire with me and under the stars on my flying carpet on the way to the next stop. I was imagining colorful feathers raining on our bodies and yellow flares from stars traveling while Janis Joplin was at full blast. The whiskey also helped a little.

In the morning, she quickly got dressed and stormed out to go to work saying 'close the door on your way out'. I had time to shower in her feminine bathroom in pink towels and lots of bottles of cosmetics everywhere, but two toothbrushes by the bathroom mirror!

A few days later, since I felt there was more of what happened to be repeated, I caught up with her during her hotel visit and asked her out. She was not available because of a work meeting. That same night, I happened to go to another friend's pub, John's, and had a Scotch after work. Near the closing pub time, there she came and sat at the bar without seeing me. John got out of the bar and gave her a massive passionate kiss. A kiss that declared an existing relationship of some sort. Being a gentleman, I left quietly, not to be seen and to cause embarrassment. Strange fruit this one too!

A birthday invitation at hers followed and I went after work to meet all her friends, as well as John, who had a guest role in the whole social interaction, like myself. We enjoyed the music of Gypsy Kings as it is always an easy party solution and while some were pouring down their Margaritas. I had some of the whiskey I took with me. At a point John came near me to say cheers with his glass and he straight forward said

- 'Hi man! I know who spent the night here...! I recognized your car, then I knocked on the door but the music was so loud!'

I smiled and said,

- ' Well John... I know that the toothbrush in the bathroom is yours'.
- 'Actually not! I never slept here as she visits me at mines!' he replied
- 'Then who is the third criminal?' I wondered.

We both looked in the room to recognize a suspicious indication. The young restaurant manager in the corner? Or the sport's boy suntanned and trimmed? No social behavior expressed any conclusion that night but it did not matter to us.

Being all merit with all the ladies and guys at the party, we did the forever challenging game of spinning the bottle. My turn never came and I did not get to kiss any girl nor I was kissed. We all laughed about it and Valentine approached and whispered in my ears

- 'Stay the night with me!'

John looked at this from a distance and winked at me, indicating that he understood. The party ended, everyone left and we had a last drink and a slow dance together which was of course 'Careless whisper ' by George Michael.

The bed ceremony started with giving me a full body massage with coconut oil. It relaxed me and almost sent me to sleep. Then, she wrapped her body around mine and spread the surplus of oil from my body on hers, which had again the Octopus effect on me and aroused every inch of my body. I spent the whole night with her and listened again to her 'aye, aye' in enjoyment of our body actions. In the morning she left again first and repeated 'close the door when you go' to which I replied 'aye, aye' to her, and she laughed. I had a shower in her pink bathroom and left my toothbrush as a third one in the glass by the mirror! The Summer went on and my first job was getting more and more interesting and with more challenges in all spectrums.

Valentina was a beautiful flirt, a butterfly going from flower to flower. She chose her flowers, all so different, but never stayed long enough to get attached to one. Spectacular colors and moves and speedy flying courses. A few months later she was sent to another country to look after her clients and explore the culture of the destination. I wondered what colors she would be wearing and what highlights would have done to her hair then. We kept in touch till now and we often talk about other things but based on the past. We met later......

THE MOUNTAIN HOTEL

In the summer of 1980, when I was still a student and had the attitude of a premature hotel manager, I walked into an office where I was acquainted with a reputable lady, an economist, named Demetra. She was running a small hotel chain in Limassol, a seaside town in Cyprus.

- ‘Good morning Mrs. Demetra, my name is Paris, I am studying in Oxford for hotel and catering operations and need a summer job other than a beach boy and a house boy that all the other hotels offered me. If you think there is something in your hotel for me, we can talk’. I said, standing up.

She was wearing glasses and lowered her head and looked at me under her glasses for a couple of seconds. She drew a piece of paper and started writing, while she said in a tone of voice declaring authority

- 'Sit down’

I did not sit down but I carried the attitude and said,

- ‘I will sit only if you have a job for me!' To which she raised her voice and repeated
- 'Sit down!'

I felt I was in for a job offer but also that there is someone who can speak my language. I thought she liked my attitude in demanding serious respect for my positioning that I wanted a challenging job. She handed me the piece of paper, in beautiful writing, stating my salary of 600 pounds, plus hotel accommodation, plus meals and spoke

- 'On Monday, you will report to Mrs. Vaki, the finance controller and you will start as a food and beverage controller, costing menus and doing stock takings and supervisions for starters'.
- 'Thank you, very much, I will do my best' I said and walked out of the office feeling successful but insecure, as I have never done costings and stock takings!

I worked hard to be on time with costings and assessing recipes. I learned how to carry out stock takings in all the hotel's departments. I tried hard to be perfect for her. She would send me a buffet menu for 50 people and needed a cost for it in one hour to be on her desk. That entailed me spending time with the chef, writing down all the ingredients needed, getting the unit purchase prices from Mrs. Vaki and multiplying by the quantity needed so that I come up with an answer and taking into consideration many other factors like labor, energy etc.
When I would present my work to her, she would look at it carefully. She had a certain look on her face I could never tell. She would look at me under her glasses in all seriousness and she would correct my numbers instantly, as if she knew my mistakes in advance. I learned a lot from her.

She was stunning and always dressed eccentrically, in wonderful and unusual designer's clothes, a challenging spectacle. She had a rare personality and the wisdom of education in many sectors such as economics, politics, tourism, fashion and arts. We talked about everything from politics to travel, from economics to trends and there was always a warm business relationship between us. She inspired me with her strong personality and for being so dynamic. She would present her views on matters, at any cost and with confidence she would position herself so right. She had an attitude to always dare do new things and she succeeded. Through our collaboration that summer, I developed a great respect and admiration. We became good friends, we still are!

In 1983, having worked a year in the hotel in Ayia Napa, I walked again into Demetra's office for a coffee and a chat. Always very enjoyable to share time with her. She suggested a managerial job now at a small and picturesque Pinewood Valley hotel at the mountains of Troodos, belonging to the chain of hotels run by her. It had a certain feel of a Swiss Chalet. I had stables with horses to ride for the first time in my life and my Prince, a Belgian breed of an Alsatian dog, given to me by a family friend, a British General of the armed forces stationed in Cyprus, as he was moving back to the UK.

I interviewed a groom called Andreas while he was riding a donkey, off to pick up cherries in the fields. He had the jaws of a horse when he would smile and although he said he knew nothing of horses he became my companion riding together. We learned to ride horses together. He broke my everyday routine, as he was the only soul having a coffee and a chat with me. The hotel was busy mostly on weekends so there were no staff or guests from Sunday night to Friday lunchtime.

I jogged on the mountains, cycled the woods and lived with the trees, the wind and the sounds of them alongside the singing of the birds and bees. The mountains were fringed with pine trees forming thick forests and lush vegetation, so different to how I was imagining Scotland. Water streams were adding to the picture with that soothing sound of the water washing around the stones as it flows. I was never alone, there were people sometimes in the forest, they were watching me from a distance. They were hiding, but I could feel them... There was a beautiful smell here and there. The gigantic, exotic and colorful birds were flying happily around and sitting on the branches of the pine trees and singing melodiously. I enjoyed the happy sounds of Mozart's compositions. Sometimes, I would pick up a feather that dropped off the tree.

This placement was a good time for my career, as I made the hotel busier through serving imaginative food and offering high standard hospitality. I claimed a good reputation for myself. I was privileged to have Demetra coming sometimes to relax and go for a walk and talk about life and all concerns. Very precious times and always an inspiration.

On the weekends my friends Nikolas and Basil would come alongside other friends to stay in my quarters and relax but for me it was great to have some socializing going at least on the weekends... Nikolas was my sister's classmate whom I met at the annual carnival festival in Limassol town, many moons prior, which was the beginning of a great friendship I kept for years. He was kind and gentle, loved sports and music and we shared many times together talking and doing sports. He introduced me to jogging and bicycling. Nikolas was a very good-looking man in the likes of George Clooney and was still unmarried. I knew of his private affairs with certain women and were not to be announced! I was very fond of our friendship and I enjoyed spending time with him. Basil was a friend of my brothers from school and I got to have a better connection with her than my brother. We used to talk and go out to dinners and were like brother and sister.

One of Nikolas' friends, Evi was accompanying another lady, Mira, whom I had previously met one afternoon in Limassol when I was visiting an interior designer for advice on furniture manufacturers. She was there with him and never stayed long enough to understand their connection. However, Mira was coming almost every week and we formed a gang of regulars spending time at the mountains. It was her that she called me one weekday and broke my peaceful routine and expressed that she wanted to escape Nicosia and perhaps come for a midweek break. I offered to pick her up from Nicosia, an hour's drive from the hotel, as I combined it with some hotel work, I had to do in town. We traveled to the hotel through the forested mountain and rain on a cold night and when we arrived, I lit the fireplace where we had soup and bread with cheese and sausages cooked on the fire. I had a Scotch and she had a glass or two of red wine. My prince was sitting right next to me and enjoying listening to our conversations.

Mira was a dark hair version of Marilyn Monroe. Black sparkling eyes, thick lips, black weave hair to her shoulders, plenty of bosom and a small waist ending to a curvy backside, a good height and posture and a beautiful sensual smile. We enjoyed the warmth of the fire and a good chat on relationships hinting to me that she was involved with my interior designer friend but not anymore. I was surprised to hear that as my mind did not go there as I knew he was married. She also discussed our personalities with my bestie Nikolas and she also said that rumor has it that me and him are a gay couple to which she said, I know better.

She gave me a kiss goodnight on the cheek and thanked me for picking her up and for dinner. I was thinking that there is magic in sharing moments with a woman. There is something in the atmosphere that comes from conversations or movements or simply the existence of two souls in a space. It is as if other powers are around the room throwing shiny dust that makes your inner world bring out colorful flowers and happy butterflies.

She slept in one of the many empty hotel rooms while I withdrew, with my Prince, to our apartment right outside the hotel. The next day, we had breakfast and she followed me on my routine. We walked Prince and she waited while I rode the horses for some exercise.

Close to lunchtime, at the lounge of the hotel we lit the fireplace and sat on two armchairs right in front getting warm. The lounge was big and had a lot of sofas and armchairs, an empty bar at the end. Empty rooms but imagining people, there are groups, talking and sipping down drinks and coffees, children playing around, background music.... But now empty, just her and myself and feeling the opportunity, a power encouraging me to do anything I wanted in there. Everything was an option from creating a mood with music, taking my clothes off, eating or sleeping on the floor. The whole empty hotel was bringing out in me this predisposition.

Mira looked as if she needed to say something to me and

kept looking at me in a different way. She was very smooth and gently forward in her ways of talking, which added to her femininity for me. She was soft and kind, yes there was something about her. I felt uneasy, almost uncomfortable at what could be unfolding, but I started pouring out stories.

Once, the horses were on the loose while the groom opened the stable gate to feed them. I looked everywhere in the forest. Hours later, I found them walking happily on the road, with a massive queue of cars behind them and with the drivers being very patient. When they saw me, they walked right next to me as if they wanted me to lead them back. I stroked their heads and spoke softly to them to make them relax with me. I walked in front of them and they followed me unleashed into their stables.

Mira looked drawn by the story and smiling she said

- 'Woah that's amazing that you have such a good connection with your horses! But I would not expect anything different as you seem to be the master of many trades!'

- 'Oh, thanks for the compliment but it's me that should be complimenting you being so pretty!' I expressed looking away at the fire, and carried on talking to be engaged as I was nervous about what was possible to happen between us.

- 'Another story that happened to me is that I have convinced the area policemen to steal, with the official Police Land Rover, an ornate wooden municipality bench at the side of the road in a village further down, as I wanted to place it in the garden of the hotel. So, one night a Police Land Rover loaded with the bench arrived here and it became my secret with all the area policemen.'

She smiled and the stories went on until she touched my hand and simply said

- ' I like spending time with you. You are different!'

That was a good platform I was familiar with, to which I wanted to say in return 'and I find you so fucking attractive', but words did not come out and smiled instead as an answer keeping my thoughts to myself. She was calm and patient. It took me a few seconds to build a sentence in my mind, which felt like a whole day and managed to say

- ' I feel that you are special too, and beautiful... I don't know what you are doing here alone with me'.

She got up, looked me in the eyes, came close to me and sat on my legs. I was feeling nervous and I could feel my heart beat becoming faster. She gently grabbed my face with both hands and forwarded those lush lips to touch my own. I got lost and drunk in the feeling of mist, I could not feel my legs but I was burning inside. I felt an adrenaline growing in my chest and moved my hands around her back and squeezed her towards my body. It felt sensational, I diverted my eyes from looking at the fire and wondered around her neck and breasts… exploring the feast.

We slid to the floor in front of the fireplace and while kissing we started slowly to take each other's clothes off. Her lips were silky soft and her neck was to be kissed. Her eyes were closing in enjoyment of the feeling of being kissed and that provoked me to do more. The light was magical, glowing a deep orange on our bodies, creating shades on the curves of her body that I wanted to touch. I fantasized I was with Marilyn. There was the sound of burning wood, but I could also hear some background jazz, on and off and wanted to cut the music off as it would take me elsewhere. Touching her curves and looking at her lips I could not resist myself to anything other than what was lustfully possible. We moved in all possible angles and sides, there was pleasure, enjoyment and happiness. Prince at one point got jealous, as he had never seen dad naked on the floor with a lady, and came to give us a lick too!

I chose to believe that I was having a weekend relationship with Mira. She kept spending time with us up there. Sex had been a part we were both looking forward to. Sometimes, she was hurting while having sex and asked if it was my fault and whether I was doing things wrong, but never got to find out. She simply smiled and said, no it's nothing, do not worry.

These weekend experiences carried on for the whole of winter season, with all my gang around us and all having fun. The next spring, the visits happened every other week, as Marilyn went to other towns and villages to explore, with her friend Evi. After sometime, she expressed that she wanted to have a break, only to find out, from my friend Nikolas that she had formed a lesbian relationship with Evi! Hard enough for a young man, just as he begins to feel a little macho overcoming whatever can be male insecurities and shyness that such a catch of a woman, left you for another woman! It did not do me any good and was not sure of trusting women even when indicating that they were happy or at least pleased with me. However, the page was turned and I have explained it all to Prince when we had a whiskey on our own around the fire on many other nights!

One beautiful morning, after I took Geronimo, my beautiful black horse for a ride, I went into the kitchen to prepare breakfast for Andreas, my groom, and myself. Andreas has gone on his favorite horse, Speedy, for a long ride, before me. He did not come back for quite some time which was not the norm. I got worried and took Geronimo in search of Speedy and Andreas. I was calling his name in the woods and I could hear my voice echoing around the mountain slopes. I followed the routine path through the trees and towards the water streams. After a good twenty minute ride, I could see Speedy standing loose near some trees. I called Andreas' name and Speedy started squealing as if to communicate attention. We galloped there and found my groom on the ground and blood out of his ears. I jumped down from my horse in despair and Andreas was unconscious. I slapped him on the face and shouted his name hoping he would respond and to bring him back to his senses. Presumably, he fell off the horse and hit his head on a massive stone, as he dropped. I called his name again feeling useless! My loud voice turned into tears, as there was no breathing and he was cold and white. I tried to put methodical pressure on his heart. He was gone! I was so upset. The horses felt the moment too, as they stood next to one another looking at me in silence. We were all friends and now in the middle of nowhere.

I remembered in the army how we were taught on how to get hold of a wounded body off the ground. With great difficulty, you lie down next to the injured body and pull his hand over your back as you bend your knees to slowly raise yourself off the ground with the body crossing yours. With extra strength I laid him on my horse back and walked to the stables. It was a horrible walk with tears in my eyes, perhaps the horses cried too. I had no answers. I notified the police and his family. People came from all neighboring villages to find out the details and spread the news as not many things happen up there. A horrific experience losing a friend like that. It was hard. I said to myself, one moment was happiness and next moment was a tragedy, no one knows what is laid in front of us and when your candle will burn out.

ELLA

Having built a reputation as a good manager, young and full of ideas, I was given a challenging job to move back to Ayia Napa, to one of the busiest hotels on a landmark beach, called Nissi. Everyone in Europe knows the white sands Nissi Beach in Ayia Napa, like everyone knows Ipanema in Brazil. I took Prince with me alongside my bicycle and we lived in an apartment above a pub. I had a full routine of sleeping from 8 to 10 in the morning and 3-6 in the afternoon. The rest of my time was allocated to work and sports. My friend Nikolas followed me some weekends as we shared time jogging and bicycling. He was then days in a relationship with a young woman that later on left him as she went on with another woman and caused a lot of funny jokes between the two of us having the same experience.

At Nissi beach there were more than four thousand almost naked bodies every day, and most looking to feel good with a suntan, to enjoy the movement in the water, to socially interact, to drink and relax, to dance and explore all their wishes, sexual too. These were the days in the mid-80s: everything was possible, you could meet everyone you liked and friendships and bonds were built. Those days there was an influx of tourists from the Scandinavian countries, the UK, Austria, Germany and Switzerland too.

For me it was perhaps the beginning of the craziest times of my life. I was responsible for eight bars, two restaurants, a live music venue and a night club and my presence with an administration role was very significant in all. I lived through this work load as a routine for months. I was 26 years of age and perhaps one's body is recharged in the sun. I was solar powered!

There was a club called Mamas which was my concept

and idea to recreate a playground for people to play with toys, nothing like sex toys, while dancing, drinking and socializing. The space was used years before as a disco, so with some renovations and additions, it became a colorful disco with teddy bears, beach buckets, light pistols and other stuff. Once with some drinks on you, all the silliness came out. Everyone needs a Mamma and they all came for her! Older men and women playing with water guns with each other and laughing their heads off, young ladies dancing with Teddy bears, some wearing funny glasses, some in a more serious disco inferno mood on the dance floor. It was the time of Boogie Wonderland! It was a place to release yourself and be someone else. Anyway, they all looked to me as someone else from what they were in real life. It was another zoo, men in skirts and fancy hats, clowns, naked women with aprons, nurses, mothers with babies, dads with pistols, cowboys and Indians, all looking to make someone else out of themselves for a while. Escapisms!

Mammas was successful which gave me the passport to be wanted to be met by many as this was a new idea in the area and creating a buzz.

One night, I was welcoming at the entrance a large group of people while inside the zoo was in full gear with loud dance music and flashing lights. An English lady approached me and said,

- 'Are you the manager here?'

- 'Yes, you can say that!' I replied in humor which she totally received

- 'Well, tell me, where can I get a mop? Your ladies' toilets are blocked. Or perhaps you store them here,' she said, opening a closet and grabbing a mop.

She went to the toilets and three minutes later she came back and placed the mop back in the closet. I looked at her and said,

- 'What is your name? What do you do here?'

- ' I am Peggy, pleased to meet you!' and gave me her hand. 'Obviously I am having fun! What do you do here?' she asked with a smile.

I smiled back and said,

- 'I am the zoo keeper but also looking for my Mamma! Come on, let's go to the bar and have a drink'.

- ' Good idea' she replied with a surprised expression on her face, and continued to talk towards the bar.

- ' I can work in this zoo as well, if you have any job. It will be so much fun!" she said.

We went to the bar, and I asked her for her choice of a drink. A double Jameson whiskey with no ice! I had a double Scotch with one ice cube!

It was the fastest interview I ever had and was the start of a beautiful and hilarious friendship in my whole life to follow. Peggy was from a very complex background with divorces and relationships of all kinds and had a forever inquisitive mind ready to explore and explode at the same time and sky was the limit. We drove to five-star hotels for potato chips dipped in vanilla ice cream, we drank refined Bordeaux wines, but loved our whiskey too. We had a great bond and lots of laughs about ourselves and everyone else around us. I was describing to her what I was seeing in other people around us and she had enjoyed my colorful birds and the music played and she was participating, asking questions for more descriptions. At that stage of our connection, she helped behind the bar and tried to entertain and looked after the crowds. We were on a daily basis, friends for life.

Another soul asked me for a job at Mammas. A beautiful black girl from Denmark, a jazz singer with a curvy body with abig bosoms, a cheeky smile with white teeth, curly hair and a flower always on her head, in the style of Billie Holiday. She worked as a barmaid but should a song have appealed to her; service was abandoned as she was in the middle of the floor dancing her head off to the sexy beat. She was every man's dream to get their leg over this one and she did not stop challenging everyone. Her name was Ebony and she was under my protection as all these men were after her and suggested various sexual fantasy scenarios to her. But I understood her more. She was so troubled by men in her life that she trusted no one and she would run a mile away from any awkward situation she would have found herself in. She had the hot looks demonstrating the opposite of what she really was, a rather reserved and conservative towards the opposite sex.

Ebony was always happy, hyper, kind and funny. She had no direction. She loved her vodka. I had to keep an eye on her! At Mammas she wore a piece of beach cloth in multiple colors which suited her and made her more exotic as she wrapped it around her breasts. She was always in flip flops and a flower on the side of the ear. That was the trademark. One of those nights, drunk after work and scared by a fat and old policeman who blackmailed her to either go to bed with him or he would call immigration to arrest her, she came sobbing to me for protection. She was on a tourist visa which meant she could not legally work. When we closed the club, I drove her to her apartment and instead of going in, she asked to sleep with me at mine and that she did not expect anything from me.

I took her to my apartment where she met an excited Prince, and made the sofa into a bed for her. She fell asleep immediately. In the middle of the night, she came to my bed. I felt her body spooning mine and her hands coming over my chest. She was still asleep and I carried the burden of a scared soul finding refuge and security in me.

She carried on sleeping in my bed, whenever she wanted as she had a key and I was her protector. I felt familiar sleeping with a black woman and I sometimes 'traveled' to Africa as if I arrived in a village and I was given a bed with a woman to enjoy. It is a gesture to honorary visitors from the Chief of a tribe offering a woman for hospitality and pleasure. I could see that as the time went on, she started looking at me differently from being a boss to a protector and to being a man too! One day as she was getting on her bike she turned and said to me ' I have never been to bed so many times with a man and did not make an advance on me!' and she drove off.

Funny they all are in so many ways, I thought. What do they really need? Attention? Protection? Sex? Conversation? One has to be there at the right time and be who they expect to be!

People thought we were a couple, as they saw her coming to my apartment at all hours and walking Prince, when I was at work. One night, while at work, I received a call by another club owner to go and pick up Ebony before the police goes there. I drove as fast as I could, to face my girl topless dancing in the middle of the dance floor but with the flower still on her head and a lot of men cheering her. I squeezed in the circle and pulled her cloth to cover her breasts, she looked at me and kissed me passionately in front of everyone. I was angry to see her drunk and in such a situation but thrilled that she made the first move. The truth pops out easier when you have some drinks! I literally picked her up, as the groom would pick up his bride, and stepped up in the car.

I drove her to my apartment. She was drunk and did not want to let me go. She insisted on undressing me and asked me to have sex with her. I said to her, 'have a glass of water and in 20 minutes we can talk about it', but she would not take no for an answer. We did have sex and it was just an act of lust for the moment. She then fell asleep and I went back to work feeling awkward, as I did not want things to have happened like that.

When I returned home, after work and tired, she made soup for us and laid the table. She had a big smile on her face. She sat me at the table and poured a glass of whiskey for me and a glass of water for her. She dimmed the lights and she stood in the middle of the room and started singing Ella's Fitzgerald 'If I give my heart to you'.

My legs were trembling as I truly lived the moment that Ella was in my apartment. She was, and I was in that smoky jazz club in the 30s. I was sitting at the bar looking at the band. There was a handsome saxophonist and a ....smell in the room, a pleasant one has interrupted the scene. She had the voice, the looks, the face that smiled sunshine to me and the heart to be who she really was. I lived to travel. A woman in front of me as she wanted to be, real. I was proud of her for having the guts to do so, her voice too. I clapped my hands and I squeezed her in my arms the whole night long in my bed.

She has stopped drinking as much as other nights, and she was at home as early as possible, forever teasing me that I am scared of her, a stuck-up manager and I don't make moves towards her. 'What sort of a man are you' echoed in my ears!

So, the plan was formed. She has received a printed invitation that I made, to a night out with me. Things were going to be my way. She perhaps thought that we were going to have a meal at home or go out for a meal and then home for sex, as per her challenge. I picked her up at seven at night and we drove to the pub. I held her by the hand, as we went in, and she froze to see the fat policeman that was forever chasing her. I insisted, all is well and to keep her hand straight and be next to me. We went and sat with him, as I had prior invited him there. I offered a drink to everyone, while he was looking at her. He seemed uncertain as to what was to follow, and so did she. So, in a voice tone of a dictator, I said to him,

- 'This is my girlfriend Ebony, and I want to ask you a favor, as a man to a man...to respect my companion. I want you to look after her when you see her on her small moped going to work. There are a lot of men that run after her, not for a good reason. I would appreciate that'.

He took a few seconds to compose his words and agreed, whether he liked what I said or not. We all cheered and I invited him to the club, the day after, for drinks.

In the car, Ella remained speechless but stared at me with a look of envy, until we arrived at our party place for the night! The amusement park! She grew a big smile on her face.It was a young girl's smile in excitment as she realized my spontaneity and madness. The flashing colorful lights placed us immediately in the mood for a party and it was not Mammas club! We went on every possible slide and bumping electric cars. We played games and ate with our fingers chicken sticks and fries and made a mess with tomato sauce on each other. We laughed so much feeling young and irresponsible all over again. I loved to see her happy. We never forgot how to be children at the Luna Park but sexy adults at home later on. She saw another side of her rescuer, boss, friend and lover...

LASCIVIOUS

Later that summer, Ebony left for Denmark, as it was the end of her holiday time in Cyprus. We said goodbye and it was moving to both of us having lived different relationships together as boss and employee, friends and lovers. There were no promises to meet again, it felt like the end of knowing each other and that our paths were not likely to cross again. As she left, I had the responsibility taken away from the role of being the protector and had more freedom to enjoy free time, when not at work, getting to know guests frequenting the restaurants and bars.

Jenny, an old repeater of Nissi Beach Hotel, introduced me to her daughter, visiting from the UK. Her introduction featured a certain facial expression implying that you two need to get to know each other. Julia, had dark skin, straight black hair and a very large pair of boobs right in front of your eyes. She was a little butch, a description I stored for women, when not so feminine in movements and mannerisms. Me being me, polite and gentle, I avoided looking at her. as you couldn't not escape targeting your eye on her attractive pair of those, which was the talk of all male waiters on the floor. We had the usual holiday makers chat while all members of their group were at the table. As they have spent lots of money, I extended an invitation to the venue with live music, for a complimentary drink after dinner.

I cannot say that I have crossed any lines other than being professional. Somehow, at the nightclub venue, their daughter kept asking me to sit at their table, to which I tried to avoid many times and even showed a dislike at the end. I wanted this relationship with the group to stay at a professional level and to keep safe distances. After some drinks and on her way to the ladies, she stopped at the bar and asked to talk to me after work. I could not look her in the eyes. I knew what that meant, more unnecessary trouble.

After work, we walked around and stood under a tree. She said that she found me very polite, attractive and interesting, but was I gay? I should have said yes, but I replied with a smile 'some think I am!' She smiled and suggested we walk towards the beach and we did just that. I was feeling nervous about what may unroll in front of me. On the way through the gardens of the hotel, there was a big palm tree, a tree that still stands there and I see it every time I visit Nissi Beach Hotel. She pushed me towards the trunk, pulled my shirt and tore the buttons off, as in the movies. She made her moves as a hungry lioness. A scene from the film Fatal Attraction. There was violence and force and it does not work for me. I grabbed her shoulders and gently tried to distance her from my body. I was recalling some ancestry powers to guide me, as to how to handle the situation. I had no reference. I did not want anything sexual to happen. I could have been romantic, savage or retaliated with rejection. I did none of these but somehow felt noble to accept it. I declared reserved and suggested a slower progression to interaction! She started kissing my chest and working her way down, as she unbuttoned my pants and started giving me pleasure. I asked her to stop. I was confused, I felt angry and embarrassed at first, but as the excitement creeped in, lust for pleasure took over my debate. The only possible option, I had on my cards, was to lose control. I had surrendered to her. She dragged me on the ground and sat on me, aiming to succeed in her plans. She did all the work and led the way. Those beautiful round and firm breasts of hers were going up and down which accelerated the happy ending.

I was worried, while she was hoping up and down that someone may pass by the gardens and see the assistant manager of the hotel, having sexual intercourse with the clients, a Daily Mail story! It was over fast enough, she then kissed me and said:

- ' Woah that was amazing, Paris. You made me so happy! I would like to continue in my hotel bedroom'.

- ' I did not want this to happen! I really have to go home to attend to some matters and my dog Prince is waiting for me the whole day... perhaps some other time' I said.

She touched my face with force and said,

- ' I will come with you then. I want to meet Prince and we can walk him together'

I wanted to leave the whole idea there and then, I disliked the word together and said in a stronger voice

- ' This will not be a good idea for tonight. But let me ask you as I don't know anything about you. How is your life, what do you do in the UK?'
- 'I am a lorry driver. I work for a company transferring goods from the UK to France and back, twice a week.'

I had visions of her amongst those lorry drivers, driving massive tracks, full of produce and stopping on the motorways for meals in gangs with those huge and rough looking men. I suppose many were her close friends.

- 'Rough life', I replied with a smile!'

I have avoided her until her last days there. When we said goodbye, in the hotel lounge, she kissed me in front of her family and my staff and said she would be in touch.

A week later I received a postcard saying that she felt that I was not open to show my real feelings to her. She would stop driving the lorry, if I would ask her to live with me, and it ended,' one of us is in the wrong country!'

Honestly... such a big step because of what happened once under the tree?

I had no type of such a situation, as a reference in my mind, to manage my thoughts nor I have met any of my sister's friends at home with such persistence to see things differently than the reality. We were two completely different people and operating totally on different platforms. During this brief interaction of a couple of days, she has managed to convince herself that I was the one, or that this is the life she would want to have. She blind folded herself and did not allow any room to consider me, my world, my thinking and certainly the fact that

I wanted to be free from any of such commitments while 'en route' to finding more in life. I hate to disappoint people. The same way, I feel when I am not where I promised to be for people. Little me was promised independence and freedom, integrity and on a course to conquer so many experiences. I had a whole world of mine around me, what would have happened to those?

I was called by the hotel's manager, Christos, to his office. Serious and experienced, as he was there many years, we were meeting once a week for a coffee and to catch up. We talked about the usual hotel business agenda and on the way out he said to me jokingly,

- 'I was told by Mrs. Jenny that her daughter is planning to move to Cyprus as she fell in love with you.'

My face must have showed my horror in an expression and I said,

- 'I hope not, as this is not something that I want in my life' I carried on and said,
- 'Something happened during their stay that I did not want to happen. I will not be responsible for her decision to move back here'.

He smiled back to me in full understanding and said,

- 'Oh, you, young people!'

One morning, as I opened my apartment door in my jogging shorts and with Prince, ready to go for our run, Julia stood there with a bag of bakeries. I was shocked to see her. My face was concerned and unhappy. I took a big breath and said,

- 'Hi... when did you arrive in Ayia Napa?'
- 'Good morning, Paris, it's good to see you. I just arrived from the airport and wanted to see you first-thing!'
- 'Oh... good, yes... I'm.., I'm on my way for a run with Prince, can we talk later....why are you back?' I asked her. She touched her hair as a sign of feeling uncomfortable and said,
- 'Well after you did not reply to my postcard....I decided to come to see you. We have a week off as UK is on strike on the French border and I came with a girlfriend of mine' she

replied.

I apologized to Prince for a few minutes as a joke and asked her in. I sat her at the dinner table and gave us two glasses of water. I sat opposite her and I could not look her in the eyes nor her cleavage, obviously proposed to me.

- ' Julia…', I said in a sincere tone of voice. ' Sometimes people meet and they are attracted to one another. You are a beautiful girl. You have a job in the UK and a life there. I am on a career growth journey and have a different plan for the future than being with someone right now. Perhaps, I will never settle with anyone. This is how I feel right now. You have an impression of me that I was important to your life. I am afraid you have to stop thinking like that and accept that I want to go another way in my life and you are not in this plan. I am sorry to tell you this….'

She started crying. I got up and gave her a hug and she was crying in my arms. I must have said ten times

- ' I am sorry'.

- ' But...I love you to belong to me', she said crying

- ' No...no...no! People belong to people, you want to enslave me not love me. If you love me you should respect and embrace my dreams and let me go' I replied with a tone of compassion.

Just like a poisonous snake, she looked at me and the tone of voice changed and the tears became poison ready to bite in my body. She slapped me twice on the face and howled to me

- ' Then why did you let me make love to you that night? It was so magical, you cannot understand! '

- 'I did not expect it, I did not ask for it, and I did not want to reject it and I did not provoke it either'. I replied in defense and in the same tone of voice.

She stormed out and she shouted

- ' You are a waste of time, I hate you... you don't know what you are missing!'

Indeed, I did not know and I never found out! It felt sad to hurt her. I could not really understand why she expected a different reaction.

THE FRENCH BISTRO

Towards the end of the summer, in 1985, I planned to change direction from an employee to become an entrepreneur and open up my own first restaurant. I remember going to the bank manager with some casual configuration of numbers on a piece of paper as a means to ask for a bank loan. I had in the bank just 600 pounds and was asking for 1,000 more being the 50% of my estimated investment those days. I hoped to have been able to pay the rest on credit terms.

When my mind is creating a new screenplay, all my senses are in full force and I become ready for everything, full of energy and excitement. That can be directed and consumed through flirting. I am not so shy in these situations, but spontaneous and dangerous. My friends Peggy from Mammas and Nikolas knew this side of mine.

I found an old farm house to rent, built of stones in 1924, in a corner of Ayia Napa. Everyone thought I was nuts to make a French Bistro out of it. Peter, a Swedish tourist representative passed by while renovating the farmhouse. He looked at me assuring me of my failure to make use of it as a French Bistro. He had visions of a French restaurant being red carpets and crystal chandeliers and could not envisage a country style farmhouse restaurant! A new annex was built to accommodate the kitchen, the walls were restored, doors and windows were scrubbed and repainted blue traditional colour. A garden was planted and additional flower pots were grouped here and there.

On the second of April 1986, we opened this bistro with authentic French home cooking specialties. We panicked as in the middle of service there was a power failure in the kitchen but no one noticed in the garden. We were excited to feature liver pates and vegetable terrines, warm cassoulets and roasted ducks, different first quality cuts of meats and fish was daily fresh in for creations. Snails and frog's legs too. The meats were mostly grilled with elegant sauces with caramelized onions and meat juices infused with fresh herbs and home baked steamy bread, cut on every table. We had Vin de table, but also many distinguished wines and champagnes of distinction. Every day we prepared a different menu, chalked on a blackboard, from where people would choose their courses.

I used to wake up in the mornings and shop at the local markets hand picking the vegetables and searching the fridges of the butchers for the finest meats. I was then making some preparation in the kitchen for the cooks to continue in the afternoon. In the evenings, I used to wear my apron and bow tie, every day a different one, bought on trips or given as presents by friends. I took orders and served our customers, alongside the staff. I loved it, as we were giving a unique experience to an audience.

On entering, you step into the courtyard under a wrought iron portal entwined with trailing vines. The courtyard featured ancient olive trees and the sculpture-like trunk of a very dead eucalyptus tree, marking the old age of the building. The aromas of mint and basil was penetrating the balmy evening air. There were multi-colored geraniums spilling out of some earthenware pots while the pomegranate trees and a lush bougainvillea has taken over a corner of the building – a vivid shock of purple and pink hues. A veritable feast to the eyes!

We had no electricity in the garden as mostly we used oil lamps and candles. We played classical music at first, but old French songs and jazz later on as the bar entertained lots of customers before and after dinner. It was all about a contrast, gravel on the ground, no electricity but huge crystal wine glasses, and superb food. On the wooden table, featuring old sewing machine metal bases, lace cotton table mats and hand crochet napkins were laid alongside old designed cutlery from Sheffield and distinguished crockery collected along the years.

There was contrast, coming from my parents' diverse backgrounds. A simple environment with gravel on the ground but exceptionally set up on the table paired with brilliant food ideas.

During this creative stage, creating menus and matching ingredient combinations, I met a girl called Joy, young and happy, a party animal, an excellent socializer, easy going with an open mind, ready for adventures and daring to try everything. She was seeing another man, very unaccounted by myself, although quite successful in business, good looking and with plenty of cash. I kept seeing her around and there was real joy as she entered any space. After all, she deserved to be named Joy, indeed. I found out where she worked and I kept sending a red rose to her from an unknown admirer. This went on for a month nonstop and no one else knew about it.

While this was carrying on, another lady, Chrissie, won my attention quite the opposite of Joy. We met at a cocktail party at Nissi Beach Hotel, where I was invited as I knew some of the repeating guests. A serious, knowledgeable lady, sophisticated, and life experienced, as she traveled the world. She was married to an English gentleman, an officer in the army. It was a couple that I enjoyed socializing with and listening to their heavy British accent, and their humor too. They often teased me of my occasional Scottish pronunciation of words popping out. Chrissie found me polite and interesting to talk to. We got to know each other well. We used to have regular wine sessions in the evenings and earl gray sessions at all times of the day. She was tall and had crazy, curly long hair and resembled Meryl Streep in the film French Lieutenant's woman. She had a deep voice and she loved to laugh and to crack jokes over everything. We had endless story telling sessions and I got to know so many things about many countries, politics and world economics from her. I was absorbed in her stories and I was fascinated by her. I treated her like royalty and I tried to be a real gentleman, always giving priority and care wherever we were going. At some point she amicably got separated by her husband but we carried on this friendship for quite some time. I used to call her a lady with tea hair.

When it was time for me to open The French Bistro, it was her that planted a meter long Bougainvillea tree, in a corner of the building, which grew and grew like her hair and I liked to think that the tree took after her. One of the persons that had a strong impact in my life and still has. She had a way of talking about small things that were so important really, like when someone gives you something, to enjoy the mannerism and the gesture prior to the present, whatever it may have been. She had a way to pay attention to all persons she came across, young or old and see through them and pinpoint some elements that make her smile, whether it was a piece of information, or an expression or an unusual word. I have adopted her ways. She showed me other spectrums in life, bonding with people, nature and I felt lifted to another level when in conversation with her.

I met Chrissie later on in life, in 1999, in London. I was honored to go out, just the two of us, instead of a hen's party! We went to a local Italian restaurant for wine, food and laughs, prior to marrying another English gentleman, Michael, a charmer and related to royalties. At her wedding I represented her family and friends giving a speech, excelling the virtues and physiognomy of my friend. Actually, I cannot remember what I have really said, as champagne was flowing for a good two hours prior. But she was excited with my words expressed and everyone clapped and cheered when I delivered my speech!

Joy and Chrissie inspired me and added the spices, the color and the taste in the creations of the food. I was excited in their company and excitement brought me creativity. They kept me on the search for new combinations of taste pairing prunes, mint and earl gray tea in an ice cream cake or sizzling duck breast with fresh raspberries and orange segments in honey caramel sauce and more! I was hyper in searching for 'things' in them, different 'things', which reflected back into my work. It is like that!But back to Joy and the flowers, as one day she came into the pub with one of the roses. I asked her

- ' Hello you, give us a smile and a smell of your rose'!
- ' Which rose would you like to smell?' she replied with wit. I blushed and yet got into it saying
- 'Well...it all depends what license I hold! I am still a learner! She smiled and ended up with both of us laughing.
- 'I was thinking.... would you like to join me to disco dancing later on?' I suggested in anticipation
- 'Sure... pick me up at 11 after my shift and let's go dancing' she happily confirmed.

I left with a thrilling smile on my face. That night we danced and laughed and were silly to all around us. She seemed to have had this effect on me, to make me follow her and do silly things. These meetings carried on other nights and other nights... We became close, there was no sign of the other man, and one night after drinking and dancing at a club, I got kissed in the car and afterwards in my apartment. The following day I sent the last rose but now signed!

She loved Prince, but my continuously unfolding craziness, too. It is a fact that different people bring out different things in you. She had a key to my apartment and my life, as we started living together most nights. For the first time at the age of twenty-eight, I started, on unconditional and temporary terms, living with a woman. A big step. New things and everything different from now on! I did not know what to expect every night when I went home after work. A party or a themed drink session between the two of us. A decorated house with weeds from the fields, a stable theme or new furniture throughout? But that was the whole fun of it. For the first time, someone else was creating a mess around me! It was the name of the game, not knowing what to expect from Joy! More food was created in new plates, colorful and with different shapes now! A decomposed Millefeuille with thin down 'crème pâtissier' with Eau de vie, featuring crusted filo pastry sheets and wild juicy strawberries dusted with icing sugar and nutmeg on the top. There was a terrine of a trio of fish, salmon, trout and sea bass, composed in layers and served with avocado, mango, orange and basil salad and more refreshing taste combinations.

The restaurant was established and appreciated by food critics too as it offered contrast and sophistication, lifestyle, character and old charm, bloody good food and exceptional wines. It was not long that I was recognized as a leading chef and entrepreneur on the whole island. Customers came from Greece and even France, Sweden and Norway especially to holiday in Ayia Napa just to experience the restaurant. You see, me being the producer of my mental travels and scenario sets, I created a stage where everyone could have a role to play. Roles in a scenario of superb night out, great food and music, positive feelings exchange and once you do that successfully, you will have more encores!

The gastronomic interest of this restaurant was forever changing for the better. It started as a French traditional bistro, but later on, with me traveling in the winter months it progressed. Once France was consumed, I traveled to the then French colonies for inspiration like Martinique and Morocco, which brought more influences and a complex development in the cuisine.

All those strong smells and vibrant tastes, the creations and the colours and shapes of on the plates were combined also with my life experiences, sexual or not, from the days back from the first kiss to Nina, Cilia, Marilyn, Ella and all others. I believed that the way we eat says a lot of how we are in bed and vice versa. I was having sex, while I was creating ingredient combinations. Sometimes, I would cook at three in the morning and share it with my partner in bed after or prior to our interaction. Even now this is one of my streaks. I would prepare a meal for those celebrating and fill them up with love through the inspiration brought to them by taste.

I was creative and never bored. Things out of the ordinary have a tremendous effect on us humans. In relationships too. Breaking free from routine. Brings an immense feeling of satisfaction and achievement, a positive recharge of the batteries, a reason to carry on.

Affected, also by what I was tasting in my travels, everything I read in books and living the experiences with all the other players. I wrote a book, as if I was in a corner of this theater and observed the people playing the various roles. The theater was my restaurant. I was perhaps an actor too like them and had a role in my stories. I could have been any of them. The book was called 'Notes and Bows'. Notes all jotted down on a scrap paper during those special summer nights as I sat back in a corner watching myself, others and life.

'... at times people inspire and affect me positively. I enjoy looking after good looking, interesting people, especially young ladies that have that sense and style to dress in a feminine way! I feel responsible to offer them the dishes that suit the occasion... Once I felt I was melting in front of a brunette with exotic mystery eyes as she elegantly had a mouthful of champagne and asked in that smooth tone of voice what would I want her to have since she wished to eat light. I asked the cook to prepare thinly sliced duck livers in honey and raspberry wine which I decorated with loads of purple mint flowers and I presented it myself. I went through a patch decorating dishes with all kinds of flowers! I felt that everybody should be happy and full of sparkles!

However that night, the brunette went off on an impressively powerful bike with a broad-shouldered man, gelled hair, black T-shirt, kind of a Mickey Rourke look alike!'

Extract from 'Notes and Bows'

The restaurant brought in many new experiences to me. Creations, acquaintances, getting to know different nationality characteristics alongside success and acknowledgements. Now being older, with less reservations, I could really come out in colours and conquer anything on my way, any subject that would attract my attention. I still did not have answers as to what exactly women are looking for in a man. Or what am I looking for in a woman, as all the time it is different, new and creative, like every plate on the menu. One thought that was very strong in me, was that I wanted to place new dishes on the menu, different, new and creative. This thought did not allow me to sacrifice my independence and lead me to be free from attachment, which I began to love.

The freedom to create dishes took me around the world, mentally but physically too. I lost myself in India and Cuba for six months and experienced and thought of everything that happens in the world through living the cultures through the people on site. I smelled and tasted everything that was new and different. I experienced contrasts and challenges. I went places and built my confidence now in my 30s and into how I come about, but as to what I am looking for in a soul, was still to be revealed to me.

OUT OF AFRICA

Through time, one gets inspired or affected by scenes and attitudes and all the other influences that come and go. I am not sure if there is an incubated attraction to certain auras sounds, pictures as appearing challenges that come and go in our lives. Those that are connected from our past existence in the world sometime, somewhere and with a different character. Perhaps, I chose to believe that I have lived before, to justify my attraction to anything Scottish, African and the atmosphere of old Chicago.

Once I worked with a lady called Angeliki, raised and traveled in different countries, Kenya and South Africa. She was forever kind and politely spoken. She would never disagree with someone and I knew when that was, as she was going quiet. We shared lots of humorous conversations and she has shown me a new way to accept everyone's ideas and position, although not in an agreeing line with everyone else. It often resulted in a statement that she did not agree with but she kept quiet until much later it dawned on me to ask her what she thought about it, to discover she totally disagreed with me. I was always trying to change people as I thought it would be better for them while she believed not to interfere with other people's wills. She taught that saying

- 'My Paris, just let everyone be. We would all end at our destinations, through our path we created and chose to walk through'.

Some evenings, we had visionary conversations about Kenyan tribes and history, but more I was hooked on their behaviours, traditions and ideologies. I was in the plots she was describing, but I looked as if I was listening. I told her that I am fascinated by them. She used to think that I may have come from that tribe and made fun of me. This tribe believed, like me, that the life force of their ancestors can come back to the life through the act of birth of a new child. Angeliki kept saying that my personality traits and attitudes were similar to those of a Kikuyu. They were like me, she said,' stubborn like old goats and stuck to their ideas, but proud of their values, like you are!' I had reasons to believe her!

I have been drawn into historical films of Africa and have been through a lot of books by National Geographic about the tribes but drawn on the Kikuyus. I loved the film 'Out of Africa', which I have probably watched twice every year and have learned quite a lot of quotes from it. It fascinated me, from the production point of view but goddess Meryl Streep, as Karen Blixen, gave a superb performance through this rather sad and real story, but wonderful while it lasted. Robert Redford, as Denys, portrays quite a bit of my status, needing his space and freedom and to come and go, sharing time with Karin Blixen. It clearly comes across that Denys had no desire to be monogamous and to build a domestic relationship, although whenever he was with her, he wanted to be with her and had feelings for her. It was just wonderful and so noble. I have been confirmed by that, since I was young and en route to somewhere unknown. All the souls that came in my life were absolutely individuals and it was more important we shared time and experiences together rather than drop in the swirl of a committed life relationship. I also loved the relationship Denys had with his Maasai warrior, always at a distance with him, but close enough to show care, respect and acceptance.

In April of 1988, when It was my 30th birthday and although birthdays for me are times to be alone and think and enjoy peace and repositioning, Joy, on the contrary, being vibrant and fun as always, had planned a surprise and insisted I take a day off the restaurant. I had no clue about these plans.

I took a day off at the restaurant. I was blind folded, feeling insecure at first, but joined in the fun later. I was driven by her, for some time, through roads and fields while the radio was in full blast with pop songs and her singing at the top of her voice with crackling laughs at the miss of tones and off-key sounds. When the car stopped and I was still blindfolded, we walked a few meters and I had to go up a few steps and to seat to what reminded me of a bus. I was guessing touching leather and the window. I could feel there was another person around as I was not exactly sure there were more feet stepping up. He, or she, did not speak at all and there were moments of worry but suspense. Joy said, it's time, and she unfolded my eyes. We were on a small three-seater, one engine airplane with a pilot who was to fly us around Cyprus and to enjoy...

A bottle of champagne popped up and the plane made its way to a short runway. We were airborne and the views through the windows were magnificent.

The sun shone brightly above us as we flew on the small plane. The sky was a brilliant shade of blue. From our vantage point in the sky, the world below us seemed peaceful and tranquil. I looked out the window and marveled at the beauty of the lush green landscape below. The trees were a vibrant green, and with their leaves, dancing in the wind. The rolling hills and meadows were a patchwork of different shades of green and yellow, creating a stunning view. The small towns and villages were a sight to behold as well. The stark white houses were like little dots in a sea of green, and the winding roads and cobblestone streets gave the towns a unique charm.

The feeling of being so high above the world, and being able to take in its beauty from a completely new perspective, was breathtaking. The sensation of the wind whipping around us and the sun warming our faces, added to the romantic feel of the experience. Being in my arms and drinking that champagne, Joy wanted us to feel as in the film Out of Africa, when Denys flew Karin on a plane, as an incredible gift to get a glimpse of the world from that height. I was so wonderfully surprised and overwhelmed and everything was so breathtaking.

All my emotions were stimulated, ending to inflame my sexual urge for eroticism. I have drawn the curtain between us and the pilot and have lived the moment, up in the sky, through unzipping clothes while kissing and touching her, till the end of these forceful powers that accelerated lust during the conduct of our bodies reaching up in the sky indeed! What an experience we both had!

That same evening, Joy promised to impress me and to cook a meal for two at our house. Prince had also a plate of cooked meat for himself. Candlelight atmosphere, African beats and pottery ornating the table and the music just like her, happy and dancy, The Cure- 'Just like heaven', and lots of Wham and Dire Straits. The two of us had a good chat about the plane ride and how we felt for over an hour around the table. We had a delicious tagliatelle with chicken and lavender cream and a chocolate and passion mousse sweet that started being savored from each other's bodies. She stopped the 'overture' right there as she wanted us to take a bath together. There it was, a warm bath full of lemons and it has been and still is, a desire of mine towards lemony desserts and sorbets.

We played in the bath until the water was almost cold and at that point, a man had to do what a man has to do! So, as with all my weapons presented, I have picked her up in my arms. While the lemony water was dripping off our bodies, I lowered one side of my waist to touch open our bedroom door with my elbow, full of anticipation. I planned in my head the scene of when the lion has the fragile victim in his hands and taking it to a safe place for the feast.

The door opened to perhaps twenty or thirty camera flashes right in our eyes and the loud voices of 'Surprise.... Happy Birthday...!'. It seemed that during all our dinner time, followed by our lemon bath play, all my friends were hiding in silence in our bedroom. And how does an 'armed' naked and fully exposed man holding naked Joy in his hands, react? He spontaneously dropped her on the marble floor, as a reflection to hide his private parts, from all pairs of eyes right in front of him, but really too late as the cameras recorded it all and I had a horrific facial expression to go with it. Thankfully, she was not hurt. The music became louder, boxes of drinks came out from under the beds and the party was on!

Joy has really marked our time together with spontaneity, out of the ordinary things that I loved and probably encouraged to bring out in her. I was also very contributing to this madness. I learned to share and be spontaneous. She was a good girl, kind and clever.

I cared about her and after a lot of thinking I decided to talk to her one evening after dinner.

- 'Joy, sweetie, I need to talk to you about my thoughts on you' I said in a serious tone of voice and received her full attention. 'You are young at 21 years old and you work at a pub in a tourist resort town on a small island. You are clever, bubbly, full of real joy and charisma. You know that I love having fun and spending time with you but life is much more than this!' .She listened carefully and said,

- 'You are about to tell me things I will not like....'

- ' Well, I want to tell you things that you may not like now but you will be grateful to me one day. I feel that you are capable of many things in life. I feel sorry you are here in this town offering not amazing job opportunities....I want you to go back to the UK and study anything you like, become someone, educate yourself a lot more, get a nice job meaning something for you. Achieve and conquer many other things, you have a big potential to grow!'

- 'So, why? you don't like what we have now? It's so much fun!' She expressed from her heart

- 'I agree but the bigger picture is much bigger and eventually more fun than this one here! Life could not always be a continuous party, in the false world of a resort town' I said and held her hand.

- 'I know you do not like what you hear right now, but if you want to really make me happy... you must go and get a job, study something you like, and we can still meet when I come there and party harder. I will be there for you whatever you may need, but it will make me happy to see you succeeding in life' I continued.

I often took this role to suggest, advise and coach people into better situations. We agreed, hard as it was to go apart and miss the fun. The condition was that should she do that, we would talk again about the next step. Three weeks later, I took her to the airport and said a sad goodbye. She had tears in her eyes as we waved to the beginning of a new era for her. We kept in touch and I kept encouraging her next steps.

We continued being in contact and I was now in the role of a mentor. I was missing her and all the fun. Eventually, she found her way to become a successful businesswoman in the UK. Now married and with children, we exchange Christmas cards but the memories remain.

THE WEDDINGS

Peter the Swedish tour representative came to Le Bistro to have dinner with a friend. We were in our fourth year of operation and he had no words to express his amazement, as to what was finally created. I have won his respect and I felt a winner after his discouraging first comments during the renovations.

Peter was very tall and handsome, kind of a Swedish God. He could charm any girl he wanted without trying hard at all. He was one of those gifted men in all ways. We met accidentally one evening at a pub and we had some drinks together which was the beginning of a long friendship and adventures. Once we went clubbing together and bought all the flowers from a man with two baskets, going around the club to sell his roses. We had a basket of flowers each and we were to go around and sell the flowers ourselves. A pound each! The winner with the most sales would have taken all the money and the loser would have to buy a bottle of champagne to share. We went opposite directions in the club and tried our best to sell. Half an hour later, we met at the bar with empty baskets. None of us wanted to count his money first, until we cracked up into laughter. We both gave the flowers to all the pretty girls in the club for a smile and none of us sold a single rose! We ended up buying two bottles of champagne and enjoyed drinking with the many Swedish girls around us that he attracted, of course!

One day, he booked a table for two at our restaurant. He made it sound as a very important event to me as he was on a date. Apparently, this was the second date he had with this special girl. He explained that he messed up, at the first one, as he went half an hour later and he forgot his wallet, so the girl had to pay his invitation. He wanted to make-up for this.

I created a special menu of four courses and printed it with the heading 'For Erica'. They had a great time and enjoyed the food. We cheated, as I told Peter in advance, which wine to choose and a few tips on the grapes and its characteristics. He ordered the wine to the waiter and spoke of it in front of her. Erica was very impressed by his knowledge on wines! Peter was forever thanking me that she was so pleased with the whole experience and it seemed to me that it was the beginning of their relationship, as she moved in with him.

On another happy night out with Peter, he had drunk quite a bit and he was worried to go home to Erica, not to wake her up. I insisted on driving him, to go home and as he was not fit to drive himself. I packed him in my car and drove him to his house only to discover he had no keys. He had to wake her up. Drunk as he was, he started calling a few times ' Liza, darling open the door'. I laughed! Liza must have been another girl he had living with him at a point. Erica opened the door with a smile ; she received a big kiss and a hug and being called Liza a few times, she put him to bed.

This story became a speech at their wedding, a few years later in Stockholm, when I was one of their best men! The wedding was at a small chapel on a hill and the Swedish priest was specially chosen as he could speak Greek and he was translating the ceremony in Greek too. The whole ceremony was simple and charming. Some friends sang a song and some read a poem. The party was hosted at an ex prison complex, in a stone-built room. It must have been the room where prisoners were let loose to stretch their legs every day when they had a break from their cells. Lots of stories were told expressing imaginary scenarios of prisoners kept there. It was a rectangular large room with thick glass windows overlooking a field ending to a thick forest.

As a best man I had to dance to the song, Zorba the Greek, a significant song marking the personification of the spirit and enjoyment of life! They all made a circle and I danced in the middle at first but then dragged everyone to dance with me forming circles.

Peter and Erica made a unique couple and they complemented one another. I was proud of them starting their life and that I was part of this plot. Weddings are nice for people to come together but I was far away in my thoughts from being the main player. Peter and Erica had two handsome sons, Simon, who became my godson, and Uno who came a few years later.

Many personalities made stories at Le Bistro. However, my staff, my people, were the heroes to believe in me and to share these dreams. They were the carriers of the soul of the place and they enjoyed the success too. Peggy, worked with me there too and pursued all our dreams, she shared the passion. She has helped me a lot as being my right hand and she was always there for me. I called her Mary Poppins! She was a good friend too, running the business when I was traveling and looking after Prince.

A man called Gregory from Greece, with whom we became close and best friends. He followed the concept of working in service. He had a particular and difficult personality, sometimes fighting with himself, but a very loyal friend. We became close and I took the respect of becoming his best man at his wedding a few months later. He married Tina, an Irish lady and had four children. Two of them, Milto and Odysseas, are my godchildren while Rosaria and Filippos are like mine too!

A tall Serbian man walked in one day, as I was watering the garden and asked me for a job. Michailo was very tall, handsome and had an intense personality. He gave the guest a valet service alongside other small jobs. We developed a respectful relationship and made all a good team. Later on, Michailo married Jelena in Serbia, I was their best man and have christened both of their daughters Tashana and Gala! How blessed I was! At their wedding in Serbia, we went through the custom of stealing the bride from her house by bribing the parents with money under the door. Then the party began.

Although, I went there with a girlfriend called Monica, there was a hottie Serbian lady staring at me and eventually asked me to meet her at the toilet. I was intrigued by curiosity, but I did not go. She looked at me unhappy during the whole party. However, when I went back a year after to Christen Tashana, we had a tete-a-tete session at her apartment.

She had invited me to dinner but we both knew what that meant. She lived in an old complex and her apartment was so dated that it was a 70s vintage style now. She had a candelabra, with red candles, on the dinner table, set for the feast. As I took my coat off, she came right to my face and gave me a passionate welcome kiss, while she was hardly breathing. We took our clothes off in the corridor like we see in films.

Mara was blond and very sexy, curvy, with a strong body with muscles. She was an actress and my first Serbian experience. She led me to her bedroom and we fought who was going to be on top! I let her win and she blindfolded me. She was touching me all over and observing my reactions. When she touched my cock, I was prepared for the action. She sat on top of me backwards and while going up and down she was massaging my feet. I could hear her getting more excited with accelerating breathing and moaning sounds as she finished fast and first, as any man's blessing!

I stopped my movements and controlled my urges. I took her by the hand, removed the blindfold and led her to the table so that we could eat while naked. She wondered why I did not want to come too and I said with a cheeky smile 'we will go back to that after dinner'. She presented a selection of antipasti followed by some kind of goulash with meat and potatoes. We had a glass of wine and a bottle of whiskey came on the table. I noticed she had a picture of a Scotsman in a kilt on her wall. I asked her ' how come...' and I could hear the bagpipes and a strong wind... she was sitting across the table, still naked and she looked like a whore in a public house back in the 1800s. I got up, lifted her in my arms. I placed her on the carpet. I opened her legs and went on top of her. It was not me, but a stronger, a violent man inside me. She did not seem to be bothered... on the contrary! When it was over, I must have fallen asleep, as I woke up covered by a blanket and it was me again.

We both got dressed and had coffee and cake with blackberries. Mara explained that she has visited Scotland and that it was a man she took the photo of. She was fascinated that men wore kilts and she wanted to one day marry one! It was time for me to go!

MESSING UP

The years went on and the French bistro was getting more and more upgraded in standards and with loyal customers and friends. On the contrary, Ayia Napa started becoming more commercial with massive tourism pouring in and less foreign clientele to appreciate all our efforts.

My Peggy left for a love adventure in Zakynthos, an island in Greece. She had her romance with a Greek and we were in touch exchanging our funny stories unfolding. New personalities came in to support the course of the restaurant. Elaine, was an English lady with finesse, style, a great figure and was very pleasant to everyone. She had the gift of the mouth and a great attitude to smiling. I employed her as a manager, and have had an incredible course of friendship with her. She has lived in India and Africa with her second husband, a geologist from Germany and had two children Sean and Karin who also became regulars in our conversational index on a daily basis.

With Elaine we started playing squash and we were forever going for walks and talks, sharing dreams of what we really wanted to happen to us in the future. She was always there for me and has entertained my exploration of characters coming in and out of my life, but hers too. My creativity stirred a buzz within certain social circles. I often created themed parties with stories, whether crazy hat parties at midnight, or masquerade parties in the middle of the winter. Once, they all had a role to perform as Zulus. They were partly naked with black faces, wore the relevant wigs and held spears. They prepared the sounds and dances in this mode to welcome Elaine at Larnaca airport. We almost got arrested by the police, for causing such a nuisance and disturbance to the flow of arriving travelers.

The themes and the film sets were live now, without the magic carpet needed as a means to travel! Some nights, after work and drinking and dancing, many of us used to frequent what we called soup kitchens, as in small eateries, open usually after hours. As drunk as we all were, we started food fights and got all the customers, even from the other tables, involved in the fun and having a good laugh. Silly as it was, many were the nights that I went to bed disgraced and drunk, to find myself in the morning covered in tomato sauce and boiled eggs! Those times were so different, as everyone blended with everyone they met and it was like one big party, everywhere you went.

One of those nights, when you were wondereingwhat may happen, I met Lara, an acquaintance from some years back. A gorgeous, beautiful blond lady with a hour glass figure, big eyes, superbly dressed, younger than me, a millionaire's Cypriot based in London. She was married to a gigolo. Everyone knew he had many relationships outside his marriage. That summer, we met at the restaurant. She was kind of inquisitive towards me and my life, going into deep conversations about relationships, a stage that many women go through during a separation. A lot of uncertainty and insecurity around her. A lot of questions as to why this is happening to her. It was obvious that she was going through this phase. I wanted to help her come out of this cloud she was in.

We often swam together, listened to music and went for drinks. Everywhere we went, she gave me the sense of wanting to say something to me but she was reserved or did not know how to bring herself to say something. On principle, little me, being sensitive to understanding the atmosphere around and the feelings of the opposite soul, I was a good listener, sympathetic and careful with my words.

One hot summer night, as we went to the club for dancing, she asked to come home with me, to see it, as she believed it would have been a very creative space. I had an apartment with many old pieces of furniture mixed with modern light appliances and big frames on the wall I collected from my travels. She herself, was an artist and an interior designer and I was talented to put things together in a space. So, while at home and with a glass of champagne in her hands, she asked me for a kiss. It seemed that it was 'the kiss of life for her' as it went on long enough, until both of us were out of breath. We got right into the scenario of boy meets girl on the chaise longue, but it was not Sade on the cd player, but Al Green ' Let's stay together'. We have invested time in showing each other care and passion during the act and endless hugs and good feelings at the end. She had invited me to spend a week in London, as her husband was going on a long trip away somewhere. She let me to understand that he would be traveling with another lady. She said that she often found another woman's pair of knickers under her bed and she took the decision and filed for a divorce. Woah! What's next, I begun to think the thread again! Would I be expected to be the replacement. I wondered what would she expect from me and although I wanted to help her become happy, I did not want any serious role in this...

Days passed seeing each other here and there and alongside the workload and social engagements. I was introduced by a loyal lady customer to a Cypriot lady living in Monaco named Georgia. She had a rather plum body with long hair, well presented in light silk clothes and with beautiful chestnut, piercing eyes. In conversation with her one night, she talked to me about her high life over there, the good Michelin restaurants around central Europe she experienced, her visits to Switzerland and the famous people she met in Monte Carlo. However, she expressed that she felt lonely and had no male interest for years to which she looked concerned. She did not seem very confident with men. I knew, from other acquaintances, that Georgia was very wealthy, perhaps the wealthiest lady I ever met in my life. She was known to be single and of course anyone would consider his options and I must admit, I wondered and perhaps dared to think that perhaps such a relationship may work easier.

I invited her for a candle light dinner. She had no clue

where we were to go. I picked her up and we drove near the beach on a rock formation. There was a simple white table, set earlier by myself, two chairs and packed prawn and orange salad, lobster mousse, fresh baguette and a bottle of Taittinger rose on ice. To impress, I used some vintage Italian plates, hand painted with colourful roses and my Christofle silver cutlery. There was a contrast which I always liked. A small cassette portable device was playing Maria Callas arias, as the flames from the candles on the table were flickering with joy to her sounds. It was a full moon with its reflection in the sea and you could see all the stars. Which film producer would have not liked that set? She had a constant smile on her face and I could almost see a glow around her head, perhaps I had one too. We felt blessed to have been able to share that atmosphere together. We talked about the beauties of the world, the great restaurants and everything that was related to the life of big spenders. Nothing connecting to emotions was spoken about. However, it took us to the next level, as another invitation suggested, to visit her in Monte Carlo in Monaco for a week. It looked like I would have had to do a bit of traveling from London to Monte Carlo!

The following night as Georgia passed by the restaurant to say goodbye, she also took notice of Lara, who happened to be at a table having a meal with her mother. I was surprised that they knew of each other! All sorts of thoughts went into my mind if they found out I was double dating! I also joined in the conversation with everyone and they explained that they were friends, from years back. They exchanged numbers to keep in touch as they were both leaving back home soon!

I did go first to London and did what every man had to, to keep the flag up and proud. I made her feel comfortable and relaxed and I was ready to have a great time together. It was an adventure and fun, as much as London can be with going out to places. London, always a Mecca land for entertainment, from bars, restaurants, hotels, nightclubs, even private-speakeasy dark rooms! I was in my element. I even thought of making my way to meet Kate, from years back, and see how she was. I would have been naughtier to do so, so I did not!

At Lara's luxurious apartment, it was all great times, cooking and partying at home the two of us as two teenagers. There was plenty of champagne and whiskey of distinction that belonged to her husband and felt good to be enjoyed for some reason! But suddenly, it all ended! The lights went off, the glasses smashed one after the other, the food was tasteless, our clothes went back on again, the music stopped and the camera stopped rolling, we both froze and all happened in a reversed fast forward mode, as she said

- 'When I get the divorce, will you marry me?'

- ' Oh, my lovely... Lara, please don't take me wrong! I am not at the stage in my life that I want to commit to anything as I want to achieve many things for myself first, travel and make savings too. It is not the right time for me' I said knowing that it was the end of the party! I left London and all the fun behind me and returned home.

One glorious morning, when the sun was bright and we had a blue sky, I woke up and wore my jogging shorts to run with my Prince. He was always so excited to see me wearing shorts as he knew well it was 'play' time with dad! I opened the door and he was so excited he shot out galloping his way to the street, when a double cabin car was speeding and hit him right in the middle of his chest. I saw the red car going right into my Prince and heard the bang alongside a dog's cry of pain. Prince was lying in the middle of the road with blood coming out of his mouth. I ran in tears and picked him up with my two hands, placed him at the back of the car and drove like hell to the dog's clinic. As I stormed into the vet's office from the way he looked at the dog and then myself, I felt my legs weakening and sat on the floor crying and holding Prince. He was lifeless, my spirited, joyful companion was gone. I was devastated and felt miserable and angry. I drove two hours to the mountains and found the spot around the hotel where we spent our best times playing in the forest and buried him with tears in my eyes. I spent a couple of hours reminiscing about the good times I had with Prince.

The first week going home to an empty apartment was sad. I did not know I had so much love inside me. It was time to move on. I felt I needed to replace a gap inside me and I tried.

Monaco was more romantic. Upon my non announced arrival, I placed a note under her front door. The note announced that there was a package for her, waiting at the entrance of the building. I rang the doorbell and stepped down to the front of the building. She came down and saw me with a bunch of flowers. There was excitement and a warm hug. Surely, the director Sharon Maguire would have liked to have filmed my welcome in Monaco and continued the following story. She drove me, in her convertible BMW, to show me around Monte Carlo town. One million splendid pictures in my brain. She has, meanwhile, ordered a delivery for the evening meal at home. Me being a restaurateur, most meaningful events and actions evolved over a feast. She knew that and it was our common area of discussion.

While she went to the hairdressers for a styling, she dropped me home to take a shower and wait for the feast to be delivered, so that the evening ceremony would begin. I placed small candles, on the floor, from the entrance guiding the way to the bathroom. I prepared the bath for both of us, remembering Kate's experience. Flowers in a vase were placed in front of the large bathroom mirror. I blew up many balloons all over the bathroom and wrote on the mirror ' would you like to live with me?'

I was almost sure I could do that, after all I have lived with Joy for a while, perhaps I can do the same with Georgia too. Her wealth contributions would have added to mine and we would have been also more comfortable in a house of her choice! We would share the experiences of all excellent restaurants, all over the world. I don't know why I did that, but at the moment I felt it was a great idea and I was full of enthusiasm for a new adventure.

As she walked in, she understood what was coming and she went through to the bathroom and laughed. She came back and gave me a sweet kiss. As she opened her mouth to say something, we got interrupted by the doorbell as the food arrived. Saved by the bell!

The door opened and a stream of trolleys, covered in white tablecloths and silver gear wheeled in. Plates and plates, covered by silver domes, a waiter, 2 golden chairs and a violinist came in to create a wonderful second set for the film! I suppose that was her answer to my candlelight dinner on the rocks and to underline to me, this is how she rolls! Fine then, the atmosphere was superb, the violinist played for us my request, Jules Massenet, 'Meditation de Thais' while the foie gras and the Margret de canard with the red berry sauce paired with a bottle of Grand cru, Domaine Weinbach, Gewurztraminer, Mambourg Quintessence de Grains Nobles Cuvée d'Or! A train of words marking an excellent wine of distinction. And the finale a Pudding Diplomat, soaked in Kirsch, an old revived favorite of mine. I loved the whole event of savoring that unfolded in front of my eyes and while holding hands across the table. The immense anticipation was when would we go to bed afterwards, but much more, to her silence in commenting on my message on the bathroom mirror!

I did thank her for the brilliant idea of the feast. I made a comment that the wine we were drinking costs 1,000 pounds in my restaurant and I could have never afforded to try it. She smiled with a thrill and proudly announced that she had a basement to show me her collection of wines, the morning after. I found it bloody exciting. A woman that can talk with me about wines and restaurants, food and that kind of buzz! I said to her that she would have to try some whiskies with me. I wanted to introduce to her, but she rejected my idea. I suggested we travel to Scotland together, as I feel I lived there once in a different life, but received no enthusiasm. I suggested we read poems to each other and there was an indication of a rejection. I felt we would have never been happy together.

The night continued gracefully and very civilized as there were no animals or red Indians in the room, but perhaps the violinist who mentally stayed somewhere behind for the melody from Ravel's Bolero which accompanied our movements in rhythm while in bed. There was not an exciting sexual plot, perhaps there was not that magical chemistry that usually one brings on the other one. Even none of the usual followers showed up in the room. No conspiracy with bagpipes, no Kikuyus, no saxophonists. Even the violinist stopped playing at the right time.

In the morning, at breakfast mode, the setup of the table was composed with the smells of freshly grinded coffee and fresh oranges just been squeezed, cinnamon and honey, toasted bagels, smoked salmon omelet with truffle oil drops and muesli with fresh raspberries. I needed a song in my head and my brain was going like a jukebox in an effort to reach through eras and genders. It was not happening, something was wrong. It stopped to classical music. Taken from Swan Lake, Tchaikovsky's ' The dying swan'! It was romantic and sad. I wondered if she was listening to it, too!

I felt Georgia was a little quiet. I looked at her and asked if she was ok. She composed a face of a judge in the 17th century with the white wig, not with an angry face but one of wisdom and said' I love the way you are, shy at first but so spontaneous at the same time. You are foolish and a charmer. I do not like the age you are! I love your creativity, charisma and your mannerisms... but cannot share them with Lara. I know you were in London prior to coming here and she knew you were coming here afterwards! '

Woah! Little me, you messed up big time and you have been fooled by both girls! She carried on and read to me from my horoscope book, she studied prior to my arrival,' Aries at the age of 30 are very immature. They may think it is time to settle down or marry. Never believe them until after 40!' I was embarrassed, we laughed, hugged and entertained ourselves with stories about our characters, everything and nothing of significance just to break the ice. There was an abundance of a mere chemistry between us.

I packed my bags and left, when it was time. We said, see you later. I came back, not wiser at all, but stupid. I felt a little 'useful', perhaps as a stepping stone for Lara to overcome her insecurities from the separation mess she was in. I thought I had made her feel like an attractive woman. Perhaps Georgia stepped on a man that gave her attention, interest, compliments and sex. She shared magical moments with me and I felt close to her at least through food and wine. I was happy to think that she is now more confident to go further and find what she wants. Not myself!

JUNE

In the years of the French restaurant, many of my regulars also became close friends and we met off season in other countries like the UK or elsewhere to share time and experiences. One particular couple made an impression on the town. Chris and June came from London. He had been a wealthy and successful entrepreneur, as money was spread in the whole town, wherever they visited, usually in different large groups of friends.

My restaurant was definitely a good ground for spending money, if one wanted the best of exclusive French wines and vintage champagne with all the gourmet foods available. There was a possibility to have private areas and extra set ups of refined atmospheres, private musicians and a lot more has been asked from me to support. Chris was a very conformed English man. He had been a specimen of a perfect scout leader, as a young man, studied accounting and made a lot of money working hard. He grew up to be a polite and kind aristocratic gentleman.

June, was a darling to me, with an infectious smile, short hair and chestnut eyes, always made to feel like a Queen by Chris and of course myself too. We connected quite a lot through art and taste and she had the charisma to enjoy taking interest in people. In conversations, she saw through me and liked me for my contrasts and whatever else I did not know. This connection was strengthened, not only through art but creativeness of the moment, allowing us to express our innermost thoughts and feelings without the need for words. I confessed to her that I may have lived many lives before and she believed me. We jokingly said we would, one day, travel to Scotland together in search...

It was a joy,' a fete', every time they came back to see us in the restaurant. We used the best cutlery and brought in boxes of champagne and wines of distinction for them. They brought in many others with them and always were perfect hosts, looking after everyone's individual needs.

The year of 1991, after my father's death, I was very low and in deep thoughts. They invited me to join an extravagant plan of celebration for June's 40th birthday. June asked me specifically to join them. She always wanted me to meet Alan, a friend of theirs, from London, who was a kind of a healer or a medium. She had a lot of therapy from him as she experinced some back pains. She felt that I would connect with Alan, should I meet him and Alan knew of myself too, apparently. She also thought that Alan could relate to previous lives people lived.

At first, I was skeptical to go, but my then close friend and Chef Costas had a word with me and pushed me to go away and to see further than what I could those days.

- 'We will look after the business' he said,' and I am sure your father would have wanted you to go'

We attended a formal Black and White dress code dinner feast, at the Waterside Inn restaurant in London, followed by a firework display. We were eighty people at that dinner, ten on every table. As we waited for everyone to stand in front of their name tags so that we all sat down at the same time as a formality, I heard a warm voice of a man behind me at the next table. I turned my head to see who had such a warm and attractive tone in his speech and he turned the same time and said to me

- ' Hi Paris, I am Alan, I have heard a lot about you and we will catch up tomorrow as I believe we are traveling together' I smiled back and replied

- ' Yes, I am looking forward to getting to know you, Alan'.

The next day twenty of June's special friends were flown on the upper deck of a British Airways' Jumbo plane to Barbados. Champagne was flowing faster than the airplane fuel. I sat near

Alan and we chatted about the introductions as to what we do in life. It turned out that Alan and Nora, had a baby under a year old born with cancer. The doctors gave them little hope. The baby was in pain and crying day and night but the cancer would not go. Medicine could not help and the doctors refused to give the child pain killers, as it had gone beyond any treatment stage.

Alan and Nora, ended up seeing people from other schools of thought, as a way to find out how to help their child to go. They found a spiritual healer who has seen the baby and them too. He looked at Alan and held his hands for a while and said to him

- ' Alan, if you want your baby to be freed, you must stop picking him up when he cries'.

A very sad and ironic way for Alan to find out that he possessed powers of healing and that when he was holding his baby, he was delaying its passing away. Alan said that in less than three weeks, their baby died. He felt that if he had any powers like he was told, to try and help as many people as he could.

He met June at an airport queuing behind her to check in. As June tried to pick up her heavy suitcase, she pulled a back muscle and he took her to the side. He had warmed her muscles with his hands, and concentrated. Five minutes later June was relieved. He spoke of many other people that he tried to help, even from some distance.

Alan and I talked for quite a while and there was a nice feeling listening to him. I told him I lost my father, and I was quite upset inside me, as I lost my reference and part of myself. He maintained that my father would not leave me and that he would be around and that I will know about it. I told him that I was attracted to other lives and times.

- 'We have all lived other lives, perhaps myself too' he maintained,' Some of us have the power to still connect with our past lives and it has to do with how many times our souls came back.'

He encouraged me to practice meditation and I would

know. He also explained that we all meditate, even in the course of the day. A thought, an impression, a feeling may be connected to our past lives and that it is the meditation that brings it back to us. It was rather deep at times, what was coming out of his mouth. Before we landed, and on the last glass of champagne, he looked at me in the eyes and said,

- ' Paris, there are many qualities in you. I feel you are more connected to your mother. She protected you, somehow, she saw you as herself, I am not sure, but there is something there. I believe that you have some powers in you, there may be a day you will discover them and use them. If you do, give it back to your friends and to people. Help as many as you can'

Woah! So much was said and sent me into deep thoughts! Is it real, seeing other things and traveling to scenarios, is that what he is talking about? Have I really lived other lives? How and what powers was he talking about?

When we arrived at Barbados airport, we flew by a smaller plane to the island of Antigua for a crazy party night. I think I danced the whole night around a palm tree or with a palm tree. I definitely hugged it! Perhaps we all did! It was humid and hot. We stayed at some colorful bungalows on a sandy beach. We had little time to enjoy anything more, as the next morning, all with a hangover, we were flown over turquoise waters, with a Virgin's helicopter to Necker Virgin Island.

Necker is a private island, belonging to Sir Richard Branson. As the helicopter landed to pick up the first group, I saw a couple with many children disembarking and escorted to the airport's hall. He had a blue jockey hat on. He looked familiar. Later on, we found out from the pilot that it was Mel Gibson, having just had a family holiday to where we were going. If I knew, I would have gone to declare being a fan, as I watched many of his films.

As the helicopter approached Necker, the island looked more and more spectacular surrounded by the shades of the blue waters washing its shores. The house appeared, as if they took off the top of a small mountain and placed it there. On landing we were greeted with refreshments and smiles by the staff. The rooms were absolutely out of this world. My room opened to the sea all around. The toilet had no door or windows, and it was looking out to the endless open. No pounds were spared in the making of everything, from elephant bamboo four poster beds with white curtains flowing to the thick cushioned armchairs and the solid teak floors. It was lush and yet so simple and beautiful as nature was in charge of everything.

June explained that we all had special bedrooms chosen by her. There were 9 double bedrooms for the couples and two of us were in single occupancy. Myself and Ann, an American lady that I have never met and was to arrive later on.

As soon as I unpacked, I ran to one of the private sandy beaches further down. It stretched for quite a while and was kissed by clear turquoise waters. There were some Albatross flying in and out from the sea and landing on the sandy airfield. I run with them. I noticed one that was perhaps following me. I played with it and changed direction and again it followed me and sat before me as I stopped running each time. I smiled and wanted perhaps to connect it with being dad saying hello, as he did have a hobby keeping all kinds of birds in our garden back in my childhood. I spoke to it...

- ' Hello Dad, if it's you, I want to tell you that I miss you and I think of you all the time'

At the house on the hill, every breakfast, lunch or dinner was served in a different tropical island style decoration, with wines of distinction and lots of Veuve Clicquot, available everywhere. Champagne and drinks were always on all beaches, in a cool box, just in case some happened to spend time on this or that private beach. All was available for us, beach sports, boats and kayaks, music to play everywhere and it was all so beautifully planned and provided.

The first night when all of us sat down on a long table full of pink flowers and colourful napkins and runners, I got to know Ann, a district attorney, based in Miami and specializing in drug trafficking cases. She was very knowledgeable about the world and I loved the use of the American language,' are you for real',' hang tight, i'll be with ya in a minute'. It made a difference, as most of the other people there were British and I was Cypriot with other ancestry influences! We spoke over nice wine and food and about our lives as to what we do but not in depth. She teased me of my accent, being Greek influenced and charming to her but she noticed some oous and rrrrs slipping out my mouth sometimes, on purpose,

> ' It is grrreat that June boookedus overrr herrre...it's absolouuutetly fantastic!'

I described to her Mrs. Houri which made me a little nostalgic and of course I said to her that I may have lived a previous life in Scotland and she added that she also lived in Brazil, but never could place when. I sang in tune to her...

'Tall and tan and young and lovely
The girl from Ipanema goes walking
And when she passes
Each one she passes goes 'ah' '

And she clapped to which I got up and bowed to her being the audience.

The next day we swam together in the pool. An albatross came and stayed for quite some time looking at us. I have said to her my story and she said I would believe you if the bird comes again tomorrow!

That same afternoon following a lunch party with everyone on the beach with lots of cocktails and champagne I have invited her to come with me to a neighboring island for exploration and adventure. We drove the speed boat to a small island with a shack on. It looked as if someone left a lost pirate there, who in modern days, was running a kind of a bar, for those coming off shore for a while, to rest and refresh. Some adventurous on surfing boards, offered us a nice spectacle, while we were sipping down our first 'Sex on the Beach'. An albatross flew close to us and she looked at me.

At the shack that older hairy man, who prepared our drinks, was called the Pirate and he had autographed pictures on his wall of my goddess Meryl Streep and of Robert de Niro. When I looked at them, he said, they all come here. Lady Diana was here too, he said. His story was that he was there years back for diving expeditions and he fell in love with the island. He stayed there, not having been back to the rest of the world for at least thirty years. He said that time did not matter and that he ate when he was hungry and slept when he was tired and every day is different. I treasured his words especially looking at my hand featuring a watch and a bracelet stating my name... as if it was important!

The following night, it was June's big night. We all got excited to be there and make the celebration happen. I wore black and white with a floral bow tie and the same pattern as a cummerbund ban. Ann was in a gorgeous black dress with a white trimming, strapless and opening up from the waist down as in the style of the 50s. Everything was superb, Chris thought of everything for us, the food, décor, and the music was superb. We even did the limbo dance after all the Sunshine and Summer song titles that existed. Most popular were the 'Sunshine Reggae' and the 'In the Summertime' but we did not miss out on the 'Walking on sunshine!' Towards the end, June and I danced a slow song and as Chris took her back Ann came in my arms and we danced under the stars. I held her from the waist and she placed her hand on my shoulder almost touching my neck while our other two hands were in harmony together pointing to the ground. We moved slowly to the song and nothing was needed to be said.

Alan and Nora were next to us. Alan winked at me at a point, reading me, as if he was giving me a go ahead, or knew what was following. There was no way for such a film set for the camera not to roll further. It was the perfect setting. We both were merit. With not a thought in my head, and being with such a respectable lady, I felt that I had to lead the way, a quite rare gesture to come from little me. So, I whispered in her ear 'my place or yours?' She looked at me in the eyes with wit and whispered back to my ear,' to both'. I gently held her hand and led her in my bedroom through candlelit corridors...that resembled the corridors of the Colosseum where torches were lit for the athletes to pass through to the battle ring. They were filled with voices of a cheering crowd, as if I just won the gladiatorial fight at the Colosseum. I was walking through to receive my prize!

In my bedroom, candles were already lit everywhere. Flower petals were on the bed and I did not have a clue about it. The candlelight glistened off the petals of the flowers, creating a warm, romantic atmosphere. My heart raced with excitement, not knowing what might happen next. There was an atmosphere spread in the room full of silver dust and beautiful fragrances of Jasmin and rose flowers. Just finding each other in the room it was accelerating to the senses. Not knowing if we would ever meet again, was even more exciting and added to the nice confusion. What a setting for a script to be written! I was gone...

The candlelight flickered, casting shadows across the walls. They transformed the room into a theater, with people looking like warriors, men in kilts playing the bagpipes but saxophones too and all dancing accompanying the candlelight. I was mesmerized by the beautiful, surreal figures as they moved to the rhythm of our lovemaking. As the music built, so did their movements, until our passionate exchange of intimacy was in perfect harmony with the light show on the wall. A moment of perfect beauty and bliss.

In the morning, still in my bed and with Ann in my arms, we had laughs as I said to her,

- 'I have neverrrr bean in bad withan Amerrrican woouman, as I'm stocktaking!'

- ' Gee... and I have not with an African Scot either!' she replied.

I smiled and said

- 'Rrright' and gave her a kiss

There was a knock on the door. It was one of the service

members who brought us in a tray of breakfast in bed. The maid had a smile on her face to see us together in bed. She said that the breakfast is with the wishes for a good day from Mrs. June!

We had 'breakfast' again! After, we loved the banana bread with jam and croissants and scrambled eggs with fried pineapple and coconut. Ann said to me,

- 'I saw you looking in my eyes last night, but now you are not. Are you shy now?'
- ' a little bit!' I said admittedly.

She got up and came to seat on my knees and stroke my head, kissed me and said,

- ' This is what I loved about you. Your shyness attracted me to find out more in you. You are a gentleman. I am sorry I will not get to know more of you..., as I am leaving on the first helicopter ride'.

I waved goodbye to her, when she was getting in the helicopter. She signaled to watch an albatross flying near me and she smiled!

Three months later I visited June in London, near Kew Gardens where they lived, and we went for a walk and a chat. We were close to each other and we could go nuts a little, starting a discussion from a flower to a plate of food and then to somewhere totally further. Variety, a spice of friendship. She asked me what I thought of Ann and I said wonderful things that she already knew. I said that I may visit her one day in Miami. She then said that Ann would be at the Grosvenor House Hotel the day after for only one night and since we were both in London, perhaps to go and meet her. Music to my ears to set up a surprise.

Ann was in London on a business trip, so I gathered that after five in the afternoon, she would be back to the hotel. I made my way to the hotel with a bunch of colourful roses and a bottle of Cristal Champagne. Romantic me walks to the reception and asks for her room number straight away to surprise her.

The receptionist looked again and again and took his time

in saying, would I please sit at the sofa and wait. I insisted that I wanted to go on my own and knock on the door, but he was adamant that I stay put on a sofa. He called someone in whispers and not a minute passed when I saw two very tall men in black that came right above me and asked me to follow them. They were sharp and strict with no facial expression. One had a wire in his ear. I felt weird and scared as I was out of my comfort zone. I asked what is going on and they did not reply but escorted me to a private small conference room and started almost interrogating me, names, nationalities, parents and then straight questions why I want to see Mrs. Ann and where have we met to which I felt reluctant to contribute more information. I asked again, what was all this about and I said that I am not feeling very comfortable in this room with two men looking like secret agents. I asked who they were. Then one of them said, Mr. Paris, if you were going to confirm your identity to Mrs. Ann with two words what would these be. I felt better as I understood that they were security men. I thought for a few seconds and there was an awakening smile on my face in saying

- 'Albatross and Scottish!'.

One man stayed with me and the other one left for a couple of minutes. No word came out in that room both ways, with my legs trembling and my stomach was tied in knots, I felt I was going to walk out of the hotel and to hell with all that. A message was wired in the ear of the man next to me, he smiled and he asked me to follow him to the lift. I felt so short next to these men.

The bedroom door opened and Ann walked towards me. I could not believe I made it to the room and my legs were shaking after all that experience. We hugged in the presence of the men in black who were still unexpressive. Ann asked them to leave us alone and the door closed. It took us only a minute to feel again as if it was us in that bedroom three months ago. She looked dressed for business in a blue suit and had red lipstick and red nails. She explained that she was in London on a high security case and that even in Miami she has bodyguards wherever she goes, hence the security check at the reception.

She asked me to stay and have a bite as she was hungry too. A table on wheels was pushed in by the bodyguards, probably having checked everything before. We had cold salmon cuts and prawns with avocado and warm bread, an orange and basil salad and a small surprise to me a Dundee cake. We drank some Scottish whiskey from the Isle of Jura instead of the champagne and she said to me 'slanj-a-va'.

I felt, she had work to see to, and her mind was occupied on her case. On my way out I said to her,

- 'Anne, I am not coming to see you in Miami as you live an impossibly dangerous lifestyle to have a good time' and she smiled.
  'but I invite you one day to go to Scotland together, or perhaps meet you in Chicago at a jazz bar, whatever you wish!'

We hugged and kissed goodbye. We never met again but I treasured the experience of a sophisticated lady romancing with me in an idyllic island. I learned more from goodbyes than from welcomes!

ZOE GAVE ME ZOE

I met this Swiss beauty who socially came with a friend of mine at Le Bistro. Zoe, was very beautiful and sexy with long black curly hair, big green eyes, juicy lips and with the figure of a model as she was, a few years back. She was very lively and always smiling and teasing everyone. She was the type attracting the attention of everyone, including mine. Zoe and I clicked as friends for years and I often traveled to Geneva, where she lived, and stayed with her, going shopping, dining, cooking and sharing time with her boyfriend too. She had a boutique, and I was often there charming her clients as to what they should try on and buy. She visited me often in Cyprus, Protaras by the sea, where I used to live. Although she lived the Geneva-life, in Cyprus she loved eating watermelon with her hands on the beach.

We were introduced to each other's families and friends. All my friends loved her for being so diversified in meeting people and for her vibrant socializing. She was always kind to all and a very giving person no matter what. It was her Karma to be so giving and many good things were coming back to her. Lots of new friends, success in her business, and a positive attitude to life, on a daily basis. We shared our problems and dreams and felt for each other as two friends do when sentimentally devoted.

Once I visited her with Elena, my then girlfriend from Greece. We stayed with her in Geneva, at her beautiful and stylish modern apartment full of art and eclecticism. On one of our outings, we visited a Mexican restaurant in Geneva. One of those places, where they scarcely place art crafts on the walls, hats and colorful throws and play any type of Mexican tourist music bought on a trip to Mexico all in all to convince you of the authenticity of its nationality. After some drinks, my hot girlfriend Elena and myself, as we do in our part of the world, we danced on the table to the song 'Tequila', what else! Lots of Swiss people were suddenly animated, a rather rare sight, and surrounded our table dancing with us, seeking a little entertainment and an escapism from their Swiss dedication to serious and monotonous life's routine. Zoe was so proud in telling everyone, these are my friends. The Swiss restaurant owner, invited us to do the same on a Saturday night when his place would be packed!

On one of my trips, I went to assist her to stage a small fashion show in her boutique which was a great success. I drunk a lot of champagne in the company of so many women. I met a Swiss shapely lady, whose name never stayed with me and who was very interested in coming with me to bed that same moment. You see, being suntanned Mediterranean and with an accent, is always attractive to some, as they make their own Shirley Valentine's stories as in the relevant film. Everyone needs to dream and it is indeed healthy. Not to dream you would be like a straight-line cardiograph.

At the boutique and during the show, I saw Zoe not happy and I was concerned. Her boyfriend, Jean, did not have the interest to support her with his presence. Towards the end of the event, Zoe noticed my flirty interaction with the Swiss lady, who in turn informed her that we were leaving and she would drive me to Zoe's home, until she would finish her job, as I was a little tipsy.

At home there was a situation on the sofa, where as soon as we entered it accommodated our bodies in various movements and that did not last for a long time, as there was no plot or chemistry. I sat semi-dressed on the sofa and she sat on the armchair next to me. I must have been so angry that I was talking, boring her, while criticizing Zoe's boyfriend that he did not come and has upset my friend. This must have gone on for some time, as I went onto the subject praising my friend Zoe, saying:

- 'Zoe is so gorgeous, attractive, with beautiful green eyes. She is a sexy hot tiger, a bonnie lass...do you know what this means?? She is kind hearted, an angel to everyone, loving and caring, a sex bomb that she deserves a real man to love her and treasure her, take her places and keep her always happy, whatever the cost, as she deserves the best... do you know what I mean?.... I wish... I wish I had her as my girlfriend!...Who is this guy who neglected her today? What does he think he is? Zoe is my friend, she is mine.... or I wish she was mine!' my words coming out from a drunken man spread on the sofa.

Meanwhile, I fell fast asleep to work off all that alcohol. Little that I knew Zoe has previously come home and was listening to me talking from the room upstairs.

When I finally opened my eyes a few hours later, I saw Zoe sitting in front of me and looking at me in a skeptical way. She repeated all my words I said about her, and spoke

- 'Paris, it is the first time I have listened to you expressing like that and I am very flattered that you have feelings for me more than I ever understood.'

It was in front of the fire place with no lights on, the trees were waving at us from the windows, we could barely hear the sounds of the leaves touching or clapping for us as they followed the soft blowing wind. Somehow, we were drawn to kiss and we kissed and we kissed feeling the beginning of a new era in this relationship.

I stopped sleeping in the guest bedroom and I had the role of the man of the house. I began to look after her, whenever I was visiting at least every month for a few days. I would arrive at Geneva and drive her Porsche to the traiteur for gourmet 'ammunitions', order wines and flowers and all would be delivered at home. I saw to all the small handyman's jobs around the house. Life was more than perfect. My little treats to her changed to sexy underwear and accessories, surprise trips, flowers and heart shape chocolates, a bottle of Lynch Bages, being her favorite, but sometimes very small things too, kept her smiling and happy. We planned holidays together in faraway destinations like India and the United States and we took short trips in Europe too. It was all great fun times together.

On my long travels to India, we made a deal that she would follow for a while, my low budget schedule till she needed her comfort, to which she would undertake the cost. So, we stayed from tents in the desserts to Palaces and from house boats to seven-star hotels. We met street people and shopkeepers but Maharajas too. I was in my element and everywhere was a story to be told. Prior to departure I repacked her clothes, as being an ex- model, she used to wear tight clothes and cat suits, evidently exposing the shape of her big breasts, and her sexy body curves, a dangerous sight in places like the streets of Delhi and everywhere in that part of the world. So, instead I packed full skirts and loose blouses, shawls and long loose pants to disguise the beautiful and feminine curves of her body for our safety too!

We stayed in the Lake Palace Hotel in Udaipur, an amazing experience. Strolling in the garden and the shops of the hotel she saw an old golden Indian antique necklace but a little out of our budget. She at first decided not to buy it, but the whole evening at dinner she expressed that she loved it and when we went back to buy it the shop had already closed. The next morning, we were to leave early for our next stop. I purposely delayed our departure as I said I had a belly problem, as one does after spicy Indian food, and spent quite some time locked in the loo. In reality, I wanted to kill time as I had arranged with the shopkeeper, through the receptionist, to open earlier so that I can buy that necklace for her as a surprise. We waited enough time until it felt it was not meant to happen.

The Lake Palace Hotel is in the middle of the lake. As our little boat was taking us to our car off shore, I could see the other boat with the shopkeeper crossing in the opposite direction going to the hotel shop to meet me. Cleverly of him who was well into the plot, when we arrived at the car, a hotel messenger called me back to say that we have not paid the laundry bill.

Zoe stayed in the car while I went to do so, but in reality, they brought me the necklace I was interested and I paid it there and then. I have hidden the velvet pouch in my shirt so that it can become a surprise later on. During our trip in the car Zoe got tired and wanted to lie on me to sleep to which I seemed distant and unconcerned to her, as I did not want her to feel on my belly the round necklace and I could not move it in front of her. Our trip lasted four hours. Four hours of not touching in the same back seat was very inexplicable to her and she got cross with me and kept looking the other way.

On arrival to our next hotel stay and as soon as I had a chance, I placed the necklace at the bottom of my bag and I became the most touchy and loving man with hands annoyingly full on her from there on. We loved India, the colours, the smells, the people and the culture. Fun times in the car with our driver and high pitch Indian singers at full blast, roads with holes and cows crossing every now and then. We traveled places went to weddings and had unforgettable moments.

While traveling to south India in Kerala, we hired a house boat with a cook and a paddler. We spent a week on the Backwaters floating over the water covered by colourful water lilies. The sides of the land forming our ways to the next turn were fringed with thick palm trees. The first day we thought we would be bored but themn we merged with the peaceful nature. The birds were greeting us, the breeze made the palm trees wave and cool us during the day and the stars shined looking down on u at night. We had our mobile phones off, we were so in harmony with the set around us. The cook was fishing our dinner and mixing it with tomatoes and curry with rice. At night we slept in a room with a bathroom, cleverly formed with bamboo weave on the boat and created more stories. This experience was not discovered by many those days and we did a few days to meet another house boat crossing us.

On one occasion we got out as the cook needed some more coconut oil and vegetables to buy from a small village of a dozen shacks, being houses scattered around the shore and under the palm trees. We walked around and we were noticed by children who were laughing at us because we were white. Some were hiding behind the trees as they were shy. One brave boy, around 12 years old, came towards us and suggested a handshake. I grabbed his hand and as I asked him

- 'What is your name', all the children laughed as I had a voice too.

- 'My name is Promote' he said with his intense black eyes opening even bigger.

-It is good you speak English' I said '...and what do you want to become when you grow up?'

- ' I want to be a pilot!' he proudly replied, and made me think of an impossible achievement. From the middle of nowhere, a few basic houses, a shack that was a school for twenty children and the dream of his to become a pilot! It felt like me wishing to go to Mars. I gave him my address on a piece of paper and a pen, and said to Promote

- ' I am sure you will be a pilot, if you study hard. Then write to me and let me know'.

We traveled by train to Punjab, and that was an experience, where we met a young man in his mid-twenties, called Murad. He was a student, back in Nicosia when I had the venue Diagorou, and he was our pot washer. When Murad found out that Zoe and myself were traveling to India, he invited us to his brother's wedding in Amritsar. When we arrived, there was a driver and he sat in the car with us. A different economy in India allowed Murad to be a land owner with servants and drivers. He lived in a large agriculture farm in a house with eight bedrooms. Our washer up was now our host, looking after us by giving orders to others to carry our luggage and prepare our room. We met his parents and uncles. The wedding took place for three days non-stop. Zoe wore a saree and she looked absolutely ridiculous. There is something about the Indian ladies carrying the saree perfectly well. Any white woman would look wrong in it, weather is the color complexion or posture, I do not know!

Zoe changed into a red dress and she draped a beige shawl over her left shoulder and she then looked stunning. There we met all sorts of relatives spread, from New Zealand to London and a million Punjabis. We danced and ate and ate again, to show our appreciation of their hospitality.

From Amritsar we traveled with a private driver to Jaisalmer where we did a camel ride for half a day almost or until our backs were hurting from the bouncing of the camels. We were met and welcomed by some nomads and had some curry cooked on the fire in front of us. We were joined by some Italian couples and one from Sweden. The nomads told us their history and what they did. They tried, as they all do in India, to sell us shawls and handmade jewelry but we were not interested. They cooked for us and played music and danced for our entertainment. It was part of the experience to pass around a marijuana pot. Zoe suggested I try and she would stay well away from it as we both did not know the effects and as we were both far away from any substances. The small pipe was passed around. It looked that all the couples had previously experienced it. As I took some puffs, there was a feeling of joy and then nothing else. Zoe was stroking my head, while I fell asleep or in a coma but with a smile on my face. All the couples were allocated sleeping bags in a nomad hut, as I found myself stretched, in the morning. We explored the nomad's life. I was feeling at home. We slept in the desert for another two days and felt like nomads, living with the camels, unwashed and eating breakfast and dinner the same curried rice. My Swiss partner began to protest!

The next morning, we had a ten-hour drive back to New Delhi. It was closer to Zoe's departure day. I planned to stay another month, after she was back to Switzerland, for more adventures. India and its people were talking to me. Zoe, asked the driver for the Oberoi Hotel, being of course an exclusive hotel as she planned to use her credit card. We looked a state, traveling from the dessert covered by sand and being dirty.

When we finally arrived at the hotel, not even the concierge wanted to greet us or open the door. I felt the problems as we looked not the normal type of Oberoi guests. I asked her for her Platinum American Express and her Swiss passport underneath the card. I put my Cyprus passport under hers and I directed my efforts to the receptionist, with a Bindi on her forehead, to negotiate the possibility of renting a room. I asked for just any room, as Zoe was very exhausted. The task looked impossible. The receptionist insisted that the hotel was full. She wanted to send us to a three-star hotel of the same company. I even asked for the Presidential suite and I was denied the possibility of it. When I felt that I had been through all the avenues, I overturned the passports on her bench, so that I did not lose the credit card and my passport at the bottom was now on the top. I turned to talk to Zoe, we have yet to load our luggage on a taxi and go to another hotel, when the receptionist talked to me in Greek, and this time with a smile! ' Are you from Cyprus? I see now your passport!' I replied with surprise and feeling the contrast in India and talking in Greek,' Yes I am, and how come you speak Greek?' She smiled and said ' Oh Sir, I have studied for hotel business in Larnaca in Cyprus and this is my first job. I love Cyprus. I will give you a nice room!' We signed for a suite and I took the pleasure to tease Zoe, almost throwing back at her the platinum American Express and her Swiss passport as I was waving the Cyprus passport that got us a room.

An hour later, when we eventually felt some warm water and soap on our bodies and dressed as the guests of the Oberoi, the receptionist looked happier and she confirmed her right decision. The room was not cheap and lived up to its expectations. We were lost in luxury with golden taps, marble floors and a huge lush bed, finally comfort!

That same year at Christmas time I went to Geneva and we had a memorial dinner, prepared Indian style from tablecloths to plates. She was busy at the boutique and she came in tired. I gave her a foot soak and a massage with Indian oils, before we sat at the feast for a Coconut fish curry, Kerala style, ending with a ginger crème brulé with caramelized lemons from Cyprus.

There was a gift on the table for her. A big, heavy,

square box. She loved presents, just like a five-year-old girl. The expression on her face was as if Father Christmas just came in. She looked surprised, excited and in anticipation.

- 'This is for you for Christmas, you must open it slowly' I challenged her.
- ' But I did not get you anything yet... I was too busy at the shop!' She apologized
- 'You are my present and I don't need more' I said.

She thought it was going to be something very big for the house, so she was careful in untying the ribbon, unwrapping the paper and opening the box which was full of lemons and oranges. She laughed, as she thought it was a joke.

- 'Can you estimate how many lemons there are and how many oranges? I asked her to take away any thoughts and suspicions of a finding.

We both made a guess and the looser was to wash the dishes. I did not remember at all what was the correct answer anyway. When she started counting the lemons and oranges out of the box to verify our scores, she came to a velvet pouch. She looked at me inquisitively. The five-year-old girl expression became a big question mark drawn on her face as to what was that. Suspense was everywhere in the room; my face was red from excitement. As she took the pouch in her hands and opened the string...she realized what it was. Her face turned into tears, so many that she covered her eyes with her hands. Then only I could explain why I was distant in the car in India and then the biggest 'I love you' echoed in my ears for many years after. I was happy and proud that the plan worked after all these months and to see her so excited. Nevertheless, I washed the dishes too!

Zoe marked a great time in my life. I had a thriving business; I was very sporty and healthy. I had her in my life, it was a loving relationship with freedom and a meaning. I was traveling to Switzerland and other places adding to life experiences.

One evening back home in Cyprus, as I was getting dressed to go to work, in my newly bought clothes and while wearing a new Swiss watch, I took a big breath and said to myself, gosh I wish that something happens to break this routine and become happier, to have a challenge perhaps!

About ten days later, one night after work, my friend Gregory from the French restaurant, drove me in my car home. He stopped at a kiosk to buy cigarettes and he tripped as he was walking in. Driving away from the kiosk he took the wrong turning and he had to reverse. He was driving slowly and no other cars were on the road except one, coming from the opposite direction. It was a big lorry and ended right on us for a head-to-head collision. It sounded like lots of metals crushing into an ugly combination. It felt we were thrown in front and stopped by a wall. There was silence as the brain was trying to process what has happened.

I looked at Gregory and asked

- 'Are you ok? Are you hurt?'

He looked at himself and touched his chest and said,

- 'Yes, I think I am not hurt, what about you?'
- 'I think I am fine, please go to the other car, they seem to be very hurt as no one came out. Go and see if they are alive' I said worried.

He did that and shouted back to me pissed off

- 'Paris... they are fast asleep man; they are very drunk!' and he walked back to my side of the car
- 'Why are you not coming out?' he wondered as he tried to open my car door which was not working .
- ' I cannot move' I said,' I don't feel any pain anywhere but I cannot move my legs...'

He tried with force to open again the car door. He saw a man who stopped to see if we needed help walking towards the scene with a cigarette in his hand. Gregory was concerned of the risk of fire as all sorts of engine liquids formed a cocktail on the road after the collision. He shouted to the man approaching

- 'Stop, don't come any closer with the cigarette! Stop right there... it's dangerous... stop!'

The man still carried on walking and Gregory knew he had to get me out from being trapped in the car.
I could hear him breathing heavy struggling in despair as he put his hands through the window and pulled me out, which no one could succeed under normal circumstances. Fear and concern shot up his adrenaline to do so. I felt a pain in my body and lost consciousness in the hands of Gregory. Pain in my waist brought me back to my senses as Gregory was shouting at me to stay awake until an ambulance would come. I lost consciousness again as I felt Gregory in despair.
It seemed that the accident was meant to happen. Someone had listened to what I wished for! My routine has changed and I was about to die! It served me right, having such a good life and yet not acknowledging it. I remember the scene as if it's happening right now.

I was taken to the general hospital in Larnaca, some 45 minutes from the accident scene, at the intensive care unit, as I had internal hemorrhage, broke my pelvis, my head, nose, hand and shoulder. The doctors gave me little hope. Zoe, when she found out, managed to get the doctors in Switzerland to review my x-rays. The Swiss doctors had more experiences on broken pelvis because of the skiing accidents and were confident that I would walk again after the operation. They accepted her money as a deposit, so they sent me an ambulance plane to take me to Switzerland to be operated on. I remember the flying doctors when they met me at the hospital and injected me with some drug not to feel any pain. I must have been asleep the whole journey on board and I woke up in the hospital in Switzerland.

The flying lady doctor handed me over to a male doctor at the hospital. Before she left, she asked me if I remembered anything on the airplane. I replied 'no' and she laughed! She asked what my profession was and I replied 'restaurants'. Apparently, she said, I was talking in my sleep and she kept asking me what I was enjoying.

- ' You kept smiling. I asked you what are you dreaming of?

You were answering in absurd words and I could not make sense of them. Do you recall at all?' she asked in a curious way

- 'yes, I think so'... I said,' there was a forest with tall green trees and a strong purple color background as the sky. There were these small creatures like leprechauns, with arrows sending rosti potato cakes to hit these men in kilts near the trees. These men were black in kilts, held knives and were cutting these potato cakes in defense and forming yellow small explosions, when the cakes were cut in two by their knives. There were sounds of drums from Africa mixed with saxophone melodies but not blending at all, I felt my father was watching me'

- ' That was very different to what I hear other times!' She replied with a smile.

It was a long operation of some 10 hours, then a three-month recovery period where Zoe and the others around me looked after me, as that was the worst situation one can find your partner to be in. I have been through a lot of emotional changes during the hospital times and the rehabilitation stage. I put my head down and had to accept the situation. I depended on everyone around me for everything, and I was not me. It was quite humiliating at times being fed and cleaned by younger nurses of both genders. I could not move. But I lived! I was blessed again!

One day I was taken on a wheel chair for some creative exercises and my first shower seating on the wheel chair, after ten weeks in a hospital bed. I asked the nurse to leave me alone under the shower and felt as if I was a fish needingto breathe again in water. Then she came back to assist me to dry as I could barely move all parts of my body. She dried me and left me looking at the pool, used for exercising to regain mobility, while I was waiting for an assistant to come and wheel me back to my room. Twenty minutes passed. I was getting a little angry as I could not move and depended on others. The door opened and a man, half covered in a blanket, wheeled himself by the pool.

We greeted each other as two comrades. He was very handsome and well trained as he had a bodybuilders' chest and arms, small waist and broad shoulders. He uncovered himself from the blankets to get into the pool for a swim. He had no legs. He slid to the floor. He placed his hands on the floor and made his way like a frog into the water where he began to enjoy a swim. I had no words. I felt I had no right to be angry in waiting for the assistant to take me back to my room! When the assistant came, I was extremely polite and smiling, I thanked him for coming. I thanked everyone that assisted me, I thanked Zoe, the doctors, I thanked everyone, I thanked any power that was above me listening to me. I thanked for this lesson in life I have received which changed my spectrum and still...

When I was in the rehabilitation stage and at another hospital, near Konstanz Lake, three hour's drive from Zoe's residence, I had a daily visitor. An 83-year-old Swiss gentleman, Harry, a retired pilot trainer, a wise man. His face was declaring years of wisdom. A month prior to my accident, we connected with Harry over lunch in Tuscany, at some close friends of Zoe's, who had a beautiful and picturesque estate, producing wine and olive oil. Catherine, her friend, had a small airplane company flying businessmen here and there in Europe. That day she flew to Florence and back in search of fresh pasta, mussels and scallops for our lunch.

Harry was driving an hour almost every day to be at three o clock in my room, to help dress me. He would assist the nurse, to place me on the wheelchair. He pushed me in the wheelchair to the garden to get fresh air. We talked for a couple of hours, as I had to be back for an injection. We bonded and had a good and warm feeling being close and new friends. We talked about Alexander the Great, relationships, airplanes, life and death, food and wars, women and love, just about everything.

He was so constructed in his talk, wise and so well positioned in everything. It felt that God had sent him to me for a reason. He had a sparkle in his eyes. He needed also to talk. He talked on how much he loved his girlfriend. It was a fresh romance. He left his wife for her. He fell out of love more than 10 years ago and he has explained to her that he loved her, but no longer was in love with her. It became a different love. He made sure she was well looked after with money and called her every day and visited her as often and as a friend now as he cared for her.

- ' It is best to go away when love is not there anymore, otherwise you will make people unhappy and have them trapped and that is wrong', he said.

'But now I want to love my new romance, I will die soon, and I want to live another entire life to be with her. I want to feel love again, I want this to happen to me as well' were his words.
Love, a word of endless meanings and an immense depth! Love the power of everything that makes the world go around.
Haris' words stayed on my mind. Deep inside me I wanted to feel like this.

I treasured my time with him. I felt uncomfortable to be carried, by an 80-year-old, on a wheelchair. I was helpless, but the same time, I was honored for making such a friend, a unique soul, Harry. I wished that this would happen to everyone I knew.

Before I was released, on our last wheelchair outing, he gave me one of his belongings, from when he was flying, I suppose. A gift of life, an old bronze compass with a message

- ' I wish you to find your way too, to what you are looking for'.

When I was at this hospital, I had another surprise, a gift of love. My beloved friends Peter and Erica drove all the way from Sweden and stayed in a hotel near the hospital for five nights. They came at five in the afternoon to get me ready for an outing. Peter was dressing me up and helping me to seat in the wheel chair and then in and out of the car. The destinations were distinguished restaurants from the Michelin guide book, all in that area. Exceptional handling and processing of fresh produce to become exciting plated combinations alongside excellent service. All the meals we had were amazing and even a glass of wine was recommended by the doctors. It was a good vintage Bordeaux in the class of Lynch Bages and dare to say Châteaux Margaux as well. Zoe joined us a few times too, as she had a long drive to come from her workplace. I had to be back by ten o' clock at night, for another injection and to rest. The nurse was waiting for me with an injection in her hand as a revenge treat for my outing. Bless them all, what a gift that was, to give me their holiday time and spend it with me this way! Friends!

It was time, three months after the operation and the rehabilitation treatments that I could walk with crutches, returned to Cyprus and the sea helped quickly for muscle recovery. A month later I was back on track with life and work. I felt that everyone around me were happy too!

Zoe and I continued sharing good times whenever we met. The airhostesses got to know us and our stories. Our times together were very special. Even lying in my arms watching tv was magical, sharing a sandwich and a juice for breakfast, going to the Opera in Graz or driving around Como, whatever it was, the feeling was the same of love and care. How can you love a woman as your sister, but also as the most attractive specie on earth for you...it was a blend like that. She was my everyday reference, my thought my only care. I wanted her, to always be happy. I was proud of her, of who and how she was and yet was hard to say I love you, but feelings were there!

With time passing, our togetherness, between two countries, was not enough to her. It was a long-distance relationship and she was now at the age when she needed stability and security in her life and not my crazy adventurous thirst to experience more and more. We went through some fading patches. I was not ready for that trip and I was not the right one for her. She was not ready for me either! There was a caring kind of love between us, romanticism, a different level of love, but there were others for us the same time. Our kind of love will always be for each other, it still is somehow. There is always a candle lit somewhere in us, for every soul we met in our lives.

This was new to me.

Not a day passes, when I wake up in the morning and I put my feet on the floor that I don't feel lucky and blessed. Life now had more meaning. I had learned to appreciate everything and every moment. I had learned to protect and treasure. I was privileged and lucky to have met Zoe in my course of life. We lived to experience, I felt wiser with women because of her. She gave me back my 'Zoe'. Zoe was my life.

CUBA

After the accident, a need to explore and live scenarios was increasing. I was ready for more business concepts to be created and equipped with more of what looked sophisticated! A word that can be so misconceived but in my world it conjured images of contrasts at different levels. My genes were interfering inside me and were fighting all the time till the amicable agreement to co-exist at a survived contrast scenario. Contrast, seemed to have been the recipe for success in my life. Something new was brewing.

Exerted by the music rhythm, the rum, the history and its exclusivity from the western world, were enough reasons to book my way to Cuba in the middle of the 90s. I arrived to this forgotten world, not knowing what I would find there and booked a room for a week in Havana at a traditional hotel with ornated Spanish tiles, large cane armchairs and palm trees all over. Scenarios known from some American movies, were unfolding right in front of my eyes. I traveled back where men wore white jackets and black bow ties, escorting ladies to the dance hall. The glamorous ladies were coming out of these long limos, one after the other, at the grand entrance of the building. Shiny skins and hairstyles of the 50s, long dresses, with their backs showing and cleavage revealing on the front, and definitely pearls.

I walked and walked the town from top to bottom and sneaked into buildings, dark alleys and back dangerous streets. Lots of buildings were empty, abandoned, but full of previous lives and happenings, histories and film sets, were in my mind. I felt the energy of Havana in me, the people's awareness of the possibility for sex, the Latin spirit and the forever looking around eyes in exploration, were like my electricity taking it all in.

I people watched and tried to see through them. The band in that colourful corner restaurant, early afternoon, all musicians showing enthusiasm, talent, love and their roots of culture through their musical instruments. They created a vibe, making your feet tap and your head to move, ending to your waist almost twirl around your core. The rhythm to dance was the start of the accelerated power to do something, to come out, reach and absorb the feeling and be part of this scenario. There is something about dancing, releasing, freeing the body provoking your inner world to becomes open to suggestions, to intake challenges and of other bodies, preferably uncovered or at least to the mind and the after effects of interactive moves interlaced to the ecstasy of the rhythm of music.

I felt constantly aroused by everything around me in Havana. I was starved for an experience, as all was so unusual, and was living a real dream as to what was in my mind before, a Hollywood production. I was there to make my own and to be the major actor in it.

One afternoon, walking around with my camera and taking stunning pictures of buildings, I saw perhaps the best looking, handsome version of an ancient Greek god on the street. He had a full muscle body, enough to make me feel an apology of a man compared to him. He had very big blue eyes, long wavy blond hair and red lips. He wore white linen clothes and sandals looking like a large version of a cupid with wings as he walked in the middle of the street. I stopped and took a picture of him with the blue sky and the old buildings as a background. As I was in camera focus, I noticed through the lens, a girl walking in the opposite direction towards him. There was an exchange of glances, a greeting that declared acknowledgment of each other's beauty. It was a greeting that showed there was no previous history between them. The God offered his hand which she willingly took. He gently pulled her right in front, in line with his body. That was a great posture of the two bodies in perfect harmony in parallel lines. The bodies became one silhouette and there was a kiss. A passionate real full throttle kiss. I took many pictures with my camera and more in my head.

I felt the sensuality of the kiss, the temperature of their bodies that had no clothes, in my mind, from the distance where I stood. She had a slim line curvy figure and she wore a strapless black dress. She had long straight black hair and dark eyes. Her face was attractive too featuring high bone cheeks and dimples. After their kiss they hugged and continued their way as if nothing happened. I took a minute to rethink the two meeting on the street, liking each other and kissing hello, maybe see you another day. Declaring attraction and the freedom to interaction seemed so easy over there. This would have been so much more complicated to the rest of the world. Perhaps a contract would have to been signed, prior to this such natural expression, simple and spontaneous act of kissing on the street.

I walked away in my pace for more visual feasts when a gentle hand touched me on my back. It was the hand of that beauty, kissed by that God. She noticed that I was curious, looking at them through the camera. She asked, if I wanted company and that was the start of the dream I wanted to produce, and live. A play I wanted to be the main actor in, a place that was before on my mental travels, but now a reality. I think I had a constant smile, big enough for the whole earth to be in my mouth.

Her name was Lucia, but she was my Carmen, my gypsy lady that was with me probably for something else, money or experience, but making me feel she was there just for me. I chose to go for the latter! She was easy with everything; she made the first move and held my hand walking, as a sign of submission. She asked me from where I was from,and I said from Greece, as few knew Cyprus. I did say once from Africa but it was hard to explain how I was thinking about my past lives to her. So, she knew of Greece and the Olympics and perhaps it was better like that, as she would have had a better idea of myself and my outcomes.

In the evening, Luxia suggested a super night club to dance to a 20 member Cuban band. The plot started in a pink Chevrolet cabrio taxi, with white leather seats, driven along the coast and as the waves were spinning on the shore and wetting the pavement all the way to the club. I was sitting at the back with Carmen in my arms and enjoying the cool air brushing on our faces and bodies in light clothes. She gently undone my trousers and shirt and kissed my chest and going down on me. She made all the right moves towards my pants to give me, of what is forever established as an unforgettable, once in a lifetime experience, a feeling not possible to be duplicated or produced again. The starry skies opened into blue colors, and again into orange and the colors were interchanging alongside my deeper level of pleasure penetrating all my body parts having my cock sucked. The driver moved his mirror to another direction as my face must have started declaring a total happiness as delivering a fountain of sperm. It felt like the Rebirth of Adam, in the painting of Michael Angelo to the sounds of Don Giovanni opera while Donna Anna seducing me and I was indeed the Don Giovanni and up there on the Seventh Heaven!

I never imagined such a beautiful woman to ever want to be with me. I was happily surprised and it help build up my confidence. That same night after a few rums, dancing and laughing we spent the night in my bed pleasuring each other and myself acting like a teanager. I saw the Greek God making love to her but it was me. When she was in my arms, I dreamed of being the handsome him... but Theoharis from my grey years started chasing me with his axe. I was running, probably my legs were moving in bed, and I was trying to run faster and faster as he was going to reach me. From a corner of a street the Greek God waved at me to follow him through the side street, a wave that had a note of confidence to safety. The feeling of danger was gone, we walked side by side as if we were good friends and I was proud to be next to him. I had the conforting feeling of being safe with him. He had a certain caring look.

Havana had exerted a power on me. I have tried to explore other areas on the island. It was interesting and educative but I have not felt the attraction to the atmosphere as I did in Havana. I have been to all famous places, the El Froridita bar, the Bacardi building and to Club Tropicana, where the show to run needed half of Havana in darkness to support electricity current for the lights on stage of the show. The opening act was the girls, Las chicas bonitas, having a sequence dance with chandeliers on their heads as in the 50s movies. I saw Ernest and further down Rita and Humphrey and cheered to Frank, Eva and Marlon of course. I was speechless through the show and sipping down rum, I traveled through times and back. I was not alone.

In Havana, I took regularly, salsa lessons, in a group with an older lady teacher. She was a 'Hermosa mujer ', the goddess of curves, with a glorious smile and passion to move those hips. After a week, she placed me next to her and said:

- ' Hey Greco, stop trying to dance like I show everyone. Carry on to dance with your soul as you do, I can see you feel other things! It is better'.

No one can take these scenarios away from my mind and certainly not ready to stop them.

THE VENUE

In 1994 and while Le Bistro was running in Ayia Napa, I opened a revolutionary all day industrial feel of high design, bar- resto -venue, in the heart of Nicosia. From my travels, from fashion, from music, from people's conversations I used to inspire me and somehow understand trends and forthcoming ones. I felt we were going away from the heavily decorated entertainment places and people needed simpler environments, comfortable and with the possibility to mix and socialize. As technology was creeping in, people were more alienated from socializing and partying. Eating in large restaurants, where there was a crowd buzz, became important. I put new ideas in a place for the capital's citizens of Nicosia.

This venue was called Diagorou 12, which was the address as well. It introduced a different buzz in town. It attracted a mixture of personalities in different routines and roles in life, like lawyers, merchants, accountants, secretaries, shop owners, fashion designers, all city people. All, with the same interest, in the development of social interaction and sexuality, to break away from their busy work lives. It offered food, drinks, music dance and a high social scene.

Housed in an old building with high ceilings and wooden floors, we kept all its charm and added anything that had to do with lighting and, ventilation exposed becoming almost a feature. It gave an industrial look. We had low wooden tables with metal chairs for eating and high tables mixed and matched for drinking around the bar. Two long bars with 5 bartenders behind were preparing all sorts of drinks. The place had a sexy buzz. I was astounded by the receipt of the crowds but also the variety of customers pouring in.

Sometimes, my fantasy saw them as happy animals, queuing to come in to meet and mate. First having dinner together, then dance and then out of control, the one on top of the other manifesting. What I saw was not an objective, my mind was constructing what I was seeing, all an illusion. My perception involved interpretation and the thoughts, the memories and the emotions lead the way on how we interpret what we see. I was ready to accept that what I see is real and weaving data into my mind.

Still, while my imagination traveled, I maintained a smile and I was the host- owner of this extravagant place in town. I lived right above the venue in a bachelor style one-bedroom apartment with large windows and wooden floors. I had a masculine feel. There was an inviting, black four poster metal bed and a large clothes rail, one black sofa in front of a tv and a record player. A real Persian carpet, given to me by my mother, was somewhere in the middle of the room declaring sophistication, class and culture. A little kitchenette, for off restaurant hours snacking, featured more whiskey, than food.

At the setup of this venue, I hired a marketing team helping to present the idea correctly, and as one would expect by spending long hours with the team, you develop some kind of relationships! There was a sexy bomb with ample bosom character, thick lips and energy that was drawn to my attention and did not take long for us to crawl together in my bed. Dina was younger than me, hot and energetic but scary jealous when during the parties I was sociable or more with other souls participating in the animal feast of exploration.

We booked a night in Athens to enjoy dancing at a venue playing bouzoukia, smashing plates and throwing flowers to the singers, as it is the norm for a night out in a place like that. We danced on the tables and enjoyed singing Greek songs at the top of our voices. When we went to our hotel, at least happy from the evenings drinking, we opened a bottle of champagne in the bath. 'Two party animals in a hot bath and drinking champagne' was the title of the chapter 'catastrophe' that follows.

As we moved our bodies to succeed the act of sex in the bath, the water started coming out on the floor. We have turned the tap on to refill it. It was somehow restricted in the bath. We found ourselves on the carpeted floor on more body introductions. We were lost in the moment and felt like we were the only two people in the world. It felt like the perfect moment for us.

We got into the bed and started having wild sex. We were so full of lust and intense feelings that we almost destroyed the room. We started throwing pillows everywhere and the bedsheets somehow ended all over the room. The bedside lampshades broke on the floor and the glasses smashed too while the rest of the champagne was spilled on the carpet. We kept going until we were both exhausted, if I remember well. We fell asleep in an awkward body combination.

We were woken up by a strong knock on the door. I covered my front by a towel, walked on a wet carpet to open the door to a very angry face, the duty hotel manager. It seemed that the water from the bath tap was still running and had reached the reception area through the corridor and the staircase! I apologized and had to close the door, as the room was not to be seen, and turned the bath tap off! The next day we felt embarrassed and paid for our damages. I think my name was on the black list from there on!

This kind of episode, although did carry on for a couple of weeks in a lot of versions, it came to an end, as one day, she out of the blue, stood by the door and said,

- ' I have decided to stop seeing you'
- 'But why so?' I inquired
- 'I have heard from people talking that you had a relationship with a man some years back.
  His name is Nikolas and my aunt knows him' She seriously said with tears in her eyes
- ' Woah! was the sex that bad?' I replied feeling upset

She left me slamming the door behind her. I was standing in the room wondering what had happened in such a short time of three minutes. She left her job too.

Nikolas and myself were pals in sports and going to bars and having interesting talks. It was great to have a friend like him back then since the mountain hotel. The conservative society classified Nikolas and myself, as a couple and a gay rumor about me that I began to carry since my nursery years it seemed! This rumor became bigger in this venue, when two boys from Greece came to work there, George and Alexander. They were young and full of ideas to interact with people and work behind the bar and being bloody good looking as well! There was a connection between them, definitely George was gay and he did not hide it. He offered his social side of him to the venue which was well received by all as he was charming and funny as most gays are.

Alexander though, one night on whiskey talks explained that he was in trouble with some bad people in Greece. He was selling drugs in Greece and left to Cyprus to be away from the scenes and the temptations of that unknown world to me. Slowly, Alexander became a good life student of mine, interested in everything I did, said and lived. He wanted to know everything and he loved listening to my stories of life and memories I had collected. I felt he wanted to be me. He was good looking, with a well built masculine body, gelled hair, very expressive blue eyes and a clean white face. I myself liked looking at him too and also envied him. All the girls were admiring him and he was receiving many invitations for interactions. I felt, I wanted to be him. There was definitely a male attraction as in liking to spend time together but not in a way that was sexual. Most of our stories were on women experiences and the dream ladies, yet to come into our lives. These conversations were making us both a little accelerated, energetic and definitely horny.

Every Night When I Was Surfing In The Venue, Amongst The Guests, I Could See Potential And Imagining Animal Faces And Birds Once Again, Also Blending In With The Music Whether It Was Salsa Or Rock. Even When I Knew The Deception Of My Mind, I Kept Seeing The Illusion. I Needed It.

One of those nights an old friend introduced me to a petite young lady with olive skin, shaved head and round brown eyes. There is something about ladies with shaved heads! She was wearing a tulip dress and a thin scarf tied on her head. She made it for me without knowing! I saw her walking in the dessert in Africa and wanted to grab her from the waist and kiss her in the middle of the restaurant. Instead, I accepted politely the introduction and the invitation to continue the night with them at an afterhours club. The four of us went there and drunk for the whole country. She smiled all along. She was chin- chin the whiskey with me non- stop. I love women that drink whiskey with me! So that was a good start! Being young and drinking seemed a regular thing to do those days, and it often got everyone in trouble. I was no different.

We danced and kissed and sung at the top of our voices. We partied hard to the point that she could not stand and I kept losing her dropping on the floor. I picked her up and sat her on the bar as she was waving her body to keep a balance and hang on in there. All with a big smile and those brown eyes full of fire.

I did not remember how we went to the next level of interaction, but I woke up, in an unknown apartment next to her, as we were born, wrapped with a white sheet. I tried to wake her up with a gentle touch and looked at her for a while. She was sleeping with a smile on her face. I got dressed in my black leather pants, a white shirt and a jacket with a tie in my hands as my evening attire and tried to find my way back to my apartment, as I had no clue where I was. I walked all the high street, when everyone was driving to go to work. I was still drunk. I cannot express the embarrassment when I walked by the restaurant with my staff waiting for me, an hour later, for a briefing meeting! I excused myself, they made me a coffee and I said yes to all their questions.

After a few hours of sleep, while everyone else was at work, Alexander woke me up to have a coffee and tell me of his experience the previous night and wanted my story in exchange. He was so happy he was finding his way and feeling sociable and accepted in a new social environment far away from what he was used to. He brought a bottle of whiskey and we carried on drinking before time to work. He was getting a little sentimental as the bottle was getting lower and at a point, I did not know how to handle this young man who started crying and hitting himself on the face. He talked about his past that he was a bad man that sold drugs to kids and ruined young peoples lives, he was blackmailed by others not to stop supplying, he was hit many times by gangs and all that resembling a Hollywood movie with Bruce Willis. I tried unsuccessfully to say all the right words. It was best to put him to bed to sleep over the drink and cover his place of work by someone else, as he was wasted. I felt responsible but close to this young man and wanted to help him overcome this. I could see all the potential in him doing something else in life. He was clever, young and good looking, a platform to build a future, I thought.

The next evening at the venue I saw two girls having a drink, it took me a few seconds to recognize the face of the girl I slept with the night before but shit...I did not know her name! She must have read my face, like the whole world can do all the time on me. She waved her finger indicating, in a way, come here I need to talk to you and then she said to me:

- 'Celia, nice to meet you', and we both burst into laughter. I grabbed her and kissed her on the cheek and ordered another round of drinks which was the beginning of a series of sex meetings, after work, mostly at mine. What was nice with this soul was that there was no pressure, no demand but just let's see what we have for one another and if anything happens and so what if it does not! What a challenge that is to a man. It was different than any other women I came close to. I was well behaved, polite and gentle, considerate and loving in exchange of no pressure but just smiles and good conversations. Alexander got to meet her too and we three had dinners at the apartment of mine and lots of laughing sessions as to what happens in the venue. It was like a zoo where animals gathered to mate that was my scenes in my brain. All kinds of animals!

One night or early hours of the morning when Celia was in my bed and just waking up, there was a knock on the front door. It was Alexander, possibly drunk, apologetic and troubled again. He asked me to allow him in. He came in and gave me a strong hug, like the one you give to someone you want to thank, or your dad. I sat him in the kitchen and gave him water and coffee. I had to listen to an apologetic monologue of why he is like that needing a reference, someone to keep him on track. He continuously thanked me for being his salvation by being close! All new to me, but my feelings for him were of sympathy and growing interest to support him. We spoke for hours, Celia joined for coffee and left. Alexander was tired having had no sleep the whole night and I gave him the sofa in the bedroom to rest while I was getting ready to go to work. He felt asleep immediately.

When it was lunchtime, I took a burger from the restaurant and went to wake him and give him food. I started looking after him, cared for his meals that he had a routine to sleep, to meet decent people, dress well and be clean, to boost his self-esteem and make him feel he had a role in society. We walked in the town, we sat in coffee shops, we cared for each other as a younger man to an older man. We had thirteen years of age difference with different experiences and the wisdom that accompanies your age. He was forever thankful and that hug became a daily necessity of his, as a mark of finding a rock to stand on. I tried to push him to go out with girls: they were attracted to him, but he was selective, which I approved of. He had stories and laughs to tell me the day after. There was so much energy in our conversations about sexual experiences that was perhaps the push to go further in exploration individually. Rumors in town were of a growing spread that Alexander was my gay boyfriend, and that's how more clientele rolled into the venue to gossip about it but it created more buzz!

One afternoon I met a couple having a glass of wine at the venue. He was Lebanese and she was from a Slavic country. He was a gentleman, very talkative and appreciative of the place, while she was staring in an inquisitive way. We felt that we would be seeing them again. The next day his lady came for coffee with a friend of hers. I sat with them and a diabolical conversation started on feelings and new people in our lives, the x-factor we are all looking for in each other and where does it all go. Woah, my brain was burning, I was intrigued by her conversation and finally to my relief I was called to meet someone else. Mina had turned my world upside down. She was new food to process. She asked of my horoscope and day and time of birth. All her questions have been answered without a response of gesture from her so that I get also to understand her. I was trapped in her intrigued world and in an investigation. She did not fail to underline, as she left that she found me exceptionally interesting and that she was sure we will meet again.

A week later she came to the venue with the Lebanese man of hers and they gave me an invitation to their wedding. She had a look in her eyes when he said,

- 'Paris, we would be honored if you can make it, it is on the 16th of April'
- 'Oh... on my birthday' I replied as she looked at me with a slight turning of the head on one side while he said,
- ' Oh, is it really!'

What was she meaning and why did she choose that date? I was trying to understand her, feeling sure that she chose the day to mark something, but what? Or was it to say on your birthday I give you a present, my wedding? Quite macabre!

A couple of weeks passed by and one day she came to see me. She sat in a cream suit and a white blouse, she had red hair, chestnut color eyes and a shiny silky white skin. My sister passing by, commented on how beautiful that young lady is. I felt that I have spent what it felt a whole lifetime with her talking. I felt we met somewhere else in a previous life.

Alexander got to know her too. He felt strange vibes from her. He also thought he would be welcome to explore her sexual world. This new acquaintance was evidently pleasantly welcome in my life. She created waves in the scene and I was begining to lose interest on Celia.

Alexander asked for a key to my apartment, only to use it when I was not there, as he wanted to be away from his friend. One night, as I went home after work, I found him in my bed sleeping and I slept on the sofa instead not knowing how to deal with this. In the morning, I found him sleeping on the carpet near the sofa and when I woke him up, he was apologetic for taking my bed and felt sorry that I slept on the sofa. He did not want to wake me up and did not feel right to carry on sleeping in my bed.

A couple of weeks passed by and while I was with Celia in bed, I could hear the front door opening and the footsteps passing outside the bedroom. As there was music and sexual activity in progress, I paid no attention till the end. When Celia left I saw Alexander on the balcony, who admitted to watching us in bed the whole time. He was smiling and said he was proud of me as I looked like a bull in bed! But I felt this was going too far. I asked for the key back and he was very sorry for doing that. He said 'I am jealous of you and I want to be like you' and gave me one of those hugs again to which I could say nothing.

The venue was becoming a routine. Its success made me proud, but my mind was stuck at Mina. I did not go to the wedding. Why did she go through a wedding? She was a question mark. That soul with whom we felt the same things together and there was so much to be answered and explored!

DELTA OF VENUS

Mina was charismatic and beautiful. Charismatic as she had control of her expressions, feelings and emotions and beautiful because God made her like that, a 'femmina' in all its context. She would attract the attention of anyone she wanted by scanning him with her eyes and closing them down, as if she invited you to go and seduce her. She would stir in your eyes, telling you a whole story in a second. She definitely had me after her as there was so many words mentioned, jazz, style, love, hate, passion, lust, sex, art, movies, history, food, wine, opera and the whole world attached to those.

We met many times and got emotionally ready for a night in together at mine. The ceremonial procedures were all done, candles, jazz legends music, grapes and gorgonzola, crystal glasses and champagne. She came in with a flowery dress, as if she brought the spring into my life and high hills. She had shiny wavy hair and smelled of a seductive scent. She sat on the black sofa elegantly, crossing her legs. Red nails, a lighter and a cigarette. She had an inviting aura of nostalgia around her, open to be explored and relived. Perhaps, I chose to see her like a timeless and transcendent myth!

I lit her cigarette and she held my hand, which I always loved in a woman, when directing the flame to the cigarette. I picked a grape cut it in half in my mouth and piled a mouthful of cheese. I offered it to her mouth. She grabbed my hand and forwarded it to her red lips and she sensually swirled the grape, making a bursting sound in her mouth. She licked my finger and was sensational. She had me right thier captivated in body and soul..

- 'I feel I know you for years, I feel we met before....' she said looking at me up and down in a seduction mode.

-' I know what you feel for a woman that you long for... I want to know your whole inner world'... she ended closing her eyes as if she asked for a kiss. But I had other plans.

Miles Davies came on with 'My Funny Valentine'. I picked up her hand and she felt the moment, we were to dance. Perfect height, two hands down and together, the other one of hers on my neck and mine on her waist and tight towards me. The dance lasted centuries and she magnetized me the moment she looked straight into my shy eyes. She started unbuttoning slowly my shirt, she striped off my tie and looked at me once more. I unzipped slowly her dress from the back and freed the left shoulder while I looked at her lips. My lips were starving for a juicy passionate kiss, but I waited as there seemed to have been rules under way.

She moved on. She had unbuttoned my pants and looked straight into my eyes. She wanted to tell me something, I could sense it. I did look at her the second time and there was the beginning of a war. I released her right shoulder from the dress. It dropped on the floor and I held her up, with her legs crossing around my body. In two steps we found ourselves on the bed. I tied her hands on the bed with my tie. I did not want her to move.

- 'Don't... move!' I asked her in a monumental significance. Her whole body became a feast to my lips. I could hear her exhaling steam, craving for more. Lust and lust from both sides... no talking... but chemistry and acceptance of anything to happen. Passion in agreement with all the body moves was in place. I felt being in the sky, somewhere in the clouds, conqueror of the whole world, just me and the Creator who make us feel like this. Mina was my soulmate in life. It was the first time I found a woman feeling so attracted to, for many reasons.

When we began to meet more often, it was always an event for each other. There was sophistication and a different buzz than all the other ladies I met so far. She was intense in all means. She paid attention to every detail and it mattered to me.

Dinners set ups were always ceremonial. One night in my apartment I set up a round table and pulled the chair for her to sit down and then I served a red wine.

- 'This is lovely! It's all beautiful cutlery, real silver,' she said as she stroked the knife. 'This resembles a set up for royalties, and the glasses are real crystal…it does make a difference in what you drink to fully appreciate the wine!' She continued
- 'I am very pleased you are enjoying it. It all comes from my mother's and grandmother's chests. Especially my mother gave me lots of unique sets like these, which I treasure' I expressed.
- 'It all matters in life, the little things too. It is interesting to me the stories these glasses have heard around the dinner tables and how many hands have changed and how many cheers have clinked marking occasions and marking relationships' she enjoyably said and lifted a glass
- ' So… for us to mark this relationship and sharing precious moments like these, Slàinte Mhath' I said clinking my glass with hers and taking a first sip of wine. 'It is important to me to have company in enjoying my table gear. It has a certain value to me honoring my mother and grandmother and thinking of them as to when they used them'
- 'This white tablecloth and the embroidery on it! It reminds me of the past too. My aunt in Bulgaria used to embroider and it is such a patient work,' she said.

Mina knew her jazz too. Music was an important element in our existence. For me, it was a carpet to travel places, but perhaps it was for her too. We spent hours and days, years and centuries, whenever we could, and we even began talking in the same way, sometimes even the same sentence at the same time.

I got to know what she did with her husband. She used him to get a visa to stay. He was Lebanese with a Cypriot passport. He met her in a cabaret where she was a dancer and did not treat her well. She saw the opportunity to become legal by marrying him. She chose my birthday for her wedding as a revenge to him, as she knew we would become lovers. So, our game was hidden from the husband. Months later she divorced him and ended with a rented apartment of hers paid by him.

I felt close to her, but yet, she was never totally mine. She was seeing other men, exploring her passion needs, but knew that at a call I would be there. She kind of depended on me for that. She needed me as much as I needed her. We both had other people in our lives but should there be a call, we became a priority for one another. It was not, I need to see you but I want to see you. It was not always a sexual need but a feel-good need. I knew the mysteries of this woman's sensuality; she needed to feel and see through. We felt we were capable for more. I was the provider and the producer of the set. My needs were different from hers and my language was inadequate to explain. I could not word it. She needed security and I needed freedom. It was perhaps freedom that excelled all the storm inside me towards her.

One morning, she woke me up. The sun was coming in from the long windows. We sat on the carpet on the floor and shared a croissant that she brought me with a card of Gustav Klimt's -The kiss. I said to her that she looked like the woman in the card. Mozart on the decks, playing the Concerto for Clarinet in A K.622- 2. Adagio, my hymn! Magical moments shared. I was lost in the beauty of the moments. My mind 'flew' away.... surrounded by the dedicated violin players, the conductor elegantly directing the black workers carrying baskets on their heads in the coffee plantation. I was elsewhere for some time! Green everywhere and a slight wind... also blowing in, the light curtains in our room.

She spoke to me about many things. One was about Alexander that she found our relationship so intense that she would not have been surprised if we were engaged sexually. Deep inside her, she said, she knew that we did not, but she said, it would have been beautiful if it ever happened! I have expressed to her my liking to the whole presence of Alexander and my immense interest to be there for him in all that he needed but never would I think of getting anywhere in those unknown fields.

- 'I feel the passion the way you both talked about each other... and perhaps you should both think to share a lady between you. It is a way to share love and passion between you through a third body.' She said, looking at my reaction.
- ' Woah... what a way to handle two men with feelings but give them the opportunity to spread it all out, how brave for such a woman.... Are you offering to do so?' I enquired with wit.
- ' No... not at all! My connection with you is different, I do not think I could do so,' she said
- 'Well, to tell you the truth about myself, I am not up to anything like this scenario and neither would Alexander, I trust. His needs are more of a supportive role and not so much of a sharing feeling. But I am happy I have someone like him in my life right now as he inspires me, being young and good looking like that'. I said with envy.

Mina and I, watched films of passion together like 'Delta of Venus' and 'Wild Orchid' all accelerating passion in us. At a point we were far away from reality. We were lost drunk in a beautiful mist.

Times moved on, and a couple of months later Alexander found his way to a woman's heart for new adventures. She met him at the venue one night, Xanthe, an actress, a very pretty girl. He was lost for a week staying at hers. He announced his relationship to this girl with the biggest hug. Now, he became this girl's job to keep him away from drugs and guide him find his way which was better for me too as we were getting into intense situations and unknown to both of us. There was love and care, respect and all that created confusion.

Celia moved to another town on a work project and Nina had found a way out to more exciting experiences and in another country. She met a handsome basketball player from

Trinidad, with an American passport, who was prepared to marry her for the papers and therefore a visa to America. We had a last date together to celebrate the new year.

It was prior to Valentine's and the invite came from myself. We went to our favorite restaurant in Nicosia, Pablo's, an Italian, playing opera arias during dinner, white long tablecloths, only candles and discreet service. She wore a red dress, strapless with black long gloves, pearl earrings, red lipstick and had her red hair cut in a bob. She looked like an actress on a red- carpet walk. I was in my black and white with a bow tie as one would do on such splendid occasions nor sad nor happy but saying goodbye with a question mark. We shared a prawn risotto with strawberries and orange, feeding each other, followed by a heart shaped chocolate mousse shaped cake, which I arranged prior. She dipped my finger in the cake and licked it looking in my eyes. We drank a bottle of La Grande Dame and shared a Monte Christo Tubo, number 2. I had a glimse of cuba and that night in the pink Chevrolet. It was perhaps Don Giovanni opera that was playing. through the speakers. We did not talk much but stared into each other's eyes and said it all. I kissed her hand and she pulled it towards her chin with a slight move of her head towards it. A sign of I need your love! I replied to the sign 'me too' and she knew as she smiled back. I needed her love and I was sorry to lose her but I sounded so selfish to myself that I felt I had no right to stop her from flying to new experiences and security that I was not offering.

To finish that night, I asked her where she would want to go for a drink, knowing full well of her choice. We went to our favorite bar, Plato's. We had a corner dedicated to us, forever drinking there and Jean, the owner, knew us well and felt the chemistry. He knew that we liked jazz and also knew our favorite song. I passed by earlier and gave him a present and said to him when you feel it is a good time, please present her with this, as a surprise.

We shared a Glenfiddich with a distinction of some sort

and while in conversation, I asked her which was for her, our best memorable moment in our affair. At the time she took to reply, I could see Jean approaching from the other end of the room with the surprise present. She replied,' the morning with Klimt and when you said I look like the woman in the painting'. And there it was, she was presented with a print of the painting of the Kiss by Klimt, the same moment she mentioned it. Soul mates forever? There was a kiss and a fulfilling happiness which led to our dance 'That ole devil called love' by Billie Holiday. There was 'flavor' around us and lots of cinnamon in all our food, and our fragrances. She gave me a book of poems, with a dedication, and called me her Cinnamon Peeler by Michael Ondaatje.

'If I were a cinnamon peeler
I would ride your bed
And leave the yellow bark dust
On your pillow.

Your breasts and shoulders would reek
You could never walk through markets
without the profession of my fingers
floating over you.
. . .'

But our journey did not end here...

REQUIEM

Sometimes, you get drawn into a routine, keeping you occupied and dedicated to your commitments. It does not allow you to stop and think which way to go. It also disconnects you with yourself as to what you need or miss or want to conquer. I was at a crossroad, not knowing what I wanted and what I was looking for, to happen to me. I was in deep thoughts and I did discover that it was not that I did not know what I wanted. All my thoughts were in a blender. I realized that I was missing that drunken feeling of being in the mist of creative relationships, a dive deep into the ocean of challenges, those that hold your stomach tight and fill your chest with butterflies, developing your saliva and wanting a new adventure in tasting a new dessert with extra sauce but perhaps on the side at first.

Bored as I was, I staged a Valentines party at my venue Diagorou 12 in Nicosia. Singles came masqueraded with masks and most in disguised costumes, in search of a partner for the night as they had to draw a number and find the same number held by someone of the opposite sex in the room to both get a free glass of champagne from the bar and who knows what could have happened. Fantastic buzz, great mysteries, some got on at first glance, magical music by the DJ. Five young Cannibals on 'Suspicious minds' and Survivor on 'Eye of the tiger' were the tunes and therefore the mood of the gathering. Looking and flirting lead its way to dancing and making up relationships of an unknown promised duration.

I was traveling with their costumes and the music to my fantasy world. There were colours everywhere, flashing camera lights, snippets of birds, perhaps Albatross, and many black people...yes warriors and... A couple, I did not know, stood on the bar and performed Joe Cocker's –'You can leave your hat on', with all expressive moves and more... as clothes were flown into the cheering crowd. They stopped at the underwear. I was watching with enthusiasm their bodies' expressions. The lights were low and the energy was high, as the combined eroticism of the music, their movements, and the atmosphere began to take effect. People around them could feel the tension, the sexual energy radiating of them, and it was palpable. As they danced on the bar, the heat of the moment grew and everyone in the room felt the power of their alluring performance. The man and woman were a force to be reckoned with, and everyone felt the electricity in the air. It was an intoxicating experience, one that left everyone feeling aroused and invigorated.

Fortunately, after they were back in underwear and to their bar stools, almost covered in their clothes, a police raid stormed in to search my apartment above, as they had a tip from someone in there that at this party, I was pairing people to have sex in some rooms above! So, we went to my apartment together to check that this was not happening, as a confirmation. They found a bottle of whiskey with 2 glasses, an ashtray with cigarette ends that had lipstick on and a cigar as proof that a couple had used the rooms from the venue downstairs and claimed that as proof. I was called to the station for an investigation! Finally, some excitement!

I have explained to the policeman carefully everything I said on a piece of paper. I claimed that the glasses and what they have seen, belonged to me from my previous night's 'experience'. They asked for my partner's name to verify the information which I could not have given it to anyone. It would have destroyed many other relationships! Some nights lost souls stay behind and need to go somewhere other than back home as they are bored and as something is missing from their routines. When they have time to stop and think they discover that they need just to talk or to feel wanted. One of these souls spent time with me that night, a well- known political figure, I was not to expose her. The Police had nothing against me, so I was released with no charges.

Myself too, I was feeling I wanted a new connection, deeper perhaps but was never sure. That night, I wanted to be The Cinnamon peeler. I was beginning to separate the words need and want!

I got in touch with Mina. I missed her and I wanted her. I wanted an X factor, a Delta of Venus and jazz and Klimt back to my life somehow. Two years passed without all this jazz! She was in Phoenix, Arizona with her Trinidad basketball player, marketing wines to restaurants. She said to me that through our times spent eating and drinking she got interested and started representing a wine distribution firm over there. We chatted on the phone a couple of times and as if I could see her in front of me with her seductive eyes and lowering them down asking for seduction, she said

- ' I miss you, why don't you come to see me?'

I explained that I was busy but I was to send her a present with my friend Elaine, whom she met back in Cyprus. Elaine was supposed to be on her way somewhere and stopping in Phoenix for a night. I gave Mina her flight details for the arrival.

I flew to Houston in Texas for a night, bought a cowboy hat and arrived on that flight at Phoenix airport. I saw her.... She did not recognize me with the hat on, as she was looking for Elaine. I went from behind her and spoke

- ' Do you have any cinnamon on you?'

She turned slowly towards me, her face shined like the sun and we hugged with overpowering excitement. There was a steel wall between us.Two years and so many things happened in between that none of us knew about each other. She was beautiful as if nothing happened for lost time. She drove me to a hotel and we set an appointment for dinner later on at one of her best client's restaurants where she had previously spoken to the proprietor chef about me.

During dinner, I was feeling excited looking at her, She was dressed in a queens gown with a crown and an entourage of ladies in waiting were standing behind her. She looked worried,

She was concerned on how to handle the situation, as she was living with the Trinidad partner there. The same time, a best friend, an ex-lover, The cinnamon Peeler, arrived just for her. Somehow, she tried to explain to him that I was very important to her life and that she wanted some time alone with me. There was no room at that moment for any other thought from us.

We had a super evening, chatting over great food and wine, and lots of others have been around us, I felt it. The feeling was the same like the past times we spent together but somehow different. The proprietor joined us and we exchanged experiences of our restaurant times and gastronomy. This time, I did look at her in her eyes. I was in search of the feelings I knew. The spice was not yet quite there as I remembered, the lights were dull and did not form any shades, the music was not heard, no one was around! I did not travel.

After dinner, we went to a Latin bar buzzing with real music, vibrant atmosphere, lots of rums and Cuba libras, colourful lights in our eyes, lots of rhythm and as I went to get the second drinks from the bar, I saw her talking to a tall, black athletic type of a man, obviously her partner, probably husband of hers. His posture and the movements of his hands while talking showed that he was not happy about the situation. I had an awful feeling, knowing I was damaging their relationship. At that moment the Dj played Marc Antony and as it was one of our classics of the past, she looked at me indicating come and dance with me now. Since her partner was trying to talk to her and her ignoring him, I saw a different scene, of a black panther wanting to save the victim from a lion who was going to eat her and leave her there to die! Suddenly, the dancing figures of the crowd became palm trees weaving in the plantation and music got louder. My eyes were interrogating the world like an agent on a mission to arrive at a strategy for data on how to process it all. My brain settled for what made sense.

I felt an extremely awkward pressure. My brain was spinning with assumptions. It perceived a must do strategy. I could not tolerate the pressure. I stormed out and not even knowing where I was, I saw at a distance a hotel sign where I had spent the night. My thoughts were messed up. I was jealous of the good looks of the black panther and of his possession. But I also felt responsible for the situation that I created. This could not continue...

'If I were a cinnamon peeler
I would ride your bed
And leave the yellow bark dust
On your pillow....'

The next morning, I went early to the airport and bought a ticket to a destination I chose from the board of departures. There was New York, Cancun or New Orleans. I called her and apologized for my spontaneous appearance and creating trouble. I told her I was leaving and if she wanted to, she could join me taking a flight late afternoon. Still, I was irresponsible and playing a dangerous game and not feeling good about it.

I arrived in New Orleans, quite upset with myself and feeling a lesser man. I booked a room in a small hotel in the French Quarter. I was up for a crazy time to make-up with myself and leave yesterday to the past. I did wrong to go to see her and upset her relationship.

It was night time when I found Bourbon Street buzzing with people. I walked around quite a bit. I went into a very busy bar thirsty for a beer and lots of shots. The bar looked lush with red velvet curtains in many places and some kind of golden chandeliers. There was an open circle in the middle, where one could look straight above the dance floor. It was my first time at a gay disco bar!

I could not believe my eyes at the sights, the combinations, and the human bodies; expressions. The hands were so reaching and achieving, the nudity was so attractive for exploration to the eyes. It was like a glimpse into a different world, one where people exist in harmony and acceptance regardless of their gender or orientation. Women engaged in full throttle with the same sex, two men and a woman aiming to share excitement on the dance floor, couples or not... what a mess and so sexy! I was enthralled.

As the lights were turning around and the strobe lights began to flicker, Verdi's Requiem was at full blast in my head. I could see the naked unicorns moving like herds of fish from side to side, the lionesses trying to bite each other's necks and tear each other apart. Two elephants joining their tusks and sucking each other's liquids from their throat. The animals seemed to be enjoying themselves just as much as the humans. They were playing and interacting with each other, and it was a beautiful sight to behold. It seemed like everyone in the room was in their own little world, where the only thing that mattered was the moment they were in. Some walked up the stairs and went behind the red velvet curtains for privacy. I could see through that inch that the curtains were left purposely open. I was staring, there was action in there. Naked bodies and movements, deep breathing and pain voices of ecstatic lust and joy. I was aroused! The sound in my head while intensely watching flesh being rubbed and kissed...the skies opened...

Verdi's Requiem,

........'Hear my prayer, all earthly fresh will come to you.
Lord have mercy upon us............
.... when the Judge takes His seat,
whatever is hidden will be revealed:
nothing shall go unpunished.
The day of wrath, that day will
dissolve the world in ashes,...
My prayers are not worthy,
but show mercy, O benevolent one,
lest I burn forever in fire.
Give me a place among the sheep, and separate me from the goats,
placing me on your right hand.

I felt like I had been let in on a secret, a secret that showed me that love, acceptance, and joy can exist in the most unlikely of places I also could.... See... and it all stopped! Now it was

Depeche mode –'Just can't get enough', everything was like when I walked in. I felt a hand grubbing my shoulder.

- 'You look like you have never been here, is this your first time in this disco?' a smiling young lady said to me.

Valeria was a Puerto Rican with white skin and freckles. Such a wide clean smiling facial expression, welcoming your best ever feelings to come out. Black hair and circle earrings. She wore white pants and a T-shirt that said 'I am a problem!' So that was a topic of the night. She was there, as her friend was a Lesbian and she made friends with another Elephant on the dance floor. Since we established that we were both straight, we committed to a challenge to explore Bourbon Street, and meet people. The motto was, one shot in every bar, till her friend would be available and join her back to the hotel.

Valeria was bubbly and interesting as she was a saleswoman but a part time restaurant host in her country. She wanted to know where I was from and I said I am now from Cyprus, but perhaps, I came from other places too. As the shots were going down and the bars were not ending, we were not sure of anything! I woke up with a two ton weight on my head looking at a white ceiling with a carved ornate circle in the middle and hanging a small crystal chandelier. I realized that was not my hotel. I turned my head on one side and there was an unknown girl next to me. I turned my head on the other side and there was 'I am a problem' looking at me. I quickly lifted my head and looked at my body lying down and I was fully dressed. I looked at Valeria again and she noted her head to me 'No!' We both smiled at each other and planned for the evening to meet again but to have no more alcohol.

We went to a restaurant for Cajun chicken and we drank juice and water for recovery. A walk in the park where I bought a drawing of a scene with people and saxophone players on Bourbon Street, from an artist called Solomon. We chose the drawing together and had a good chat about music. I tried to explain how music and my imagination takes me elsewhere since I was a kid to which she said 'I am a problem'. We went to the jazz preservation hall for a concert, a temple of culture where nobody talked during the musician's performance in full enjoyment. Respect!

I walked her to her hotel as a man on a date and gave her a kiss thank you. The night did not end there but in her hotel bedroom. It was intense and wild on that bed. It was perhaps not just myself but I was performing through vivid images of the naked bodies of the gay bar, At a point it felt that they were there in our room! I woke up the next morning looking at the white ceiling with a carved ornate circle in the middle and a hanging small crystal chandelier. I did not have to look at my body lying down, as I was feeling, I was definitely naked!

MARTINIQUE

In 1998, and in exploration of more French gastronomic influences I went to the French Antilles, the islands of Guadeloupe and Martinique. First in Guadeloupe for a few days. Exotic, turquoise waters and beautiful people.

Being quite athletic at the time, I have booked two weeks in the club Med concept in Martinique, where people from all over the world and of my age frequented the concept of all-inclusive with many sports activities. The hotel bungalows were spread on a white sandy beach. A central building with bars and restaurants hosted all visitors and where you were likely to see everyone as during the day you were busy with a smaller group based on your chosen sport.

I was a favourite in men aerobics, as I had stamina and flexibility, but not so brilliant in basketball, as there were many taller men. I have tried pursuing wind surfing as I thought I was not bad at it, but the wind in the Caribbean kept changing. I spent more time in the water than surfing above it. Others were very skillful, surfing so well and changing direction in the strong wind, a spectacle to sit and enjoy.

I was asked by a tall Spanish man called Pablo, who saw me disastrously on my board, flying in the water, to surf next to each other. I built enough courage to be seen as if I knew what I was doing. We stood on the surfboards and we did perhaps surf for less than a minute in the high winds which took us straight in the deep blue sea, now looking black underneath me. At the sudden wind change I was nowhere to be seen. I 'flew' right in the deep waters. The unfriendly colour of the black waters twirled me around and I could see from under water my board going away from me for more than ten meters. I felt something touching my leg like a slime rubber and I panicked swimming vigorously towards my board. In a splits of a second, I sat crossed legged on it while my heart was pounding louder than the wind. The shore looked like a line in the horizon beginning to feel lost in the unfriendly sea. I must have spent twenty minutes drifting in the currents and wondering of Jaws appearing around me for a feast. I was scared and did not know what to do. I was cold in the wind and started shivering. Finally, Pablo with a lifeguard on a boat came to my rescue with a smile on their faces. I was disgraced, but relieved. I got pulled back all the way to the shore. We have then established that I was not suited to extreme sports!

At sundown, they offered drinks on the grass overlooking the sea and a classical soft music accompanied the sunset. The sun was setting, spilling its golden light across the sky. Its rays were like a blanket of warmth, enveloping the land in a peaceful yet vibrant hue. A feeling of contentment washed over me, a sense of peace that comes with watching something beautiful. I felt a connection to the world around me, like I was an integral part of this moment in time. The sky was a vibrant mix of colours, from deep oranges to pale pinks and purples. I watched as the sun slowly slipped away, leaving behind a canvas of colours that seemed to change by the second. The music that was playing in the background added an extra layer of emotion to the experience. 'The Arrival of the Birds' - The Cinematic Orchestra. It was a dream. It was a melody that seemed to weave its way into my soul, calming my mind and filling me with a sense of serenity and joy.

There is so much in the sunsets marking the end of a day. It is melancholic to me. It always makes me think of the days to come, when there will not be any sunsets. Many of us sat on the grass and took it all in. It is in stillness that we realize the truth of our oneness and free ourselves from the delusions of consciousness. I stayed there for some time. I was far away with the music up there in the sky, a cloud or a star and thinking

about what is really up there. I felt so small and insignificant compared to this vast sky, but at the same time, I was filled with an appreciation for its beauty and its power.
There were two ladies, looking like mother and daughter. They were introduced as Eva and Sarah. Eva smiled and asked

- 'Where are you from?'
- 'Well from many places but I live in Cyprus!' I replied
- 'Gee...where is that' she said in a strong American accent I made it easy and funny saying
- ' Well, awrrrright, ame actually of Scottish ancestry, and grrou up in Grrreece', to which she said,
- ' I know Greece is in Europe, so you drink a lot of whiskey?' and I put my accent on again
- ' Aye, I was rrraised in the Highlands drrrinkin whiskey!' and laughed.

I did not think they got it, but it did not matter!

We got talking and I invited them to dine together at the Grill restaurant an hour later. At the restaurant, handsome and ' braw' Pablo came to see how I was, and asked him to join us. As the night progressed with conversations of all sorts, Pablo took Sarah on a proposed walk, leaving me with Eva to entertain. Eva was living in Brooklyn, and she was a typical American, plum shaped lady with concerns of her long nails and curly hair with the Jewish classic nose to match. She was at a sports-oriented holiday camp but had no interest in moving at all. All she wanted was to get sun tanned and drink wine. She was in a business network with other Jews in Brooklyn, and living in a lush apartment, as she described to me.

The mornings were busy with sports and exercises and in the afternoons, I was lost in walking from beach to beach out of the hotel, to discover the area, and the culture of these islands. I went to restaurants and hotels and found myself in the town, where I watched the people walking and interacting during their daily routine. Slim postures of women covered in colorful shawls and colourful tied up turbans on the heads. Shiny skins smelling of vanilla and coconut and nutmeg, drifted passing by me and I closed and opened my eyes…to…

I could listen to the sounds of African drums and saw hundreds of these colourful shawls waving in the wind to me. There was a bonfire in the middle and barrels and barrels of rum in piles everywhere. I could listen to the African drums in the background and seductive, lusty, voices and deep breathing. Dark skinny men, topless, wet from sweat, were shining in the light reflection of the fire. They wore hats, and had a jar of rum in their hands, pouring into the glasses of all attending to the celebration. The women held baskets under their arms filled with colourful exotic fruits and offered them gently to the mouth of everyone, looking into their mystic eyes. Everyone carried a passionate expression. Now, the African drums in the background were accompanied by seductive, lusty voices and deep breathing.

There was Pablo and Sarah kissing around the fire. She was completely naked and her nipples were touching his body while his hands held her neck for that kiss. They were free from everything. They surrendered to the mist of lust. I saw the most beautiful silhouette of a woman further down and walking close to them longing for participation in their delegation. I was drawn closer to her. She had big eyes and a long neck. She was wearing an orange and pink shawl and had velvety skin round earrings and a colourful stone necklace. She was breathing fast as she looked at the act of passion developing right in front of her. Pablo picked Sarah up and her legs crossed right behind him. Their curves were outlined even more in the light of the fire. Pablo looked masculine with the grandeur of an African body and she had an aura as an interpretation of a sexual Goddess. I was turned on. I extended my hand to the black woman looking at Pablo and Sarah and longing for attention. I was inviting her to take it. I wanted to take her with me, to my quarters, feeling like the lion who found its next pleasure. I saw a drop of her sweat coming down her neck slowly and I wanted to stop it with my tongue. I nodded hello and said to her ' Wĩmwega' which is hello in Kikuyu, thinking that she may have heard this from her ancestors but... she disappeared and everyone else. I was back from my set and felt let down in the absence of adventure.

That same evening, the same four, Pablo and Sarah, Eva and myself, sat together for our dinner. We were chatting over wine and having a good time, sharing various stories. Pablo and Sarah obviously coupled up, as they were looking at each other in a more familiar way. I wondered if they knew I saw them around the fire! Eva kept talking of how impressed she was from the Phantom of the Opera show and music throughout the dinner and she invited me to her bungalow to listen to it over a nightcap. Knowing very well what that meant, and having no desire to live an experience with her, I have gently declined the invitation with a silly excuse. The second night and the third my excuses were evidently showing lack of interest to pursue any of whatever interaction she had in her mind. It probably made her more determined.

One night, she slid- opened the door of my bungalow and she came in covered in a white sheet. She was the Phantom but there was not going to be an opera from my side as I said,

- 'That's lovely Eva but I'm really not interested in any adventures and no offense to you'. She said nothing and left the room.

I was upset with myself for not finding anything attractive in her and ended up hurting her. It was an awful feeling, I just could not, and I was jealous of Pablo getting it off with her beautiful friend. I thought of trying to go to hers, but I was not feeling any sparkle. No sparkle, no fire. This could have happened If I was very drunk and everything around me looked and felt wonderful and sexy.

The next morning, and feeling sorry for her, I asked her to walk with me through some paths in the dense palm trees ending to The Salinas beach, where it felt like the Blue Lagoon from the film. I think she walked just two hundred meters. Then she said that she got tired and we sat on a stone for her to rest and light a cigarette. I tried to talk to her about the slavery times and the people brought in from Africa to work on plantations around these islands. I tried to talk to her about the agriculture on the islands but she was not interested in these sort of topics.

We could hear the birds on the trees and we saw a turkey walking by, in the greens.

- 'Gee what is that?,' she said .
- 'That is a turkey!' I replied
- 'Oh,' she said, 'I thought turkey was something we bought in the supermarkets!'

I smiled at her for being so American and thinking of the sight of her in the supermarket looking at a fridge with thousands of prepackaged cuts of turkey breasts in cellophane with a big sign saying Turkey and a price tag!

We walked back and as it was our last night we went to a disco party on the beach, staged for all the departing guests. We managed to all dance with interchanging partners. Sarah was the right size for me, not too tall, feminine curvy and we would have been a perfect pair in bed. But it was never to happen, she was taken. There were a few slow songs at the end, when Eva asked me to dance with her, and I just did that. Sarah requested for her, 'The Phantom of the Opera' as the finale, and as Sarah Brightman was on her high pitch, I got kisses from Eva. A kiss that went on and on trying to make me feel like her Adam perhaps. The kiss began to feel kind of ok. I was beginning to get a hard on and considering submitting to the idea of actually having sex together. The song ended and I grabbed her hand and walked towards the beach where we kissed again and I could see that she felt happy that she got male attention and lived some romance. But I felt no connection.

- 'How lucky we are to meet on earth and on such a beautiful island, and to romance... ' I expressed'. 'I believe that we should show sexual abstinence as this will stimulate our brains to remember us holding hands and our kiss and treasure this moment for the rest of our lives. If only we had a few more days perhaps to build it, it would have been better!'

I carried on and she seemed content and spoke

- 'Perhaps visit me one day in Brooklyn!'
- 'Yes', I replied 'yes, let's do that' which saw the end of the night. And me and my big scenario final words came out
- 'The Phantom of the Opera is there in my mind!'

I sometimes bring on the charisma to convince me of a situation!

Indeed, in six months' time or more, I decided to visit the old friend of mine Basil, from the times of the mountain hotel and close to me and Nikolas. I was on my way to Mexico for the holidays and stopped in New York. Basil was living in Manhattan on the second avenue at a small apartment overlooking the river. First time in New York and it was all so grand and exciting. Everything was so big. My first impression of New York was in the taxi when I was interrogated by the driver as to what I do in life, where I am from and what am I going to do in New York. I replied to all his questions and at the end he said

- ' Gee, your English is so good, are you kind of educated or something? '

I explored the bars and the areas of Soho and Village, went to museums and exhibitions, looked at the American girls and got confused. Who is an American finally? It was such a fusion of different people. I visited fish markets at midnight, great restaurants, even on the World Trade Center while it was standing. Approaching Valentine's Day, I called Eva in Brooklyn and joked that the Phantom of the Opera is in New York. She asked me to visit her one afternoon. My friend Basil was to be left alone and so I booked her an Adonis of a man hunk as an escort to take her out, as flirting was missing from her life and seemed a normal thing to do in New York. Everything was up to her of the outcome of this experience and I felt I was being a good friend.

Eva was happy to welcome me and my flowers. Her apartment featured lots of cream leather and gold trimming, a super large tv, thick carpets, lots of candles, reclining armchairs, some massage chairs and at a touch of a button the library split in two and a bar appeared. It had a feel of the 80s, a rich Jewish apartment in New York as in the movies. She presented me with a Scottish bottle of The Dalmore King Alexander III. She choose it as the name was Greek, she said! I drank quite a bit of it with pleasure and enjoyment and we talked about Club Med in Martinique and our dance. Apparently, Pablo and Sarah met in Spain for a holiday and she indicated that Pablo kept her friend very satisfied. I thought that I would not expect anything else other than that from 'braw' Pablo!

I relaxed enough with my whiskey and she gave me a cigar too, from Cuba, which brought memories of my unique experience of the Cuban young lady, enough to place me on the platform of what was going to happen next. She led me to her bedroom with a four-poster bed and thick carpet. The music was one of a saxophone boring tune of either a supermarket atmosphere or a boring porno film of the 80s. Whatever, I blocked that out.! We kissed and took our clothes off and she said in my ear,

- 'Show me the Phantom in you!'

'Alright', I said to myself, awakening anything Scottish in me. This could be the beginning of a horror movie instead!

There was no connection but just the animal instinct. It all went smoothly and it was again the case that a man had to do what a man had to do, ending two satisfied bodies for two different reasons. I guess, Eva was feeling attractive and happy conquering her Phantom of the opera finally and little me that has traveled miles and had no sex for some time and feeling the conqueror of experiences but happy to give pleasure to a woman. Simple as that!

When I went to Basil the next morning, we went through her experience, I had arranged for her. She could not believe how handsome her date was. His name was Philip and he had a charming smile, a great body with perfectly styled black hair. She felt comfortable and relaxed in his presence, and it showed as she was glowing. The two of them decided to go for dinner and drinks at a nice restaurant. Throughout the course of the evening, they talked about everything from their lives to their dreams. Basil was surprised at how open and honest he was with her, and it made her feel even more at ease. He talked to her about his escorting experiences meeting women, which made her more sexually interested. As the night went on, the two of them got lost in conversation, not wanting the night to end. They left the restaurant hand in hand and went for a walk around the city. Basil felt a spark between them as soon as she saw him.

She invited him to her apartment. She felt a wave of excitement and anticipation course through her body as she slowly made her way across the room, unable to take her eyes off him. Philip did everything right, as my friend was forever thanking me, and she was looking forward to her next meeting with him.

LAS MARGARITAS

After New York I flew to Cancun and wanting to escape commercial destinations, I arrived at an Island of the coast of Mexico, recently opened for tourism, Cozumel. I do not know what I was looking for and if there was anything to look for but there I was in a small hotel with a pool where I knew nothing and no one.

I thought about attending the welcome meeting by the travel representative. She told us, as inquisitive tourists, about the area and what there was to do on the island. I asked her about many restaurants and she was going to drop some cards for me later on and she did so. She was petite, dark skin, black hair and sparkling eyes. When she brought the cards, I was upfront and asked her perhaps to join me one night to try one of these places and asked for her name, Juanita.

I worked on my suntan and walked the city searching for bars and restaurants, visited shops and felt the Mexican culture at a small local bar, café with homemade tequila and a garlicky version of guacamole. Only locals were there. When I returned to the hotel, Juanita left me a note saying,' be ready at 8 o'clock'. I felt that this was my style of gesture leaving notes for a date, but here it was, the opposite.

At eight o'clock she came with her moped and asked me to sit behind her and as one does, I placed my hands around her for support. She was cool about it and off she drove on the winding road towards the center to a restaurant with live guitar music. We sat talking and eating whatever she ordered as the menu was not in English. She was working at a nursery in the morning and as a rep in the afternoons. She had many brothers and sisters and it seemed there were strong family bonds. The trio of guitar players came to our table and sang some romantic songs for us, although she was embarrassed and asked them politely to go away as the mood was not for romance. The band insisted she sing with them, since she was Mexican. She was not shy and she had a good voice which was an amazing experience. We laughed and shared margaritas with everyone there, us, the band and the waiters. Some Americans further down have sent us more Margaritas to cheer the new Mexican singer! We crossed hands holding our glass of Margarita and we drank together like in marriage. She loved that and we did it again and again!

She dropped me back to the hotel and I thanked her and said to her I had a very good time. Perhaps we can do it again and she said spontaneously, tomorrow be ready at eight o clock! She must have liked my company too, if she was open to this and obviously there are no other obligations if she was available for two nights in a row. Definitely not a man in her life.

Eight o clock it was and I sat in front of her on the moped, while her hands extended on the stearing from my sides.

We went to another restaurant, with more Mexican style decorations and not as simple as the night before. There were colourful table cloths and fresh flowers on each table. She wore a dark green dress up to her knee, simple and sweet. She had some make-up on and a small gold chain around her neck. The food was better and a jar of Margaritas came on the table which I drank in 3 minutes, excited as I was feeling we are going to have a good night here! The music became louder and she grabbed my hand and we danced to a Mexican song in a kind of a valse type from side to side. We giggled and laughed when I missed my steps and why not. We ate and drank margaritas again and again, but my pace was faster than hers and already beginning to feel tipsy.

We went back on the moped and she kept going through a path which ended at a beach. We took our shoes off; I rolled my pants up and walked the bay next to each other up and down. Half way through I held her hand which she squeezed as a sign of approval. We looked at the stars and started naming them as Mars, Galaxy, Milky way and when I ran out of chocolate names, I started naming them like flavored Margaritas. This one is Lemon Margarita and the big star is Strawberry Margaritas and although I was a little drunk, she was entertained by me. Oh, she was so pretty and everything was so smooth and euphoric, it was the moment I pulled her towards me, looked her in the eyes and gave her a kiss in the mouth when I saw her tasting her lips afterwards in thirst of a longer one. We must have been kissing for fifteen minutes standing up, when my body needed to lie down, but she implied negatively with her body language. She held my hand and we walked further down and we kissed even more.

My hands began to slide down but she put them up again. She looked to be loving kissing and feeling lost in each other's arms. She had her eyes closed when our lips were exchanging kisses and she was breathing heavier. I held her hand and we walked back to the moped where there was more kissing. My lips were hurting from the kissing and I thought I developed extra muscles on them. She drove me back to the hotel where there was a long kiss goodnight. I looked her in the eyes and said to her, 'Juanita, come with me to my room' to which I sensed she felt uncomfortable, and said eight o'clock tomorrow, be ready.

So, there I was when she came with a wonderful black lace dress with short sleeves and all her hair was up and she had turquoise with gold earrings and lipstick. She looked like a star that fell from the sky. She was looking at me and could read my enthusiasm for seeing her again. I kissed her hello and said to her that I was driving the moped and she would tell me where to go. She held my body with her hands and I could feel her resting her head on my back as I was driving. She was completely relaxed with me.

We went to a bar, an animated bar full of music and sombreros for everyone. Tequila shots were shared around and we had some tacos and many Margaritas. We walked out of the bar and drove to another beach following her directions. The kissing carried on and the hands were allowed to feel and touch but not everywhere. I tried to touch her breast but she moved my hands away. I touched her knee and went up but there were boundaries and she moved my hands on her shoulders. She was a little girl in my hands. I felt ready for the plot at any expense, and started making the moves to make love to her on the beach. She was not letting me further my dreams for the night. So, my mood started dropping and I asked why she doesn't like me to do so. She was shy, she looked in my eyes and lowered hers and said to me,

- 'Paris, I have never been with a man and I am a little afraid'.

Oh, a twenty-eight-year-old beautiful girl and a virgin, what a responsibility! I gave her a hug and said to her,

- 'It's all right, it's all fine and I gave her a big kiss again.

We walked a little further on the beach and we sat on a rock looking at the water and the moon reflection in it. She wanted more kissing and it was not doing me any good, as I was ready to undress her and take her to my paradise. Instead, it came out as a frustration and I said to her, Juanita,

- ' I love being with you... but I cannot carry on kissing like that as I am a man and I need more of you. I want to explore your body. So, please drive me back to the hotel.'

She seemed understanding and determined to her positioning. So, she drove me to the hotel, I gave her a massive kiss goodnight, I smiled and I pleasantly said to her

- 'You know my room number'.

I went to my room and had a cold shower, not only to clean off the sand, but to really cool down from the emotional roller coaster. I turned the lights off and lied down when there was a knock on my door. My face lit up. I felt I became a pinball wizard game machine that hadjust got turned on! I opened the door, now in my boxer shorts and she looked shy and perhaps scared. I held her hand and as she came in, she took her shoes off, as the heels were making a noise on the marble floor. We said nothing. I tried to be her and feel what she was going through. Scared of the unknown, attraction, inquisition, should I not, is it going to hurt? I felt a responsible role overtaking me.

I was tender and softly kissing her lips and around her ears and I said to her

- 'Do not worry about anything, just relax and let me take you with me, we will feel the same. Do not fear it will not hurt you and if it does, it will hurt me too'.

I was the best self I never knew I had. I have hidden all possible male beastly elements creeping out when having sex and got into a mood of making love with the responsibility to guide this soul to heaven with me.

I started off by gently caressing her body, exploring her soft curves with my fingertips and tracing circles on her skin. I wanted her to feel comfortable and relaxed, so I took my time and kissed her softly, making sure that she was ready for what was to come. My lips trailed down her neck and shoulders as I moved my hands along her body, exploring her. She gasped, as I kissed her neck and chest, sending shivers of pleasure through her body. A beautiful melody. She felt my hands against her, tracing paths of pleasure on her body. Her skin was soft and her breathing quickened with every touch. I smelled something beautiful in the room, as if someone brushed by me. I did not stop, I moved my hands down, lightly brushing her inner thighs and exploring the softness of her skin. She was so responsive to my touch.

I could feel her trembling with anticipation. I moved in with my hands, exploring her and bringing her closer to the edge. She moaned softly and I could tell that she was beginning to enjoy the pleasure I was creating.

It was very warm in my room. I touched her between her legs. She moaned and writhed, her body now begging for more. I felt someone was in the room, I took a glimpe of my Greek God seating relaxed on the chair and looking at me with a sense of approval of the scene. I looked again but he was gone. I smiled to myself.

I was aroused but in control. The moment I gently entered her, she felt a slight twinge of pain, but as I continued to move gently and rhythmically, her discomfort began to subside. She closed her eyes and savored the warmth of my body against hers. With each passing second, her pleasure grew as she experienced something totally new and exciting. I was patient and controlled myself to pace. I could feel she felt the sensations rising from her core, as I increased my pace. As we reached our climax, there was a feeling of an incredible sense of satisfaction and fulfillment. She looked at me with her big eyes and a smile, as if she was in the sky amongst the stars. She had a bright face of awakening. I was proud.

My time on the island was over and It was time to return to New York and meet my friend Basil. Juanita was sad and came to farewell me at the airport. I gave her my telephone number, so far away. I promised to call her and invited her to visit me whenever she wanted. Sometimes, there is no way to continue a soul connection. An experience becomes a memory and stays strong inside you. It is connected with the pure feelings you shared at that time. This one was a different exploration. It cannot have an ' encore'. It all started with margaritas.

MADAME CLAIRE'S

There was a time dedicated to frequenting this fascinating country full of smiling faces with an easy life flow and time passing as ' evely day is the same, same but different!' The motto of the day! Late 90s in Thailand, Bangkok, a fascinating city for me. Perhaps it is like London, and New York put together but Milano and Hong Kong too, Bali and the whole of Indonesia, all together.

Buddhism accepts everything, everything goes, just comes from any organized civilization and you will feel relaxed here as nobody notices what you do and nobody cares but in a nice way. You can be whoever you want to be, play any game you want to in Thailand and certainly I had seen people doing stuff on offer all the time and felt mostly sorry for them! My visits to Thailand were mostly for exploration but also to purchase many arts and crafts, as meanwhile I have opened a couple of Ethnic concept stores in Nicosia and in Ayia Napa.

My traveling took me also to India, China, Hong Kong but mostly Thailand.

I was more open to spiritualism. I was becoming in line with Buddhism atmospheres and some friends were underlining this in me. Acceptance, tolerance, calmness and mindfulness were new elements in me and taking over.

I loved Bangkok especially when I was recommended by a friend to meet Christophe, a French man who was a creative caterer and concept developer in Thailand. Every time I would arrive, I would have a list of places to go and what to see and what to eat. I got to explore this town more than I knew any other city in the world because of him.

I had great interest to experience new places and it

inspired me, as I also started creating different concepts for other businesses and how to present something else to the public. I visited markets, designed T shirts, bought Art crafts like jewelry and statuettes and visited hotels, bars and restaurant of contradictive charm and sophistication following Christophe's lists. For me this city was like New York and London put together as one could see the forthcoming trends of Asia to the rest of the world.

On one trip his chauffer, a Thai lady, very sociable and playing loud party music in the car, took me to stay at Madame Claire's studio. There was no sign outside the door but she stopped and gave me a signal to indicate, go through that door. She smiled and greeted me, see you later Mr. Paris! I rang the bell and a small flap opened so that I got to see someone's eyes staring at me. He spoke Thai at first and then English and asked if I had a reservation. I confirmed that Monsieur Christophe has booked a room for two nights for me and after sometime the door opened into a dark wooden room with a varved wooden Thai old sofa. I sat down until my presence was acknowledged by this young Thai girl in purple attire and bare feet who opened the door into a bigger very impressive room with a high ceiling. The walls were covered in green marble and framed by an ornated gold sequence in panels all around. A massive purple velvet curtain separated the room in half and I was guided in the other half room where there were some short chaise longue so that one could rest his back but his legs were still on the dark wooden floor. Bowls with warm water came filled with flowers and towels and two young pretty girls gave me a feet soak for a welcome, while a gentle faced boy served me a green tea with some sugar in it.

All was so proper and civilized blended with the sounds of a harp piping through the speakers. It felt I was entering a spa. Everyone was smiling and there was a calm feeling all over, but one that made you anticipate what was in the next step on your way to the room. Another young lady, so petite and feminine, came and greeted me the Thai way and the gentle nodding of the head and asked me in Thai, but indicating well, to follow her. Two muscular grand men, in dark green Thai fishermen style pants, topless and with dragon tattoos on their bodies, have pulled sideways the curtains so that I could make my way into what looked to be the perfect set for a Roman orgy. The dragons were moving on their muscular bodies. The column carried on being featured and ornated in green marble and gold, holding the glass roof panels allowing in the sun rays into a dark green oval play pool with steps all around. At an elevated area, some lush purple velvet floor cushions with trimmings, and low gold tables were available for anyone wanting to spread and relax around this area. All was so stunning, and I was smiling inside me thinking of Christophe and his idea of sending me to experience such a novelty. All around the elevated area there were the doors leading into the rooms and number three with the name Joy, in gold engravings, opened for me.

It had beautiful dark wooden floors and a large four poster bed for the prince, as I felt once again, with lots of cushions in velvet and gold trimmings. There was a sofa with a green marble coffee table and a small bar trolley with crystal decanters featuring whiskey, other alcoholic spirits and glasses. I thanked the girl for the assistance and I spent perhaps the next few minutes looking and absorbing the details of the room and planning my day in Bangkok. As I came out of the room, my camera started rolling the new film clip, perhaps of Madonna called Erotica 2. A european looking, stark-naked lady, emerged from the pool and the topless big Thai guy handed over a towel to her. She dried herself and sat on thick floor cushions fully exposed. I pretended I did not focus on her, but it was obvious, as my head kept turning in that direction. So, Christophe has sent me to a nudist hotel to experience it. I wondered if I was expected to run around naked as well! No, no no! I have never been exposed to nudism!

The door of another room opened and there was a naked man with his private parts dangling right and left as he went and sat next to that lady. The music was mystic and there were smells of burning incense sticks. Although I wanted to stay on and observe more to satisfy my curiosity, I had to attend a meeting with a shopkeeper to arrange some purchases, which was the main reason for my visit.

On my return at about seven o clock, I still had to be seen by the eyes behind the sliding frame. Just as I came in, the music was playing loud and there was now a party going on around the pool. There must have been about fifty different naked shapes of bodies, some looked at me in a funny way as I was dressed and some perhaps in not such a funny way. Some were dancing in the water with a glass in their hands. Definitely club house anthems at full blast, an edition mix of 'Touch me' feat. Casandra -Rui de Silva! Woah! What a party tune, I wanted to stay, but I would not have taken my clothes off and joined in. I was embarrassed. I went into my room and I was really intrigued about not being out there. It was unlike me, as party animal scenarios, and such setups for my mental travels, were my own thing! Now it was happening in reality and I was not a part of it. I felt the battle inside me, a challenge contradicting my shyness and inexperience.

My mind was made up to go for it. Live every minute of life, I said to myself. I took my clothes off and wrapped a towel around me, went out of the room, dropped the towel and soaked in the pool! I was looking around and around for flesh of all sorts and most were at the edge of being wasted. I noticed some suspicious actions with a straw at a corner as well, there was a drugs table but this was definitely not my thing. We moved to Bob Sinclair- 'World hold on', indeed, hold on, the tune!

A young man swam next to me and introduced himself with a big smile and a certain provocative look on his face,

- 'Hola, I am Julio from Argentina'
- 'Hola to you too! My name is Paris, I come from Greece, Cyprus!' I replied
- ' Good, join me to the bar for a drink...' he said with the same provocative look on his face, insinuating more.

My masculinity was threatened and I felt insecure. So, I said,

- 'No...I'm going to my room'

Julio composed a pleading facial expression and spoke

- 'Come on brother, let's get to know each other! This is Thailand'.

That was definitely not for me, I paraded like a ballerina, being my natural walking style, as if I felt comfortable and I have done that before. I went back to my room. I put on the TV, I could hear the bass from the party, still wondering and intrigued, perhaps a little upset for not being out there...

There was a knock on the door, I wore my pants and opened the door to see Julio and Birgitta with a big smile, all the way from Sweden! I smiled, as I felt better that there was also a Birgitta on the scene, to balance things out between Julio and myself. I was happier now that I was not the target. They asked me to join them. There was no way I would, having clearly seen the size of Julio's gifts! I was not to stand naked next to him and become a comparison! Instead, they came in without giving me a choice, and spread on the bed. Birgitta was quite drunk, but so was he.

They started interacting through the 'pre theater meal deal' for sexual intercourse. There was so much flesh, I was aroused of course, and felt jealous of Julio in his proud presentation of manhood. They were performing on my bed and at one point Julio was looking at me as if he wanted to say 'here man join in, this is life ! But 'Insomnia' by faithlessness, I can't get no sleep... .insomnia please release me...! Woah, Paris what a mess you are in, aroused and shy, sex in front of you and invited to join in, but not quite there, what a mess you are in! My heart was pounding, I could feel the blood running through my whole body, I was hot. I thought of Kate, if she would have been there with me! I thought of our sensual kama sutra experience and felt it in my body. The black panthers were there running around the scene. I got out of the room and went back into the pool. I looked around for potentials.

There was a big fat man together with two Thai girls, elegantly sitting naked on the lush floor cushions. I caught the eye of the one. She looked with interest back at me while standing in the pool. I felt I needed to be macho and release all that was gathered inside my head, my belly and further down. I waved my hand with a composed welcome smile, indicating come here, join me. She came close and she said to me' I am afraid of the water, come out you!' Blamie! was the word, how do I do that. She was petite but nice, sweet and with a cool figure. I manned up thinking, no one knows me and no one will ever see me again. Dripping water, I walked out towards her in whatever grandeur I could put together, and she said

- 'You look suntanned!','did you go to Phuket'?
- 'No' I said 'I live in a sunny country'.

We got a drink from the bar that did not matter what it was, and I gulped it down in one. I got refills again and again. I asked her to dance to Daft Punk- 'Music sounds better with you!' She liked my moves as top trained in the clubs of Ayia Napa, and she brought me a couple of shots and suggested,

- ' We buy a couple of lines of white stuff in the corner, my flend is there'

Instead, I suggested to her

- 'Why don't we go to my bedroom here?'

Whether she understood me or not she had no time to react as we walked in my room of Joy, to find out that Julio and Birgitta were probably oversexed and unconscious on my bed. At the sight of them naked she thought we were for a group orgy, and she smiled at me and made her way out.
I shouted in despair,

- ' No please wait, it's not what you think' but it was too late.

She walked back to her friend.

I spent the night on the sofa in my bedroom dressed, as the other choice was to lie down on the bed next to them, but I did not trust Julio. I woke up the next morning crippled on that uncomfortable sofa and found a note with a telephone number with a heart shape next to it and the name Julio!

KOH CHANG

While on travels, still for French food exploration, I traveled to Cambodia savoring the leftovers of the colonization by the French. But their art and love for the silk and their presentation of interiors ended up much more interesting to me. I loved the people although I felt that they were not so easy going as the humble Thai people. I visited many historic sights and, on my way, back, I decided to stop at Koh Chang as those days it was opening up for visitors. I stayed in a hut on a picturesque white sandy beach with palm trees. On a sunny day, seating on the beach and looking at the sea, you could see forever- yourself, your time on earth and reposition yourself.

Tin huts built by wood and bamboo with a fan in the middle, as basic as nature intended us to find refuge in a shelter. A bigger hut further down was the restaurant, THE restaurant. Simply, five wooden tables put together by hand and some palm tree cuts forming a stool. The menu was everything with pineapple, coconuts and whatever fish was caught on the day together with sticky rice. The first night I went fishing on a small boat with the couple owning the restaurant and we caught prawns and lots of unknown fish to me. He tied himself with a belt around the trunk of a tree and went up to cut some coconuts for the juice and the flesh for the food.

It was a wonderful liberating feeling to be barefoot and wearing almost nothing day and night and eat when you were hungry and sleep when you were tired. I felt like the pirate I met back then in the Virgin Islands. Liberation makes you feel calm, peaceful and empty, ready to conquer, to feel and experience. Empty from anything you must do and be able to behave as you like. There was rarely anyone in the beautiful sea and I wondered why there were not so many tourists going around the island, only to find out, from an info leaflet, that the Island had for years malaria and only lately it has been opened for visitors to come and everyone expected it to rise into one of the popular future destinations. It seemed the norm to me to be somewhere before others or just one of the first to be there, like in Cuba. This was in my actual life events, in locations and in status as well.

After the catch of the day was brought in, I casually had my dinner in a bowl sitting on the steps and looking at the sea. I was invited by some Italians in a group of six where we exchanged experiences and views through our travels in Asia and it was interesting. They were all handsome and a happy bunch of young people adding spice to the exotic atmosphere of the set. Further down, there was a mixed group of people noisier than our table and ended up dancing to some techno music with Thai words. They were drinking Thai whiskey and I did not refuse to try it when they approached me as at a point, I was left on my own. I drank with them and got introduced to Tawan, Fan, Mahe, and other sounds that sounded difficult. There was also Claudio, an Italian guy with long hair who seemed to be the boyfriend of Tawan, a Thai guy looking very feminine and had a clean, innocent looking face to go with it.

With a few drinks my eyes were evidently interested in what looked to be a mixed origin girl called Fan which meant Sky. Her exotic looks felt like she had just dropped from another dimension, indeed. I got hooked by her aura and her feminine moves. She had short hair and thick lips, firm body, plenty on the front and with a Brazilian figure of a samba dancer. Her eyes were shaped with a circular orbit and had that come to bed look. Almost a hypnotic look. At one point I smiled at her and she openly came and sat next to me all in a good spirit. She was smoking a joint she passed on to me which I tried too, for the first time. I was quite far away from anything that could be weed or cocaine so far in my life. It was not in the culture of mine, perhaps my upbringing, perhaps my friends and through what I have tried to do with Alexander, I was so far away from this whole world. Whether I felt good or mellow or nothing I do not remember.

I kept on smiling to Fan which was enough to give me a sweet kiss, as we were sitting on some steps, talking of nothing and everything and looking at the calm sea. I felt that I knew her and we had been together somewhere before. I was relaxed with her and I was feeling myself. Meanwhile, Tawan and Claudio got engaged in hugging and Chi, a Thai girl came and sat next to Fan.

The music became house music and more to my liking and I asked Fan to dance with me. Who would not dance to 'Show me love'- Robin S? I was staring at her while our hands and legs moved in a sequence to match the beat and rhythm of the music, penetrating our bodies. I was a little drunk or more, under the sky on a sandy beach somewhere in the world and with a bunch of stoned young people and not a worry in the world. The restaurant was closing and Claudio asked me to join them in his hut, as they will all party, so I dared to join them as it seemed to be an adventure. Music was played for dancing and to be merited. 'Plastic dreams' – Jaydee, and more underground tunes from there on. The feeling was one of hugging and kissing as everything else prior to building up for this succeeded.

Tawan came close to me with a look on his face, indicating a sexual proposal. I was relaxed and confident to handle anything but also felt good that someone showed me preference. He touched my swimming trunks right at the front and while feeling his warm hand he said to me 'come with me'. I felt completely taken back. I was unprepared. I had no idea what was going on and was filled with confusion and became upset. I felt violated but invigorated. The touch was gentle and kind, I was conflicted. On one hand, I felt like I wanted him to stop, I was ready to push him away but on the other hand, I wanted him to keep going as I was looking at everyone having pleasure in dancing, hugging and kissing. It was a cocktail of embarrassment, shame and excitement. Dead scared, I said to him

- 'it's not a good idea' but I did not sound very confident in that.

- 'But I want to feel you all over my body and I will show you things you have never experienced'. He said, still touching my excited cock.

Woah, it's true, I have never experienced that! My heart was pounding, I felt Kate was going to appear and take over of what I wanted to happen but I retaliated in saying with a smile

- ' It's not a good idea'... sounding more confident.

He kept touching my front as Claudio came close to us and strongly as a wild lion pushed me away while he started kissing him which was the right time for me to escape. They carried on kissing, and Tawan was lowering himself on his knees, and sucking Claudios testicles and looking dramatic and appealing. Looking away, I got a glimpse of Fan kissing Chi passionately. Oh! I could not stop looking at her and wanted to be Chi. My chest doubled in size from the pumping of my heart. My inner world was penetrated with steam of lust. It was an electrifiing atmosphere that I wanted to explore. I purposely walked to the door and I was looking at them kissing and feeling wonderfully aroused. On the bed, there was the other one syllabus named people. This was a version of a real boy and girl, already nude and at the first chapter of having sex. Seven people and one invitation from the gay boys and alone in the middle of the room. I was ready for an experience.

Fan took a look at me and whispered into Chi's ear who moved over together with the Thai couple to make friends and participated in their threesome. I was totally overwhelmed that I was a visual participant to an orgy. It was like we dropped in a circle deep in transit to another dimension and another circle further in. It was another world. A world with no rules.

I made my choice for my desires, I was free, not attached to my shyness but on the contrary with a lot of madness. I was excited almost released from a prohibition zone or out of my cell. I walked with confidence to Fan as I felt welcomed. I wanted to hunt, conquer and succeed. I started touching her to ascertain her reaction. She responded and pulled me over her and we kissed passionately. I whispered in her ear

- 'Come with me in my hut'
- ' It's better here between friends' she replied.

So, when In Rome... I have completely undressed her and myself in the same room with the others been occupied in their courses. I was free from any inhibitions. I went through her whole body, warm and firm and with her breasts in my hands, we had of what it felt the end of the world inside me. I had a glimpse of Kate in my arms as I was seeing another dimension. Volcanic explosions and lava running through our bodies while listening to her breathing and exhaling fumes of joy. I turned around and saw everyone else in red and gold steaming lava covering parts of their bodies while enjoying the touching and penetration of each other with lust and anticipation for fulfilment. Ecstasy and passion led us to the seventh sky where stars were shining and flowers were all around us while we had big smiles on our faces. We looked at each other with joy of sharing the experience.

It could have been the joint and the Thai whiskey, it could have been my lustful mind intrigued by Tawan and Claudio at first that made me give myself totally to Fan and then dropped in the hands of Hypnos, the God of sleep. Hours later, I woke up with Fan in my arms and Tawan at her end, but with his hand hugging us both. Claudio was with Chi and the other Thai couple were gone. I woke Fan up, gave her a kiss, I said to her I had a heavy head and I'm going to my hut if she wanted to pass by later.

I fell asleep again, stretched on my bed alone. Hours later, a knock on the door brought in Tawan with a smile and a bowl of fruit. I got up and said,' thank you Tawan', who so sweetly came close and gave me a warm friendly hug and said they were leaving and Fan is waiting to say goodbye. I wanted to have Fan in my bed at my hut and feel once more everything and more from the night before. I met her out in the bright sun, we hugged and kissed goodbye and ever since kept the memories of this magical night locked forever in my head. I became more open to processing people's preferences, thoughts and behaviors while exploring myself face to face with challenges and different experiences.

TOTAL CHANGE

In the 2000's the atmosphere in Ayia Napa began to change as real clubbers were pouring in, the likes of Ibiza and Miami. They were pursuers of good house music following DJ trends, they knew their drinks and drugs too. My gourmet searchers were becoming less and less and my French restaurant was not any more on the must visit list of the tourists. The new tourist wave was interested in fast food rather than gourmet experiences. I needed to diversify and bring a change.

Having traveled by then to India, Cuba, Caribbean, Africa and most European countries I was inspired and I was feeling a trend of fusion food, ethic influenced music, ethnic fashion wear remixed and re-edited for the millennium. I have turned the same farm house hosting the French Bistro into a new concept. A concept as a platform, where the visitor can be in any place of the world he chooses. Hence GURU was born, a concept bar, restaurant and more bringing a message of global symbiosis. A white palette where ethnicity slashed colours, tastes and smells, sounds and vision here and there. All together a beautiful painting, blending in world food, drinks and music, cultures and feelings and sieved through all the senses. I was drowned in overflowing powers to present my new set. I have given in all my creativity and inspiration and presented a new concept for Cyprus. It featured, a Drinks Garden with a DJ, a low seating sensual lounge with lounge music and a small intimate restaurant.

The restaurant was very sexy in blue and pink lights, white tables and with silver frames on the tables featuring part of naked bodies together, sensual but unidentified. All was left to your imagination. It was named ' Love Bites!' The menu cards were made from various sensual photo cuts resembling Dali creation. Mirror balls down the white dome sprinkled dots everywhere, causing a three-dimensional effect. The waiting staff all in white and with white masks on their faces and white angel wings. It was a place for two to savor food as the beginning of a sensual evening ahead. I saw myself as a visitor there from where I could have gone everywhere and hoped the same for others too. You did not need to make conversations, just look and feel anything that your imagination was capable of!

A huge white tent with thin transparent white curtains dressed in a reflection of blue fluorescent lights formed the shell of the low seating lounge. Lush white cushions around Moroccan copper low tables on thick coconut carpets. In other elevated sections real pastel green and pink leather sofas gave the visitors options to either seat comfortably or even lie down on the carpeted floor. A display of real paintings inspired by India's Kamasutra, Japanese Geishas and Oriental women dancers were displayed as a background on the far end of the lounge capturing the multi ethnic cultural and mystique mood of the place. As the music was romantic and exotic and the white curtains were dancing in the tones of the summer breeze, the candle flames were following the tempo and all the senses of the visitors to this plot were explored. A large handmade, Moroccan clay deep dish, in the middle of the floor featured plenty of white candles and burning incense of sandalwood and patchouli adding the fragrance to the summer mist flowing in from the sides of the tent.

There was shisha service, head, shoulder and back massage service, exotic cocktails and small bites served Middle eastern style in copper small dishes. The staff were very discreet, softly spoken and part of those paintings on the wall. It could be the case that suddenly, a ballerina dressed in light whites would perform around tables, as if no one was there, like a happy butterfly or like the white swan of my own Swan Lake composition. No words, just music and her, movements of curtains and flickering lights, white everywhere and everyone could choose the colours and create their own painting.

The front party area had 3 white bars with beautiful and highly trained staff performing all sorts of ethnic inspired cocktails. Blue and orange lights dressed the white floors and glowing on everyone's faces as they were moving around to socialize or dance to the sounds of researched music mastered my various DJs. Fire shows, dancers and flirty teasers dressed the evenings randomly. It was full of happy people of all shapes and outputs, postures and poses with lots of sexual potential. After all whoever was there was in search ofa flirt and an adventure. When I had time, I was seeing my fellow Kikuyus, the gentlemen in gray pants and gelled hair at the bar drinking martinis but the Scottish pals in kilts also partying in these sets! It was like a fanfare in my mind, a big party in reality and another one in my head.

I did it again and this new venue, Guru, became a must go and must have experience. Famous DJs pouring in Ayia Napa clubs those days, having tables booked in the lounge. Many media sources like radio stations from the UK and Cyprus, fashion magazines and newspapers, had tables booked for the whole summer season. Visitors started dressing up Guru style with lots of ethnic bohemian outfits and colourful bead necklaces and turbans on their heads. For those that were in the mood to become someone else there was a room full of accessories and stage costumes, hats and outfits. Many were coming out as belly dancers or 'hippified' with colourful shirts and bands on the heads and many other creativities. This made many people enjoy and mark the night as a favourite. They had the possibility to be other people. I felt that I was staging many film scenarios, just like in my travels.

Through all this success, I formed a music label called Mukta Music and bought all the rights to music played at Guru and created about ten CD music compilations dressed in photographs of the venue and all was a super memoir for people to buy and take with them. Some of these compilations were distributed worldwide.

I made many friends from visitors from all over the world, politicians, influencers and some famous artists as well. Many friends became regulars too. Mary, a beautiful lady who was born in South Africa, married for some years and had two children in their thirties. She was inspiring to me, sophisticated, simply stylish and elegant. She was always there for me to exchange views and we became the point of reference for each other. We knew of each other at different stages of our lives since my times at the mountain hotel. Our acquaintance developed into a valuable friendship. Our conversations had depth and value and from that stage on we were quite close. She loved dressing up with her friends and seated at postures around the bar.

The central bar was the socializing bar where one would meet everyone as the happy mood of the place made you feel you were in a cosmic party anywhere in the world. Cosmopolitan as it was, Mary met a man from Italy that was looking exactly like her as a male version, when you were looking at them. I gave them space to get to know each other and after a few drinks and during their conversations, I saw her slapping him angrily! It was quite unusual for Mary to do so! Later on, when she was leaving, I asked,

- 'But why this slap him on his face, was he rude to you?'

- ‘No, I liked him so much but I did not want to like him! I am scared and not sure I want to a start an adventure and I reacted like that. I gave him my telephone number with wrong numbers to avoid him’. She replied but not convincing me of her choice.

Poor lad, he came back to me the next evening asking me so politely for the right number. I had a chat with him, he was pleasant and kind. I felt that he would be nice for her, so I risked giving him the correct number of hers. They made up and had a great time together for a couple of years. I think Mary still has a small candle lit for him. Sometimes you need to help people see what you see and live what you know that they will enjoy. Just give them all a push!

I made friends with a young lady as one of those in my travels, an unusual looking colourful bird dressed in turbans and huge circle earrings, red curly hair with a baby girl personality, innocent and joyful, easy and welcoming and mostly open to everything and new ideas. Kia became an associate of the new venue and a personal friend of mine but also one that was absorbing life inspiration by someone older and more experienced, like myself. She was kind and supportive of all my ideas and a good carrier of the Guru 'disease' as it seemed to have been. She was spiritual and could read my inner world and understand my values and personal policies, the complexity of my character and my attitude towards other people around me. I was giving everyone everything they needed, love, care, interest, knowledge, guidance and all willingly and expecting in return to see them all succeeding. She called me her Guru and at a point, she said to a close friend, she believed that Paris was a 'God', in her efforts to say how much she saw in me. I was told that, and I felt more responsible!

Lots of charismatic personalities worked for us, many were the new experiences I had. One guy had blue short hair and was softly spoken in the politest version of masculinity. There was no aggression in him. He was lost in his life and was trying to find a cushion to rely on and someone to push him to stand somewhere on a floating raft that was going somewhere. I named him Pet. He loved his name and my attention. I made sure he was fed and that he kept to his time table commitments. I spent time with him talking and philosophizing. I even went jogging with him every morning to give him some exercise too. He was my Pet, I tried everything on him to show him directions and gave him small tasks to do and rewards after each one. He did fine but never really took a seat on that raft. He was perhaps weak and a little lost in drugs of some sort. He is now in London and found a cushion. A powerful and dynamic lady that seems to have enough ' love fuel' for that raft going somewhere.

Mara, an Indian girl with the most beautiful eyes, olive shiny skin, worked behind the bar. She was elegant and had those beautiful feminine hands as if performing an Indian dance but preparing for you a Cuban Mojito. A feast to the eyes, she gathered many men around her bar all asking her out after work. She was handling everything well and eventually found interest in my Pet. I saw her bike outside his apartment in the mornings and one day later she hasd some blue highlights in her hair.

A tall Cypriot manager, Panayiotis had the looks and the size of a Rock star and was a rock to depend on. He was the man who always saved the day, while other characters were to add to the entertainment. He was loyal to me and to the concept and he was learning everything on management techniques from me. Perhaps, it was his beginning to form a base. A strong enough base to later on move into management, more educational courses, is now a hotel manager.

There was a tall muscled young guy, sun tanned and topless in white fishermen pants and huge white wings welcoming everyone with a big smile. Erik was from Latvia and he was a woman's dream to look at. He added spice and exerted a sexual appetite for women and for some men too, I suppose! When he moved on to another country, as they all do, this beauty element in the concept was replaced by two Slovakian boys, young and fresh on the scene, with nice bodies and everything so well placed on them. Always smiling and with the hungry eyes for girls, they added a sparkle to the place while serving drinks and socializing. I loved them both, Stefano, flirty with no limits, a Calvin Klein model for underwear, and Kamil, sensible and clever, a blue eyed blond handsome God. When they left and years after, as they became responsible men, Kamil got married at Guru and Stefano came too. It was a happy reunion. They now call me Uncle and I love to see them when they come back to me!

The same year there was Kin, a nineteen-year-old beautiful Latvian girl, a model that was abused by some fashion designers with the promise to make her famous. A story heard so many times. She was naïve and scared which contradicted her looks and anyone could see her potential. She worked at Guru as a waitress. Everyone tried it on with her, but Peter another Slovakian young man succeeded to have a summer relationship with her and protect her from all the dragons that wanted to eat her. Peter was a carpenter by trade and had an uneasy brain. He ended up at Guru that Summer in search to travel and learn waiting and bartending. It was his first experience in this profession. Peter had dark hair and green eyes. He had one hand tattooed and something on his back. He was deep in his thoughts and had a lot to say in serious conversations. There was something very individual in him and he was protecting it perhaps out of insecurity. I wanted to be closer to him and go places in the profession. I wanted to show him more ways on how to think and deal with things but he was not letting me close. When he left, we lost touch for a while, but then he came back in communication. He became a bartender and a bar supervisor, a manager and partly owner of a brewery pub in Ireland. He kept traveling the world and now he is married in Switzerland and working as a manager somewhere. I'm so happy for him.

A black Congolese/Cypriot man, Alex, was a fast and professional bartender. He added diversification to the exoticism of the whole venue with his spectacular looks. Alex was deep and spiritual, mysterious, kind and exotic. There was a lot of respect between us.

There were nights when we had face make-up in black and white, different on every one of us, and tribal jewels with colourful beads and ropes around our necks and hands, heavier on women and all added to the white uniforms. There were nights when the staff went out in uniform and these outfits to night clubs after work. That was enough marketing as we presented a picture out of reality with all nationalities, beautiful people and dressed in white creative clothes, fruit of the loom! But the personas that I met working with me were endless... and they gave me so much.

Bing was a Chinese boy, tall and handsome and he wore white Chinese silk flowing pants and shirt. Always bare feet, he was in the lounge offering head and back massages, finding the pressure points he needed to press over the clothes of the clients and make them feel relaxed. He was quiet, reserved and observant. I wanted to know what he was thinking but he was well trained not to allow anyone to know. He was wise! One night I asked him,

- 'I know you are watching and recording everything. I am happy if you are using everything for you to learn from people too'

- ' Yes, I do, thank you!' he replied standing with acquired dignity and looking attentive.

- ' Yesterday, there was a man who asked for a back massage service and you chose not to offer it to him. Is this right?' I asked.

- ' Paris, I can give massage to visitors when they will enjoy it and when they need it. This man from last night gave me negative energy and no respect to our work and the surroundings! He talked loud and disrespectful. He was not ready to receive my energy!' he confidently explained.

- ' When you do a back massage for me, do you feel I have negative energy?' I asked.

- 'No, I feel you are tired, you need my hands but I know when you are angry or upset too, I feel it, we connect. I feel your energy, you are a strong man' he said.

Some nights when I was coming in from a long trip or from Nicosia, he wanted to treat me in a quiet corner and managed to relax me and revitalize me. He could stop a headache and he could send you to sleep. He always stood at the corner and you would have thought that his eyes were closed but no, he was the manager of the whole place, assessing all situations and everyone was known to him. He grew up in the forest in North China where they believe that when you die you become nature, so you need to grow in nature. His father was a general in the army so he grew up very disciplined and wise, so wise that he knew everything in advance and kept quiet along the way. There was a lot of respect between us and I made sure everyone awarded him at least that. I wish I knew more of him.

Nicole was also from China, a very researched girl with attitude to dressing creatively in white. She had the personality to back everything up. She had a porcelain skin and she was very attractive. Nicole was proposed by men on a daily basis and she was laughing in describing in detail what silly men were promising to do to her, money too! Instead, she was a good person, kind and considerate, enjoying service and socializing and going home every night. She was on her own mission and she was misconceived by men as being open for everything they wanted. I liked her a lot, she had a witty sense of humor and we often went out for a drink somewhere quiet as I was interested to listen to her growing up in China and the political system of communism that was so alien to me and especially at Guru where nothing was conformed with conservatism and restriction. We kept in touch for years!

Sabu, a Nepalese girl, first time away from home to study for hotel operations in the area. She came in flip flops in casual clothes and greasy hair. She learned everything from me about looking after herself and how it is with men and women relationships as in the use of language, service protocols and correct manners. She learned about cocktails, food, the Mediterranean life and she was a sponge of everything new to her. It was interesting to study her along the four years she stayed with us at Guru how accustomed she became to western mannerisms and way of thinking. She would greet the ladies to make them feel welcomed before their partners and she would recognize the host to always address him. She helped the ladies in the powder room, she opened wines and served cocktails always faultlessly. She went out with visitors to cafes and restaurants to eat and to clubbing with different people and nationalities. She was a true carrier of the Guru philosophy and culture. She was like my own daughter, and when she left for America to further her studies, she was wearing a blue business suit and Prada sunglasses! A little princess! I am very proud of her, still. Now, still in contact, she is married to an American and like a father to her, I keep asking ' when are you going to have children?'

Romi was a tall young man from South India. Handsome with rich shiny black hair, a smile and the gift of the mouth when talking in English. He was trained as a chef with me and he was trying his best. He was eager to advance, humble and polite. He was loyal and respectful to me and the Guru concept. He saw me as his father, sometimes, when I was tired, he would massage my legs as he used to do to his father back home when he was back from work. I supported him to all his dreams to learn more about the world and his profession as a chef. It was also time for him to go, and further his experiences. He is now in London as a leading chef in a chain of restaurants. I met him years after in London with his wife and his boy twins. He brought everyone out, as it was important to him for his children to meet his Guru. He took a picture of me holding the two babies, screaming their heads off while seating on me and in my arms. Later on, they visited me in Cyprus. The kids now are little boys and when they visited me, we played and hugged and this made me so happy. They called me uncle. It is rewarding to see people that come into your path that they grow and reach goals and their dreams. Romi keeps calling me Guru and asks for my blessings on his knees whenever we meet. Lately he bought a big house in London and he called me to visit them, proudly to show it to me. I am a happy uncle and very proud of him and his course.

I have a special part in my heart for them, I am feeling proud of all and I have learnt so much too from their beautiful souls. I may have given them all a direction a thinking, perhaps not always right, but I gave them all I had. They gave me back respect and taught me patience, acceptance and persistence. They learned at their pace, accepting everyone else and stayed tuned into their goals. I feel that I learned many more things from them, more than they know. I have put everything I had inside me in the making of Guru, and I have taken much more back through the people that came or worked there and are still coming!

This venue was a human platform for souls to park and recharge or re-invent themselves or simply play. They never left me. People go but what they leave always stays. I am one of those too.

An Indian Canadian young lady with the name of Amira walked in one day to ask for a job. Her eyes were green, her skin was dark with black long wavy hair, a super body as she was a Yoga fanatic. She was well spoken, kind, polite and well educated. Her smile was a winner too. She was a bonny lass', a stunner and I gave her immediately a waiting job as her looks would add to the place. I liked her but I was distant at the beginning, as the boss always needs to be, but close in matters of work procedures. One of my close friends started dating her flat mate, I was asked out to join them for a drink on several occasions. It allowed us to get to see each other outside work. I started seeing more of her inner world and I was liking it a lot. That was the beginning of a joyful ride full of teasing acts and lots of humor.

There was chemistry. I felt as if we were in an affair although nothing happened for a couple of months. We said enough, we were ready for each other. Our silence was a complete perfection of our feelings as we could feel its vibration when looking at one another. Everyone in the venue could see that something was going on between us, perhaps some thought we were having a relationship before anything indicative ever occurred. One night we went out to a club and as I drunk a little more, she suggested I stayed at theirs on a sofa but that did not happen. I slept in her arms the whole night and I felt that she kept looking at me while I was fast asleep in dreamland. The next day she said, I slept with a smile on my face and I apologized in return. She teased me that it's good to smile and don't apologize! I said,'nye, I apologized for sleeping and not!' She laughed and she said ' you are welcome!'

The days were approaching when she was to fly back to Canada, the venue was busy and we were all tired. I had other commitments in other places and I was not holding up very well. I for some reason walked out of the venue as a family of Scandinavians walked by. They had two children with them, their girl looked at me in the eyes and walked towards me and clutched on my legs. Her parents apologised and gently pulled her away as she looked at me and offered me a polo mint. I took it with a smile and she walked away with her head turned back looking at me. She had red curly hair and felt familiar. I smiled at her and waved goodnight.

One of those nights, when I had no energy to drive home. I decided to sleep in the lounge of the venue. Everyone had gone home, and I made myself comfortable on the cushions and the carpeted floor. Amira came knocking on the door. It was a knock-on heaven's door for me! It was a different knock, a real one that meant let me into your world. She was beautifully exotic. I managed to look deep in the eyes. I wanted to explore her through, I was not shy! The music was ethnic, almost tantra, which took us around the world as smoke and dust, water and air. We gave ourselves to each other. We touched each other's bodies. We tasted each other's saliva and sweat. We felt the heart beats and the breaths. Eros, the God of Carnal love, blessed our naked bodies and wrapped us in red and blue silks to intensify our sexual desire. We reached the drowning feeling in pleasure and fulfilment. We have spent one of the most beautiful nights in my life, in a perfect sensual set that I created and it was real this time.

On her last day, I waited for her to say goodbye, but instead she sent me a note with her flat mate.

' It's hard, I cannot do it.
It's better like that
I will always keep you in my heart'
Amira

Later on, I had an email from her saying how much she missed Guru and her time there. I sent her a quote by Rumi, since I got acquainted from Kate's books back in the London days. It said,

'Goodbyes are only for those who love with their eyes. Because for those who love with heart and soul there is no such thing as separation'

Guru was a place that perhaps all the people from the past had come back, some still on their own, some with new partners and some came back for me. I was there in all my versions, as in many people from my past lives but as different nationalities, a Cypriot, a Cuban, an Indian, an American, a Thai a Mexican and I was a boss, a man, a father, lover and everyone that added in me since my gray years. It built a name and it was franchised in other towns too. My staff were my people, real strong personalities and they have been able to play a role in a very demanding environment, quite spiritual and with high performance standards.

At a later point, a young man from Greece added spice to my life by offering me the opportunity to explore my fatherly instinct once again and keep him under my wings. Alexandros applied for a job just as he has finished his army service and needed a challenge. He was young and tall with an athletic perfect body. He looked like Henry Cavill, the Superman. He was very handsome and polite and was drawn by everything new, by everything that was happening and wanted to learn it all. I gave him my world I knew of, looked after him with advices and coached him to one day fly away and reach his dreams. There was an inexplicable energy between us and I was inspired too, by his daring courage as a young man. I envied him and I was jealous of him. I wanted to be him, as he was exactly the opposite of me when I was his age. He would jump off the plane, ride a bicycle between towns, swim for hours in the dark blue sea and run from here to New York. He played hard to get from the herds of girls after him and he was capable of everything. He could become a manager of Guru as he was keen in learning and absorbing technical information, but management theories too. He was good with money and calculations as he was budgeting for his own needs. His looks would have opened many avenues for him. I could see his full potential that he did not know. Sometimes it is like that and you can 'love' and care for someone and want to be him. It happened to me once before.

As he was very successful with girls, we got to hear all the funny sides of his stories. He also knew some of my adventures too. He wanted to be me and I wanted to be him. Indeed, I would have loved to be Henry Cavill for a Saturday night! When you give things to someone you will also learn things back. I felt younger with him, while listening to him about his Muai Thai techniques, his technological awareness, his underwater fishing experiences and more. I listened to his new ideas and thoughts representing the new generation. One day it was the right time. He flew away to take his course, like all the others. A big job opening in real estate. He was now equipped with wisdom. I wonder if he is now thinking like me!

In 2002, I was approached by an English business man, a customer of Guru, who wanted to invest in a concept of Internet television as in video on demand powered by a company in the US called Narrowstep. They believed that someone like myself not being technologically aware I would be ideal to market this new idea of presentation on the internet. They flew me to London to train in the quarters of Narrowstep on how this platform works. I understood absolutely nothing. My job, though, was to market this tool as a presentation to the world as everyone would have access to it. So, they wanted to create a pilot program on Cyprus, a window to the world. I surfed governmental institutions, ministries, municipalities and the private business sector too. It became successful at first, a needed tool to show the total Cyprus product to the world. Tourism, business, political concepts were all shown on the platform. Almost two years later the English businessman abandoned the idea and I was left with an index of useful contacts.

So, with some clever lads, we created a film producing company. Close to my producing skills and scenarios, we then grouped with a couple of internet technology wizards, camera men, film editors and offered film productions and social media solutions. So, more channels for creativity. We started traveling to other countries of Israel and Lebanon for productions. We represented a crew for the international channel Fashion TV but also created a Lifestyle platform, resembling Fashion TV, on the internet for Mercedes-Benz. We had a designed tv platform on the internet showing fashion shows, parties, designer interviews, Mercedes-Benz adverts and interesting destinations to travel all at a high life level. We got to meet fashion designers, media influencers, politicians and definitely many models. Some real ones too! We did a lot of films for the Cyprus Government and some corporate films for private companies. I had the role of the producer of the concept and the final film edit.

Guru lasted for fifteen years. As the avenue in Ayia napa, closer to the sea was heavily invested and shops bars and restaurants made a dynamic new entry, figures showed it was time to go. Less visitors were circulating around the Guru area.

Guru saw many young people of different ethnicities contributing with their personalities and skills along these years. I became more complexed, deep in my words and have explored my spiritual side. I needed to feel more of an individual's importance. I was calmer and receiving everyone's warmth and welcoming their presence in my heart. I was myself but as many other persons and carried with me unexplicable thoughts and ideas that did not know from where they originated. I was beginning to feel the connection with others that were 'rich' and interesting, pure and beautiful. I needed to see through them. It was an art of self- realization I became a human platform myself... and knew there was more to find out!

TIBET

Mercedes-Benz internet platform gave us the opportunity to get to know many fashion designers of international fame as well as singers and artists. One day a famous fashion designer, Aphrodite Hera, asked me to film a show of hers, sponsored by L'Oréal International in Beijing, China. I took the challenge and I went on my own with a camera. The show was held as per Chinese scale, for some three thousand people, invited to this fashion and hairstyle show. Some two thousand people were involved in the production of this show from hairdressers to light and music engineers, models and designers. The show was magnificent and Aphrodite's clothes exhibited an opulent ethnic Indochina culture, of heavy embroideries and colourful patterned materials with hairstyles to match and impressive big jewelry pieces. I was also impressed by the opening act of models parading in red light flowing materials of various designs with a display projection of red shapes of red oil. A team of dancers in Chinese black clothes performing dance maneuvers between the walking models flowing to the dreamy music. I think this team was featured in the opening of the Olympics in Beijing.

While in Beijing, I contacted Nicole from the Guru years and we were happy to meet and catch up. She had a boyfriend from Kenya who grew up in Holland and I met him too. He was not of Kikuyu origin but one of an unidentified tribe to me! Nicole took me around to impress me of the culture of her country that she was proud of. She was now a journalist for a big newspaper which was always her dream job. To express her own views, as much as she was allowed! She was still dressing up in creative styles as I knew her, with unmatching colours and patterns but with a big bow on her head, this time. I was happy visiting one of my Guru girls and seeing her in her own environment and growing up with her dreams.

China seemed to me quite diversified offering everything and fast, so fast that every day it was different and nothing the same as yesterday! It was exhilarating and inspiring. The buildings and their scale, the Temples and their grandeur, arts and creativity, food and people, so many impressions. All was impressive, unusual, new and yet quite close to me.

One of the best experiences in China was when Nicole took me to a traditional tea house. There were many separate rooms with a table for two. It was laid with porcelain cups and tea pots on a wooden tray. A specialist Chinese girl, dressed in red silks embroidered with flowers, was moving her hands so fast and handling the porcelain and the hot water pouring from a big pot into the tea pot and washing the tea leaves first and all those movements were judged by Nicole as no porcelain is to touch another piece and make a noise. Some expertise there! We were enjoying our tea and conversation with Nicole and suddenly I could see from the door being slightly open a monk walking in the main waiting room.

The monk had a shaved head and dressed in yellow and red drapes, as everyone from Tibet seemed to. I stopped listening to Nicole. There was a power with inside me. I was drawn to him, I got up and went in front of him, greeted him with my hands and a bow of the head and said 'hello'. He got up and replied with a hello and gave me the same respects. I asked him from where he is coming and he politely asked me to sit with him. I felt he was open for conversation and he had enough English language to do so. There was a strong connection in the air, I felt I have been in that situation once again. Nicole approached and it seemed not proper to sit with us, so she excused herself and went off with curiosity of my reaction. I thanked her and arranged to call her later.

Lima, was a Chinese priest of a certain temple in Tibet. We sat there and shared more tea. He wanted to know where Cyprus was but again, he was happy to relate easier to Greece and he knew of the Christian Orthodox religion. He wanted to know a lot about me, my life, my routine and he got confused when I said to him, I have a bar selling drinks and food and people dance there too and it's called Guru. He was in Beijing on a mission to collect donations , through a small network of wealthy businessmen for some renovations at the temple, which sounded a regular happening. We went for a walk on the busy streets of Beijing and I saw him having a glimpse of a big road display of an advert for women's bras, showing a woman wearing one, which kicked on so many questions. I asked him of his life and background and our conversations were endless.

Lima invited me go to his temple in Tibet and spend a few days, or as long as I want, but may have to do some light work or give a donation. He talked to me about the temple that had many children and he was sometimes teaching them. He did not like the fact that the children had to wake up at five in the morning to pray seating on the cold concrete floor. He felt that a lot of procedures and traditions are old now and should be more flexible to modern thinking. We took the train and traveled for two endless days.

On the first day, the landscape was mainly flat, with occasional rolling hills. We passed through small towns and villages, with people going about their daily lives. The scenery was beautiful, with the sun setting in the horizon and the mountains in the distance. On the second day, the terrain began to change. We were surrounded by majestic mountains, with snow-capped peaks and lush valleys. The train passed through tunnels and over bridges, providing stunning views of the rivers below. We were also able to see traditional Tibetan villages and monasteries, with colourful flags and prayer wheels. As we continued to climb higher, the air became thinner and the views even more spectacular. We could see vast plains and wide-open skies, with mountain ranges stretching into the horizon. The sunsets were breathtaking, with colours of pink, orange, and red. The journey was filled with beauty and awe. It was an experience that will stay with me forever. It was also very tiring being on a train for two days, at a point I could not even talk to anyone...

Lima had a laptop and I challenged him,

- ' Lima, can you access porn with your laptop? I mean nowadays anyone at the temple can see anything they want to'.
- ' It is difficult in China. But some can. If your conscience allows you to do anything you want, then you must not be a monk,' he replied.

I showed disbelief and repeated

- ' I feel that nowadays monks and priests can watch anything on the internet and I am sure they are intrigued to do so.'

He simply smiled. If Lima, bright and modern as he was, was denied, of what it seems to me a natural expression of a human body to be touched and the need to feel interaction with another human body, and the need of the body to release fluids from your geneticals, surely this is not possible. I could see his interest and I could feel him wanting to listen to me about my life and routine and relationships with employees and friends and slightly on relationships with the opposite sex.

He was interested to know about my Guru in Ayia Napa. We saw the map and I showed him Cyprus. He said with a surprise,

- 'It is a very small island!'

He has never been to the sea and he said,

- 'Perhaps one day I will visit you there.'

I had visions of a monk from Tibet in his colourful robe walking down the party street of Ayia Napa next to the Toga dressed party people and the drunkards who would probably think that he wears a nicer party outfit! They would have taken it off him in exchange for their hotel bedsheets!

No, it was not to happen and I did not want that responsibility!

When we arrived at the temple there was so...so much to take in! A breathtaking experience from the building and its huge ornate doors, the whole aura of respect and tradition, the sounds of the ticking bells and the children's voices... to the chanting monks and their grandeur. It was set against a backdrop of snow-capped mountains, with intricate carvings, paintings and gold accents. Its entrance was guarded by two giant stone lions and decorated with colorful flags and banners. Inside, it was a wonderland of statues, murals, and hand-crafted artifacts, each with its own unique story. Everywhere we looked we were surrounded by the beauty and mystery of this ancient place. The temple was so grand to me, and much that it sounds disrespectful, I saw it as a venue with bars serving cocktails, and in another area, steaming fusion food, prepared by chefs in monks' robes. There was great acoustics and grand set ups for customers to lounge and party too. It was just like my venue Guru but different colours!

I was introduced to the main 'Guru' monk and showed respect to the spiritualism that twirled around him at a mere glance. I was welcomed as a guest and followed their routine. I was given a cell, similar to the Thailand's mountain spa experience, but with a comfortable bed and a wash basin. I was also given plain clothes loose pants and a shirt, Chinese style, looking a little like Bing's outfit at Guru.

We woke up at quarter to five and helped two hundred boys to get dressed and be on time for prayers. They looked at me as if something went wrong with me at birth. Yes, they sat on cold floors but so did I. Then it was breakfast again on the floor, a kind of bread and tea. Then it was lessons on Buddhism and theories and mathematics again on the cold floor. The children had a little time to play and run around and then back to prayers. I followed Lima and his routine for three days. I was present during all the lengthy prayers. I was beginning to feel priestly myself and it exhilarated my spiritual inner world.

Other priests of different ages worked in cleaning and

preparing food, others went to work in some fields and brought back vegetables. Many people brought to the door bread and other local products as offerings.

The last evening, the head monk asked me to join him to dinner around a table. There was a metal dish with rice, bread and vegetables with a kind of a sauce, especially cooked for me. We drunk tea and he asked me of my job, my lifestyle and my religion. He looked as if he had his eyes closed but you can never tell. I answered filtering everything to decent material and I talked to him about my parents and my childhood too. At a point he asked

- 'May I ask you, why have you not married to have children? I see you love them '

I felt in a difficult situation to make him understand how I enjoyed being free and how much I wanted to travel and experience people and life elsewhere. Like as where I was at that moment. But I replied looking down,

- 'I have had some relationships with women, but I did not feel ready to commit to marriage. I still want to travel and explore the world, there is so much to do'
- 'Travel is good, when the mind is good… when family is good then the mind is good' he wisely said to which I noted.

He was sympathetic, polite and he smiled at me but I felt I came across as problematic.

- ' You seem to be good person, lots of good spirit and energy, big heart, lot to give!

  You patient man, I saw you watching the young children yesterday! Patience is a charisma.

  Now, you ready to become a Buddhist!' he said smiling but with eyes still looking shut.

I felt like saying to him, I am a Buddhist and a Guru and I have my own children. But instead, I asked him what I was dying to hear.

- 'Osho, what is your opinion on karma and past lives'? And he replied
- 'Karma is the law of cause and effect that governs

the universe. Every action we take in this life has an effect on our future lives. Our past lives.... have also shaped our current life. We are all here to learn lessons, and the experiences of our past lives are meant to help us in this life. Sometimes we can feel a connection to places we have never been before, because we may have experienced them in a past life. Our souls can remember these places and experiences, even if our conscious mind does not.'

I found his answers so vivid and truthful to me and I opened up from excitement and asked again.

- 'Osho... I believe that I have a connection with some other places, perhaps I lived in other places. I feel like that as I am drawn to anything connected with these locations. My mind wants to think like that, my mind wants to see more on these...sometimes I am in a cloud. I see life in different dimensions. You think it can be like that? Can someone go back?'

He smiled and opened his eyes looking at me saying,

- 'It is possible... you have such a connection from past lives, perhaps more places. It is why you feel familiar with some elements in this life. Only, you can feel this. Only you can know. Meditation, when you... ready, can help explore the inner realms of consciousness, potentially allowing you to journey back into past lives. For some people, past life memories, are only accessible through a deep meditative practice...I suggest you experiment with meditation to see...when ready. But I want to ask you, can you feel the presence of other souls around you?'
- 'Woah. Yes,,,yes and I think I am ready! So, I can see who I was! And how will I know it is me?'

He did not answer that but he asked,

- ' Do you remember anything from past lives?
- 'No, I do not remember anything, only that I feel familiar with some places or situations. There is a feeling that I

cannot explain' I said.

- 'That's okay...Sometimes we need to take the time to uncover our past, so you can explore it when you are ready. Find some clues first. Perhaps recall any memories you had from any of these places you like. Perhaps one day when you feel ready to practice meditation'. He repeated.

I smiled and since, I got him to talk, I said that I miss my parents that died, but I feel they watch over me all the time.

- 'It is natural to miss those who are no longer here. But remember, they are still with you in spirit. Even though they are not physically here, their love and guidance remain with you always.' He explained.

- ' Also, I'm afraid of death, and I love life'. I expressed in a confessing tone.

- 'Fear not, for life and death are part of the same cycle. Each moment of life is precious, and each moment of death brings new beginnings. The cycle of life is never-ending, and each moment is an opportunity for growth and transformation', he wisely replied.

He looked intensely into my eyes and asked if I thought I was a good man in my life so far. I was skeptical and went a little shy looking down, but I opened up to say,

- ' I always try to do the right things but as human I can be weak'.

Since he had his eyes opened, I built enough courage and said,

- ' I like to imagine situations and see people in other dimensions and I have fun like that. Sometimes I feel it is not an imagination. It is not simply inside me and it does not stop there. It can be during intercourse. I also met many women and with some I got involved in relationships of different values and I have not always been a very good communicator, as I am confused as to what women are looking for'.

I did not know if I was understood or taken seriously or he began to dislike me. One can never say much about Chinese facial expressions and with closed eyes as we think they have. He took my challenge and replied,

- 'It sounds like you have enjoyed life so far and have taken pleasure in certain experiences. It is good you can imagine anything that gives you entertainment. But are you wiser? Remember that in order to live a truly good life, we must also be mindful of our actions and how they affect others. We must strive to do our best, to bring better into the world than harm. You have been trying to do your best to live a good life. Perhaps you have not found what you are looking for in life, because you have yet to answer the question of what is most important in life for you. It is only when you can answer this question that you can truly understand what it is that women are looking for in a man and in life. Perhaps practice a nonattachment in romantic relationships it would be easier like that to follow the path of enlightenment, Discard all things in life that can cause pain, so one must detach from the idea of a perfect person and instead accept a partner unconditionally. You will when ready!'

I valued his sounding of wisdom. His last words stayed with me. Only when I can answer to what is important in life for me, I can truly understand what it is that women are looking for in a man and in life! What is important in life for me? I kept asking myself. I was also bothered by the mega word - unconditionally. He was correct, I was not ready!

Precious times in Tibet, with Lima, the Osho, the conversations and the respect. The Osho was so spirited. I felt privileged to have been invited to speak to him. His eyes were so full of wisdom, and his words so full of truth. I will forever live the memory of the spiritualism in the grand temple and the Buddhism prayers. I loved the children and their bright eyes; I loved observing their joy and innocence. I wondered how many of them will make it to become real monks or whether they will be destroyed by indulgence to technology and the modern world they are denied now.

Lima said nice things that I was destined to give people nice feelings. It is a blessing to be able to give. He could understand that I was advising, coaching people. He said these people are your children but I believe some more people made you be like that.

- 'To give means you have, give to everyone everything and more will come to you' he said.

Spending time at the temple was the most rewarding experience of my life. It was a time of awareness, reflection and contemplation. So precious, I could not share them with anyone for a long time. Or perhaps I was not ready to do so!

RASTAFARI

In 2003, on another occasional trip to Bangkok, I started exercising meditation with a group receiving guidance and read some books. I was absorbing quotes and methods for self-realization.

The same year, I made friends with a Thai girl from Krabi. She was living in a big wooden box, by the river in Bangkok and working on silver jewelry. Nin, had black Rasta hair, tied back or up, however she was styled, she looked stunning. A beauty spot on her cheek made her sweeter especially when she smiled. There was something very calm about her. I have been a loyal customer to her for a couple of years. My contact was obvious and I was sure she felt that I wanted to get to know more of her and perhaps differently. Many foreign visitors, in Thailand, are after some kind of disrespectful experience in her country and I felt that I carried that stigma in her eyes. Sex is an industry in Bangkok, with the lady boys, the Cowboy bars, the cabarets, but you also see some older men with young girls or boys which is not a pretty sight and especially for Thai people as they look down on these people being foreign visitors! When I started thinking like her, I withdrew my questions as to when can we go out and have a drink. A year later, as I paid my debts for buying some silver rings she said,

- ' What are you doing later today? Do you have any plans? I invite you to a rock bar I have a friend working there'
- ' I have nothing to do later, it will make me very happy to show me this rock bar'

I replied hiding my enthusiasm till I walked away out of her vicinity and cheered ' yes..yes.. yes..' with my hands up in the air and everyone looking at me as if my favourite football team scored a goal!

That same night, we met at her box on closing time and we went for a walk across the river. We took part to this sweet ceremony alongside many other people, of releasing lit lanterns, as they believe you are releasing the negative energy and you make a wish for good luck and good fortune to come. She wanted me to experience this. She was so beautiful holding and looking at the lantern of hers and I could see she was releasing it praying for better things. We released our lanterns the same time and for me it felt as if we bonded at that point.

We went to the rock bar and she introduced me to a friend of hers, Asnee, who was the head waiter. He looked after us serving us the beers and some chili crisps. He was kind of funny with a nice smile and he was teasing her, in their language, and making her laugh. She was sweet, her face was lit up!

We had a couple of beers and good conversations about the rock music and what we like. Of course, me being older and into music, I won the quiz in conversation, the respect and two more beers! We talked about our beliefs, our hopes for the future, and our dreams.

- ' If two people are in love...have you ever been in love? Would you know how they know they are in love... What is love? Can you answer this?' I asked her feeling very excited about this chapter. She looked at the ceiling thinking about it and spoke

- 'Oh... so much to think and answer...love can be many things and different to many people. Love in films is different than reality. For me love is when you accept your partner for who he is, and treasure what he is not. Love is when you are happy with your partner whatever the situation is...love is wanting to be with your partner and care and touch and there is no one else' she replied and reversed the question to me.

- 'For me love is...love is.... caring, sharing, feeling excited, help...scary! I liked your answer more than mine,' I said shamefully and we both laughed.

We explored our feelings about life and the world around us. We discussed our values, our understanding of what it means to be alive. Our conversations were deep, meaningful, and often quite profound. It was a unique connection that I had rarely experienced before. The spiritual connection between us was tangible and powerful, and I felt blessed to be part of it. She opened up in front of me and I felt a whole new world in her.

I felt my heart racing as I looked at her, and I found myself wanting to kiss her, more and more with each passing moment. I was so in awe of her beauty and her intelligence and I was captivated by her aura of her presence. I could feel a good energy between us and it was intoxicating. I wanted to spend the night in her arms.

On departing, I thought we would have moved into a kiss goodbye. I felt a spark between us, but from the body language, I did not feel the encouragement. My desire for something meaningful and spiritual was clear. My urge to proceed to more interaction was evident too. But she took it up a notch, guiding us to a spiritual plane. There was a smile and gratitude for spending time together. I felt some waves of soft air elevating us off the ground, a euphoric feeling, joy of sharing that smile.

Then, there was a sign of hope! She wanted me to be at eight in the morning, outside her box, because she planned something. Oh well, perhaps then something may happen. Such a sweet girl and so pretty and a killer smile, with her beauty spot, walking along, all recorded and stored!

The next morning, I was there at eight, and she greeted me with a cup of green tea and a ticket. She had sent me to the buses and I had to figure out where I was going. She promised me that she will be there when I come back and she will be waiting to see me. OK Mr. Paris, here you are, something is happening. I felt a superman!

I got onto the bus, confirming with many Thai people, I was holding the right ticket. There was a woman with three chickens tied upside down and very live in a big bag, next to me.

One was looking at me with its eyes and said ' who the hell you are? Mind your business'. The bus was almost full, there was a lot of talking and noise from the streets and with the shaking, I fell asleep for a while. I woke up in higher levels where only the roaring engine of the old bus, struggling to reach the top, could be heard. There were fewer people on the bus, as while I was asleep, some may have got off.

I wondered where I was going as two hours were spent in the bus. Now, the scene was beautiful, with the endless palm trees and thick jungle vegetation all around the mountain roads. Another half an hour later, the bus stopped at a place of what it looked the end of the world. Five shacks hidden here and there in the trees, and one bigger that had a better roof with metal sheets. They all left me; the driver had stopped the bus, as this was his last destination. I wondered as to what did she want me to do there.

I knocked on the door of the bigger house. An old lady, with no teeth, opened the door, looked at me and said Pale? I thought she meant me, so I confirmed Paris and she smiled confirming back to me that she had no teeth. I followed her into a small room that looked like a jail to me. Just a wooden floor and four walls with no window. She smiled and she gave me a bunch of clothes to wear. Thai fishermen pants and a top, a couple of thick towels and a thin foam mattress to place on the floor and she locked me in. Right, I said to myself, lets live this experience too!

The place was quiet, so quiet that I could only hear the sound of the water traveling in a river very near me. I began to understand that I was there to relax, feel and think to myself. It was a place to come to a complete relaxation. I changed clothes, probably looking ridiculous, lied down on the wooden floor and stretched my back and my whole body after the bus ride.

Perhaps half an hour or more of calm breathing and on and off dosing off, the door opened and the old lady indicated to follow her. There were two, not so old ladies now, and a man, all in Thai clothes like mine and all greeting me with respect, bringing the palms together and lowering the head down, the Thai way. To their surprise, I awarded them the same way.

They laid me down on a wooden flat surface and all three of them started discovering knots, bundles, blocked veins, disfunctions and disabilities of all sorts on my whole body. They started working on all my joints on all parts of my body. He even touched around my testicles, very close to all, but I trusted them as they inspired me, they knew what they were doing. At a point and after of what it seemed a whole lifetime, they somehow folded me and he pressed on my neck, I think I was out of life itself. I must have slept for 4-5 hours and they were all three there when I woke up. They were still greeting me, no words so far.

The girls left us and he placed a big towel in front of me, indicating to take my clothes off and he then wrapped me well in it. It felt safe to follow him to the next room, where there was a round wooden bath filled with water and lots of green leaves. I sat in this warm bath, which was not clear, obviously some special natural spring water streaming down from further up the mountains and he began to wrap leaves on my body. He encouraged me to close my eyes and relax, which I did. I was in the hands of the doctors of nature. I also thought that if something happens to me, no one will ever find me there!

The magic bath ended on another flat wooden bed and now all three of them were dripping hot oil on me and were massaging into every muscle and every inch of my body. I was in heaven. It was perhaps seven at night, when all was finished. They took me to another room to eat as I really felt hungry. There was sticky rice in one bowl, fresh fruit cuts in another and some tomato and cucumber slices. I had tea and water and I was locked back in my cell.

Being lost in that world, I found it soothing and comforting, and it helped to open up my energy and let go of any negative emotions or thoughts. I felt completely relaxed and at peace after my treatment. My mind was clear and my body felt light and refreshed. The experience was a reminder of the importance of self-care and taking time to nurture my body and mind. This was her gift to me.

At five in the morning, they opened the door and gave me back my clothes to wear. The old lady walked me to the bus and smiled goodbye, showing me again that she had no teeth. I was back to town to see my girl, Nin, and I needed to thank her for offering me such a rejuvenating experience.

When I met my Rasta girl at her box, she had a smile on her face, as I was so relaxed. I got her hand and kissed it. She looked at me in the eyes and spoke

- ' Explore what brings you joy, and be liberated by the beauty of your own truth. Live every moment of truth'. I showed appreciation and replied
- ' But you feel what brings me joy! '

Insinuating that her presence and what I needed to develop, was the beauty of my own truth. She took my hands and brought them to her face, quite unusual for Thai people, and spoke

- ' I feel you are special and want to keep our connection elevated to another level'.

We left it to that until next time.

Nin, was my unusual and precious Thai connection. She wanted me to understand everything and connect in a different way that I was used to connect with the opposite gender. This, was another level. I promised myself to keep this kind of contact behaviour, full of respect and love that crucified any thought from anything else happening leading to a possible sexual interaction at the time. Perhaps I was to discover something else, something I did not know existed. Our contacts were built on mutual understanding and admiration, transcending any physical desires. This was new to me and it carried on from there on.

For a whole year I tried calling her from time to time, but I was unsuccessful, as her phone was not working and I thought that she may have lost her phone or changed her number. The next year, I went full of excitement back to Bangkok to meet Nin. Her wooden box was locked and somehow looking abandoned.

I was covered in dust with street rubbish thrown outside. I asked around about her at other wooden boxes where there were painters and craftsmen, but none of them, had any English to understand me.

I wanted to find out where she was. I was anxious and desperate to know. I thought of Asnee, her friend at the rock bar. When I went there, he was not in. I sat and asked for a beer waiting for him to come. I was looking around, and memories were brought back, of her face, talking and of her smiles to me when we were last there.

I saw Asnee walking in and I got up to talk to him. The bar was busy with people talking and laughing and the music was on. At first, he did not recognize me, and I spoke

- ' Hello, Ansee...perhaps you may remember me? I came last year with your friend Nin'. Suddenly, he seemed to be overwhelmed by a wave of gloom, his face became a mask of sorrow. I felt this was not a conversation I wanted to have, as the words he was about to speak seemed to carry a weight of sadness.

- 'Oh yes that is right I remember you...... Nin is not with us anymore!' He said very sadly.

- 'Oh no! I have lost Nin....How what happened she was so young!' I said in despair

- 'She was visiting family at Krabi when she was swept away by the tsunami. She drowned....'

The thought of my beautiful girl battling in the raging waters.... was unbearable, my eyes were full of tears. Her life was taken, and all that remained was a memory. I was filled with sadness and disbelief that she was gone. I felt like a part of me had been taken away and I could not believe that I would never see her again. It felt insane. It was unfair. I was so shocked that someone so kind could be taken away so suddenly.

I must have walked all the city of Bangkok thinking of her and holding onto every sentence she said. I thought of her face, sending me on the bus that morning and receiving me back. My memories forced me to go to the river that same night. I lit a lantern and released it, like that night when I watched her face. I made a wish that she would be smiling, wherever she is, and that God, whoever he is, is looking after her. I prayed thanking her for everything. I was very sad. I watched the lantern drift away, until it was just a speck in the night sky, a silent reminder to live 'the moments of truth'. She would have liked that!

TRUTH OR DARE

With the years passing and moving on, getting older, more mature and with great experience in my professional field, I was beginning to close all venues needing my management. I felt that I needed to do bigger things. I could not be tied up in an operation. The clientele was getting younger and uninterested, but no, it was the opposite. I was older than my clientele and they did not care for what I had to give them. Trends, life, everything changed as technology crept in. I had less tolerance to managing day to day operations. I felt established as a professional and I had nothing more to prove to people about my professional abilities. Everyone knew me of being ahead of my times and this gave me a great postioning in the market of influencers and creators of new concepts. I started, offering consultancy services to hotels, bars, restaurants, property developments and sometimes to professional people on developing a concept. Everything needs a concept, a direction a reasoning. It took on as my charisma of giving birth to ideas, sensing forthcoming trends, sometimes creating them. Businesses are in need to differentiate and upgrade.

It is like a curse to be observant. You cannot relax. You always look around and you absorb. You see on the street this stunning girl that reminds you of one, in that exotic island that you have as a reference, and that you could take her and make her a model out of Vanity fair magazine or else! I could make her a Hollywood star. To spot the handsome guy behind a bar or elsewhere whom you may inject with marketing knowledge and make him an ambassador of a brand or place him in a film set! So much potential and talent out there! I'm people watching all the time and I'm never alone and bored as I imagine films unfolding in front of my eyes.

I am a mental traveler and I create the environment and the mood I want to be in. I see other things… if only they knew where I'm going in a minute! It comes naturally to me. It is like a woman that dresses up to go out and about. She cannot wear red nails and lipstick, a mini skirt and high heels and talk shy and have no direction! I would expect her to be fully confident and back up all that appearance with confidence and with an attitude of a winner! I could help her to do that and back up her whole presentation.

People need a concept, a day needs a concept, a team, an effort, an organization, a home a life needs a concept too! I could help define that and draw decisions and colours and sounds and all the senses are directed through a concept. It needs a strategy and I could do all that.

At a seaside hotel in the area of Protaras, while redesigning the organizational structure, a woman was recommended to me, by a friend, for an interview, as they needed a marketeer. Elizabeth wore a black dress and she had long wavy blond hair and blue eyes. She was a very beautiful woman and certainly out of my league, not only based on her looks, but also because she was not available as she was married and with children.

I talked to her briefly as to what the hotel needs and sent her to the director for an interview, but have asked her to come back and let me know of the outcome. A few days later she came back and explained that the director did not form an opinion as to her hiring and she was still looking for a job. I suggested she help me organize an event, as I was involved in a film production and event organization to which she agreed to meet me a week later in Limassol. Her responsibility involved the organizing of some 13 models arriving from another country to a hotel where there were crews for makeup and hairdressing and all girls had to be made up and ready at the venue a certain time where a

Fashion TV party was staged. There were film crews, caterers, fashion shows, bartenders and waiters, security people and I was responsible for the whole event. Events with shows are like tv shows where seconds matter and one delay, adds to the next one.

The girls arrived five minutes later than expected and delayed time kept adding on. It all went well and eventually at 4 in the morning we had a drink with Elizabeth to rest our feet and enjoy the success. A few other events were staged after this and Elizabeth was hired to help me out. She was sociable and inquisitive, as many questions were to be understood on my thinking and planning. Through these events she also met Kia, who still believed that I was a God, and they became good friends too, hanging out together.

One evening Elizabeth came to one bar I was managing in a hotel with an infected red eye and looking quite cute! We were looking at the sea and people walking up and down in groups. She asked for my advice,

- ' I am in a dilemma. Do you think I should accept this teaching job at a school in Nicosia? I have accepted this offer a month ago and the starting day is tomorrow! I am also concerned how to go to the school with an infected eye'! she ended with a smile, feeling sorry of her looks. I smiled and replied,
- ' I feel I want to push you to go. Live the experience, to live life and make something different, to make stories, than living in a small area with limited options. Especially, you are so young, in your thirties! Your children will soon be leaving home to follow their dreams. It is time to do more things in life and explore more avenues. People should take all the opportunities that are laid in front of them, or choose some if they have a lot.'

She did so, moved to Nicosia for the school days and she shared an apartment with a Greek friend of mine called Leila.

Our film production offices were in Nicosia, so I was in the same town and sometimes, Leila and Elizabeth, would invite me to taste some vegetarian food they cooked and have a chat. Two girls in an apartment, washing lines everywhere, make-up and nail polish at every table.... very feminine scene of a film. The weekends, I was back to my little house by the sea, as did Elizabeth, back with her family in the same area.

Most weekends, she would call me to catch up and to join me at my favurite place for swimming. There was a rock I would go to first and wait for her. We would place our towels and bags on it and jump into the sea from it. Sometimes, I would dive from it and she took pleasure in teasing me of my ballerina legs, as they formed prior to descending into the water. We had many talks on that rock. She would bring a boil egg for me, to be my breakfast and we called it our Egg and Rock.

Elizabeth liked to talk a lot! She talked about her family and her seven-year-old children at the school. Whenever I would get a slot in conversation, I would talk about my friends, past experiences, and about my mother. I was opening up to her and I felt relaxed about it. We got on well. It was very pleasant being around her and having her around me. It almost became a norm that once a week we would swim and I was looking forward to our Egg and Rock time together. It also became a norm to meet once a week in Nicosia, where she was staying or going out to a restaurant or bar to which I was looking forward to.

I remember those days, as a 'freelancer', I was seeing a couple of girls and having a good time with no strings attached which was the best thing for a 50-year-old man. I was a confirmed bachelor, living alone but never lonely, busy with work and successful, free to keep traveling the world and experience more and more. I was not looking for anything else in my life as whatever I had was plenty. That was also the times when I started exercising meditation on my own and there was a good feeling afterwards.

Socialising with Elizabeth and together with different groups of people in bars and restaurants, loving food, talking and laughing, carried on. She was charming to all and everywhere she went she was making new friends and different connections. She promised everyone to meet again and to call each other and she really wanted to. In reality, the next day she was drawn here and there by her routine. She could never really keep all these promises she gave. Sweet though! I was always intrigued with the fact that she was so available to go everywhere she wanted, and there was no partner with her. Naturally, I took the position of being her escort and to protect her, perhaps in a group with men making moves and she seemed to have been enjoying my presence and my role. She looked confident when I was around.

At the end of the night's outing, I would always escort her to her car, and we would kiss on the cheeks goodnight and that became a norm too. She was always nicely dressed, stunning, beautiful and sexy, and attracted the eyes of everyone when entering a room. I felt proud standing next to her, although illuding myself as there was no any mere indication of being my possession. A few months later, I noticed that she was going out with some other men to restaurants, casually and for socializing. I knew two of them, and they were married too. I knew they were both after one thing. I did not think it was proper, I did not like it and I was concerned which I expressed to her. She was forever denying these men's possible intentions which looked a little naïve to me. I knew her character, she was enjoying the conversation and the company and that was all.

Our meetings went on for perhaps more than a year. Through so many topics of conversation, I then begun to feel that she was kind of interested in me and I almost thought that she even began to like me. I could sense that and I was surprised. She was interested in what I had to say and more interested when I was expressing how I felt with this and that in the everyday life challenges or at work. It was not enough to say something, she started asking how do I feel about everything we talked. It was like she was getting to understand me more and analyze my actions and thoughts. This feeling was growing, I was confused and I was debating within me, what is going on here? It is not possible, and I always stopped it in my mind. I admitted to myself, I was jealous of the two married men being after her, I wanted to protect her, but why? And why was I upset?

One day, while we were swimming next to each other, she asked me

- 'Paris are you gay?'

I laughed and said,

- 'Many think I am and its best they do so! '

Little that she knows, I said to myself!

- ' Are you seeing someone?' She asked.

She knew I was, but I said

- 'Does it matter to know?'
- ' No, you are right, perhaps I should not be asking!' she said as she dived in the water from embarrassment.

I was sure that she was beginning to be keen on me, to start thinking like that, and trying to find out my sexual preferences. Probably, she must have been also wondering, why through all that socializing, I showed no interest or made any provocative comments, as it would have been normal. It was the pattern of a beautiful woman becoming interested in me. I did not feel threatened.

I remember one night at a bar by the sea, in Larnaca town, there was a DJ playing and we went with Kia who was lost socializing and dancing with some guys on the dancefloor. Elizabeth and I took an Old Fashion cocktail in our hand and we walked out by the sea to look at the full moon and there was silence. A silence that declared emotions, but not talked about. Something was in the air and we shared it in equal portions. We just looked at each other in the eyes. I lowered mine first!

Our communication and social meetings became more frequent. A few times after dinner with her and Leila, I slept at their apartment in the lounge on a sofa, not having to drive. There were some feathers on the floor. I had mixed feelings being there. One night Leila had her boyfriend, Peter, staying with her. He was from Slovakia, a dancer but more like a stripper. We all had dinner and a few drinks they went to their bedrooms and I slept on the couch. There was noise of a sexual activity coming out of their bedroom. It felt kind of strange, perhaps an invitation to my senses.

In the morning Elizabeth left to school and Leila with Peter left for a trip and locked the main door by mistake. When I woke up and made myself a cup of tea, I realized there was no way out of the apartment as they locked me in! I rang Elizabeth during her lesson at the school and she was going to run home in an hour when her lesson was finished. Having nothing to do in their apartment, I tidied up all the girlie mess, washed the dishes, cleaned the fridge and the bathrooms, swept and mopped the floors…. Until it was time to be freed! Since then, the girls decided to lock me in, every time I stayed over!

Elizabeth loved the mountains of Cyprus. She asked me to plan my time off for a trip to the mountains for a night. My mind started rolling,' how come, and shewhy will not be going to her family that weekend, on what excuse and what can happen in the mountain between us. Are we going to sleep in the same room? How are we going to sleep?'

With all these thoughts in my head we arrived at the mountain hotel where she booked a two-bedroom apartment. First, we went to the restaurant to have a meal. I was so concerned as to what may happen later at the apartment that she reserved for us. She seemed cool as always. While eating and talking, my mind was on another level thinking of later. I probably drunk four carafes of red wine on my own. I cannot remember what we talked about and how we drove to the apartment. I only remember dropping on the bed and with the whole world spinning around me, until I fell asleep. I was very uncomfortable. She took my shoes off and covered me with the bedcovers and slept in the other bedroom, as I discovered the morning after.

Loaded with a hangover, the morning after, we had a light breakfast and we went on a mountain bike ride that she organized. I was strong and did all the distance, with no problems compared to Elizabeth struggling on those hills. We drove back to Nicosia and I dropped her home with a friendly kiss, and felt a relief for not being in any embarrassing situation. I was now sure she liked me, lots of gray areas but was anticipating that something may surface soon.

A month later and during Christmas, she brought me some Christmas homemade goodies and we had high tea. I found her skeptical, perhaps troubled and as if she wanted to tell me something. It was not coming out in the open, whatever she wanted to say.

She went out to meet a friend of hers for some drinks and she returned to my little house to talk. She was tipsy but serious, I was standing in the kitchen and she was near me saying

- ' I had a couple of Mojito's with my friend and I discussed with her my situation... I took a decision I want you to know...'
- 'Ok... what's happening' I said in anticipation
- ' I am going to get a divorce' she announced in a monumental significance.

I remember I sat on the kitchen bench as a reaction to distancing myself.

- 'But why? What's going on? Are you not happy?' I asked
- Well, there is nothing wrong in my marriage... I am happy but there is something missing, I want to do more things... I don't know... it is time....I have no problems, but no I will get a divorce, she was not making any real sense.

I felt upset with the situation that she was going through a divorce decision because it was probably confusing and quite emotional, whatever the reason was. I remember, saying

- 'You need to be sure why you are getting a divorce and certainly I should not be the reason'

I don't know why I said that, as I had no right, but I was sensing something that involved me, and she spoke again,

- 'No, it has nothing to do with you, I am doing it for myself'
- 'Ok then, just be sure, it will not be easy, I am sorry. I will be here if you need me,' I added.

During that period, I got a little lost as my mother was

not well. I used to spend quite some time looking after her. Meanwhile, a couple of months later, Elizabeth got her divorce papers. She called me and sounded shocked and upset, but pleased and skeptical, perhaps insecure too. A not so good cocktail mix! She expressed that her children have stopped talking to her.

There was still a Lebanese man around her, always showing off his fat wallet and taking her to expensive restaurants. I did not like that and I made sure she knew about it. I called her,

- ‘ Hi, I hope you are well but listen...I know that the Lebanese guy is still around and you go out in Nicosia with him to restaurants. What is it, are you attracted to him?’
- ‘ Sometimes, but we are just friends, and what has it got to do with you?’ she challenged me
- ‘I want to warn you, he will use you and discard you and you are going to feel sorry for yourself. He is still married and he goes out with anything that has a pair of legs, is this who you are?’ I expressed strongly in an effort to protect her.
- ‘Ok then, we will talk later bye’ and she put the phone down.

She did not like me telling her off and we were both upset about our little argument.

Her children, now in their mid- twenties, did not like the new status that the divorce brought to the family and this upset her. I expected that with time everything would find its course.

Elizabeth was determined to carry on with her life and further herself as a person. I knew, from past experiences that she would need a stepping stone. I had, in the past, this experience and I became their temporary solution. In this case, I felt it was different and I made a point of contacting her every day so that she knew I was there for her. We met and went out a few times with friends, in an Italian restaurant in Nicosia, I have set up for a client. I was back to my gentleman’s escort duties and it was a pleasant feeling to be back on track and meeting more regularly now!

One day she called and invited me to her apartment for drinks, as Leila was on a trip to Greece. 'Scared' and shy, I did go and took a bottle of Scotch as a soothing ammunition. Her lounge had a different feeling than the other times. Now it was lit only by candles, and there was a spread of bites of cheese and sausages, dips and breads on the table, in front of the sofa and a bottle of red wine. There was soft music and burning incense sticks smelling of jasmin and vanilla. I noticed a couple of feathers on the sofa.

She wore her blue jeans tucked in her brown boots and a red shirt that suited her well, with her blonde hair. We sat next to each other on the sofa, nibbling and enjoying the wine and talking about everything and nothing. We got perhaps drunk on wine and continued on whiskey . I always loved a woman drinking whiskey with me!

I recall that we played the game truth or dare, where we had to take a piece of clothing off, should we not know the correct answer to a question. Well, I kept losing and after the pants and the shirt, I was in my socks and boxer shorts. I remember that, as I turned my head to say something to her, she kissed me on the lips. A soft little kiss. I looked at her in her eyes, just for a second, and placed my hand under her chin and gently guided her face to me, where it became my answer to her, with a massive emotional kiss and from there on we cannot remember, till this date, as to how it happened and how we ended up in bed. There was a war! It felt we had firecrackers in the room, disco and strobe lights flashing in combinations.

The next morning..., I shall never forget, as there was an awkward, different atmosphere in the apartment from the night before. We were both shy to look at each other. The previous night's crime set, was obvious and marked by clothes thrown here and there on the floor. She wore a beige negligée and while she tried to reach the tea bags from the top cupboard, her legs stretched and her back side silhouette was formed in the rays of the sun coming in from the kitchen window and showing a glow around her and her blond hair. A picture stuck on my mind. We had tea, said nothing of importance, gave her a kiss and went out of the door. I leaned on the wall waiting for the lift thinking 'oh what have we done'. Apparently, she leaned on the door as it closed and said 'oh what have we done!'

Days passed and I was thinking why she does not call me or should I? I called back to see how she was and perhaps to meet and go out. It's that stage when you don't know what were the thoughts on the other side. I was well received and we met again and again and had drinks and dinner, danced in her apartment and had also intimate pleasures in the bedroom. I was still shy but she was too. I somehow managed to have quick glimpses of her in underwear when dressing or undressing away from me. A beautiful picture to stimulate my brains and other parts but could never talk to her about it. There was a feather or two in her bedroom randomly appearing out of the blue.

I had, at this point, stopped seeing other girls, as it seemed to me, I was in a relationship with Elizabeth. We did not talk about it. Since, I could not carry all my usual characters with me in her apartment, I have been asking her in bed 'What is your name' and pretending that we just met, prior to having erotic pleasures. She got into this role. With time as she was running out of names and nationalities, she ended up gathering names from wedding party seating plans so that she had handy plenty of appealing names. She was Kirabo from South Africa one night, Amina from Morocco, Lucy from Canada and Brigitte from Guadeloupe another night. And the plot goes on, 'same, same but different' every night!

We arranged to escape the city and spend a long weekend in another town of Cyprus, Paphos at a Yoga hotel, as she was practicing Yoga. The hotel was basic but at a beautiful part of the island combining steep hills covered in foliage sinking in the blue sea.

At sunset, we sat on a sofa, at a nearby taverna on the

beach, and shared a bottle of rose wine. Our feelings were a mix of joy and contentment as we watched the sea turn from a deep blue to a brilliant orange and the sun dipping below the horizon. The warm breeze wafted across the beach, bringing with it the smell of salt and sea, and the sound of the waves lapping against the shore. We held hands and talked, exchanging funny stories, our dreams and our hopes for the future. We laughed teasing each other and the time seemed to stand still as we enjoyed each other's presence and company. It was magical.

It is moments like these that you begin to feel those inexplicable things. The bottle of rose wine was light and sweet, and it made me feel relaxed and carefree. We had some whiskey shots. We needed to warm up as it turned a little windy. As the sun disappeared and the stars came out, we watched the lights of the taverna twinkle in the darkness. We finished a second bottle of wine, and then we walked along the beach, hand in hand. She could see that I was happy and skeptical at the same time and she challenged me to talk. She was searching for heart shape stones on the beach and started giving them to me.' This one is white and nicely shaped, but this one is gray and a happy rounded shape and this one is nice on this side....' All sorts were offerings to me, so many versions of her hearts!

Everything was new to me. I was feeling butterflies in my stomach and a sense of exhilaration in just looking at her. It was a transition into a feeling of deep contentment and comfort. A sense of security and knowing that someone is there for you. Also, in addition to the physical and emotional connection, I was experiencing a strong sense of admiration and respect. She could see I had things on my mind, I always do. So, I wondered, could it have been love?

I explored the newfound emotions with a newfound openness and willingness to take risks. I was no longer scared of the unknown and I felt brave enough to take chances and put myself out there. It seemed that before meeting Elizabeth, I was driving in the mist not knowing where I was heading.

Somehow, I was not confident to talk about my feelings and could not show all my emotions. I felt responsible for this beautiful human being in my life.

I felt like I was discovering something new about myself, I was becoming a bigger person and I was excited to see where this newfound emotion would take me. I felt she was ahead of me and being a strong woman, she was ready for more. She was more experienced in handling the emotional part of us.

When we went back to the hotel bedroom, there was a bottle of red wine from the management. Elizabeth filled the bath with warm water and some fragrant herbal soap and created a perfect environment with candles. We both got into the bath and shared a glass of wine. We felt drunk by the alcohol but more by the happiness. We started kissing and the scenario moved into the bedroom, for starters on the bed. The main course was more creative by the chef, as he slid open the cupboard and gently pulled her in with him. As uncomfortable as it could have been for our bodies in that cupboard, I still do not remember how we moved but we must have been successful as we both enjoyed the heavenly interaction between a man and a woman that God so well created. Dessert found us on the bed. I expectedly fell asleep and she decided to cut my toe nails, with the aid of small scissors, as they needed it. Thank goodness carefully and successfully after the alcohol, I had them, ten in place! It seemed that she totally relaxed with me and truly enjoyed my diversified nutty mind! This was the beginning of more crazy happenings.

SPEAKEASY APARTMENT

A week later, Leila left to Greece and Elizabeth needed to move alone to another apartment she chose. This was in the old town of Nicosia at an area where many foreigners looking for asylum to live, many illegally. The whole area was so ethnic, not clean but with lots of spice shops, barber, butcher shops and second hand clothing shops.

She called me, supposedly to ask me to use a room there as a store for leftover furniture from my venues, and split the rent as it was out of her budget. I stormed down there, signed the contract and within two weeks, I furnished it and equipped it so that it would be ready on time with the opening of the schools in September.

When all was ready, I invited her to a sweet, little Greek taverna in a corner of the old town to eat and catch up. We walked to her new apartment to present it to her. It was a place of old charm with high ceilings. As you entered the hall, there was a long dark wooden dining table featuring two grand crystal table candelabras with dark green long candles. The floor was patterned with dark black, white and mustard color Moroccan styled tiles. Tall doors led into her bedroom with a vintage metal iron bed. In the corner I placed a round makeup table, with a double face round mirror, hanging from the ceiling. She had this idea while getting ready to do her make up with her friends sitting opposite sides and enjoy a 'Sex in the city' talk prior to going out. There was a separate boudoir, where I moved all her clothes, enough for all New York, and kept a drawer and a little rail for mine as well. There was a tv room with a large sofa bed, featuring also professional cd players and speakers. On the wall, a large inspiring painting of an old Indian Kama Sutra pose of a couple, exposing body parts and facial expressions in an artistic Indian way. She also added her disco lights and a bubble machine in this room for her girlie parties.

The kitchen was my domain and well equipped for the gourmet dinners. It also featured a black metal bench bar with three Moroccan wooden stools on one side and with black metal bar shelves at the back, hosting all possible drinks for cocktail making. There was a flashing 'Bar' sign and drink slogans on the walls. It featured a wall mounted cd players of Muji design, and usually played gutsy rock or any dance tracks with a strong bassline in the likes of Gregory Porter- 'Liquid spirit'. It looked like a professional hipster's bar.

The whole charm of that apartment was a small veranda fenced with high cream color curtains for privacy with a white sofa and an Egyptian copper table. An old white fisherman's table with two rattan armchairs chairs was our dinner for two, a speakeasy corner, for candle light dinners. That was a new beginning in our lives. There were some feminine touches of her things here and there and a large Marilyn Monroe screen in one corner of the hall. The whole apartment was a scene from all my mental travels, a film set with contrasts and extreme colors. Every other travel existed in there from Martinique, to Thailand, from New Orleans to Cuba.... the Unicorns, the elephants, the colourful birds, the red Indians, Sarah, Billy, Ella and all that jazz, Scotland, Africa and Chicago, The cinnamon peeler, and everyone and everything was there somewhere with us, but Elizabeth did not know yet!

We both loved the place as it was a contrast from where it was situated in the buzzy ethnic district with lots of police hanging around for immigration or drug related reasons and through some steps, an unassuming door would bring you in transition to another world. It was just like a speakeasy place during prohibition times in the U.S. It felt like that! In the background we were listening to Louis Armstrong and Duke Ellington.

The days were passing one by one but none was the same, all different. When I was alone in the apartment, I started exercising meditation but have never told her about this. It relaxed me and made me eager to understand myself, her and us. I had learned to close my eyes and go in the dark to find the light.

Some days, when I was alone, there was music when it was silence, and there were parties when no one was in that apartment. I knew about them, as I kept finding feathers in the rooms and on the balcony. They were not careful. It seemed that some Scotch whiskey bottles were moved around!

Elizabeth was bringing i stornies of her school children. It was like watching a continuing series and she was talking about them with enthusiasm and love. I got to know all the characters and their scenarios. She was giving everything to them, but to her friends too. She would go completely out of her way to please anyone that needed her help. She was sympathetic to all in need or trouble. She had nothing bad to say about anyone, even to those that treated her badly. She had the charisma to put things aside and to deal about the emotional side of things later, and perhaps on her own by rising above them. I loved that in her.

Dinners at our speakeasy balcony with music was the highlight of the day. We had wonderful art de table each time themed after Kenya, Morocco, Asia, France and Greece. We chose relevant genders of music each time so that the others, in the apartment, would enjoy it too!

We had our intimate moments everywhere and we were making stories of love. She liked touching my skin and saying how soft it was. She would smell my body, as she was convinced, I had my own scent, a pleasant one I hoped! It did not take long for her, to discover, how much I loved a back rub and it became a regular session. She could ask me for anything to be done at that time, and she would have got it. She often prepared a candlelit bath with fragrant oils and scents of sandalwood, patchouli, or lemon with cinnamon. She would bath me, like one does to babies and shared a glass of whiskey with me in the process. She gave me a reason to feel I am special. She made me feel like a pasha, a king. No one has ever loved me so much! This was important to me.

I loved seeing my hands touching her face and her perfect body. It was turning me on. She was my girl. She was all the women in my life. All these thoughts were in my head and with time trying to digest how much my life and my thinking had changed. Meanwhile, our bedroom was making stories of these two people meeting with passion and love. We were writing our own history.

We saved money and started traveling together to the Greek islands, Hydra and Spetses for a couple of weeks in the summer, exploring everything there, but each other too, by living the moments. Moments of sharing happiness that could not be the same again. We traveled quite a bit to London to enjoy the warm and wonderful family of hers. She had two sisters Anne-Marie married to Marc, Caroline married to Adam and a brother called Mickey married to Kate. They all had children in universities. I was very fond of them all. Her mum Pauline was a superstar mother living with Mike, a partner younger than myself. Her dad was also called Mickey but have not met him yet.

Living in Nicosia made me content at the time. I quite enjoyed the fact that someone expected me at home, whenever I was coming to town, as I sometimes stayed in other cities because of work. I still had a little house by the sea, in Protaras area but I enjoyed going into the Nicosia apartment and looking after it. I would prepare a vegetarian meal, for when she would come back from school, to share a good time. My destiny was to look after her and I was doing everything I could for her, without her knowing. It was my pleasure. Planning ahead, creating scenarios, buying her new clothes, smelling and tidying her clothes and underwear and having all her favorites in the fridge. All the little things were taken care of. All these actions and behaviors were new to me. I seemed to be getting distant from my bachelorism. I was beginning to like it. I was falling in love. It was daring, scary and new!

Most weekends we were traveling back to our seaside little house to swim at her favourite beach but also to the beach of the Egg and Rock. She kept collecting for me all sorts of heart shape stones and she was snorkeling into the deep sea to do so.

On her birthday in May, she did not want any party and wanted to be just us. She insisted on this, but I knew better. She loves parties for any reason and happy times is her drug. She probably did not want any fuss over her or to take time from her friends. I planned a surprise party with all her friends. The plot was that we were having dinner, just the two of us on our speakeasy balcony. A day prior, I gave her a written invitation to dinner, with a four-course menu written on it, to reassure her that there would not be a big event. I asked her to wear her red dress as she looked so pretty in red. I was to wear a suit. So, on the night, we were eating the main course of the romantic dinner, I have planned for the two of us, and music was on a romantic mode. She felt that was the whole birthday treat.

But no, the front door opened. One by one, all her friends walked in, each with a hat of Elizabeth's as I distributed to them earlier on the day and singing happy birthday. Elizabeth screamed from joy, immediately got up and started singing and dancing with them. Food platters came from neighboring restaurants, as per pre orders. It was a super party in the end and she finally thanked me for it. She said, while kissing me, I was dangerous, if I would be able to hide such lengthy planning, with fifteen or so friends of hers involved. She did not have any suspicion prior. Hm…Perhaps she was right!

Parties were regularly staged in that apartment and it was Christmas throughout the year. Presents and surprises expressed our love to one another. We were building on this relationship. We were two different people. Our conversations revealed our hopes and dreams and we were to work together to make those dreams a reality. We created space to learn from one another, growing closer and stronger. We were both, the architects building on togetherness. It was a new experience for me and I was the one looking at myself from a distance and wondering what is the next step.

One night, we were merry from an outing at a restaurant. It must have been two in the morning when she remembered that she had to prepare some cuts of many cloth materials in rectangular shapes for the children. They were to sew two matching pieces and fill them up with soft foam to become cushions, as presents to their parents. So, there we were, each with a pair of scissors in our hands and trying to cut the same shapes. It was impossible as we could not concentrate from the drinks we had earlier.

We had the giggles, so much that our sides hurt as we tried to cut the material correctly and not succeeding. We ended up having all sorts of shapes and sizes and none of them seemed to match. Still, we couldn't help but laugh at the absurdity of it all. It was happiness, it was funny, she was wonderful, I was excited about us.

The next morning at the school, she gave the children two pieces of material, both with different patterns and certainly different shapes. They had to do the best they could and the parents were thrilled to get odd shaped cushions from their loved ones.

BERBERS AND PARAGLIDERS

I had my own moments in the apartment where I played my music and went places and met whoever I wanted. Some spoke to me in Scottish. There was a Black man, handsome with broad shoulders...

The old town of Nicosia, where the apartment was, was full of people from various countries. I made friends with many of them. They thought I was different as I was friendly and made conversation unlike most Cypriots they had experienced. If only they knew what fun it was for me! Just as I was to go for a little stroll around the neighborhood, it was enough to see some aliens from Mars, the elephants and the lions, some were black now, and talked unknown languages. I was near Taj Mahal, The Pyramids, but in the North Pole too and the Himalayas. There was jazz! I could have been exploring anywhere, all my choice!

Christmas time, and when the schools were closed, it was the time to travel together with Elizabeth. We choose Morocco and I have booked a few interesting riads to stay in Marrakech and in Fez too. Steeped in history but amazed by the architecture and the colors of the interiors in the palaces we stayed, she was Nadia and Fatima in bed, and we had lush layouts and private gardens enjoying our mint tea and cakes with dates. We went to the markets and bargained for plates, of course, handmade and painted in vibrant colours. We did the tourist areas too visiting historical buildings and museums. We traveled by car which was rough for me as I get dizzy as if I am in a boat on rough sea. The trip took us through the Atlas Mountains meeting all sorts of people on the streets. Fez was more exciting with its narrow alleys leading to the same place as we got lost again and again.

For New Year's Eve, we booked a tree house in the desert. Two camels and a guide were leading us to this endless desert where the adventure began. It was New Year's Eve and the day before a sandstorm moved mountains of sand. We had the feeling of being lost and I was beginning to be concerned. The camels were hungry and, in temperamental, I was ready to be sick from the riding. A helicopter flew right above us at a point and made me feel the contrast on being on a camel and lost. It was pitch dark when the guide managed to locate a single tree at the end of the desert. At a point we stopped, the camels sat down and we jumped off them.

We walked closer. Indeed, there was a big tree with lots of wooden steps leading to a kind of a yurt Moroccan style. A young and very enthusiastic man, has welcomed us with a big smile on his face with sapphire eyes. He showed us into a little room built with mud which was a restaurant for two and then into our little Yurt up on the tree where we would rest on the last day of the year. There was a mattress on the floor, dressed in colorful Moroccan patterns and with candles lit everywhere. There was no door as an entrance but a colourful thick blanket blocking the light at least. It was basic and so exotic, a contrast, I loved it!

The man was starting to cook for us and the dinner was in an hour. There was soup from camel's head and then cous - cous with lamb. I had to cancel his excitement as Elizabeth is a vegetarian, so it became cous - cous with vegetables and hummus with bread which sounded great to me too. Definitely, no soup on the table! Wine was present too and we loved every sip of it.

By the time we ate, a bonfire was lit outside and we sat around it while some Berbers came with their instruments and their kind of darbouka and performed for us. I was examining the Berbers, proud and full of mystique. The sounds of the camels with heavy breath as they troted in the loose sand. I had visions of Berbers on camels, their cloaks billowing in the desert night wind as they traveled from one oasis to the next. The stars shone brightly overhead, providing a beautiful backdrop for the nomads' journey. I could almost hear the sounds of the camels' hooves as they galloped across the sand. I imagined the Berbers stopping to rest and admire the vastness of the desert, the way the sand seemed to stretch on forever. They would take a moment to appreciate the beauty of the moon and the stars, and feel the peace that comes with being so far away from the hustle and bustle of everyday life trading in the markets or defending their territory.

The fire we sat around flickered and danced like a living being, providing us with warmth and light in the darkness. I looked away from the fire and saw the silhouettes of dunes in the distance, illuminated by the moonlight. The stillness and loneliness of the desert was both exhilarating and calming.

I kept thinking about the life of the Berbers, and how they must have seen so much of the world in their travels. I wondered what secrets they may have kept, and what stories they could tell. The stars twinkled above us, and I thought about how small we were in the grand scheme of things. We were just specks in an infinite expanse of sand, but I knew we were all connected by something much greater than ourselves.

Off I went in dreaming as the drums were beating like my own heart. I was with the Berbers on a camel, wrapped in black clothes, my head too. I held a Shula knife. We were fighting against the nomads that came to steal our goats. I was a brave one and had fought them off. As we were all on our camels one pair of eyes caught my attention. Olive skin and bright green beautifully defined eyes, those that make you dizzy to look at them straight. I felt drugged by this woman on the camel with us. She looked at me and went the other direction on her camel, I turned around and tried to catch up with her speed but hopelessly I tried hard. It was impossible. I could not reach her. I wanted so badly to see her again... and back to where I was around the fire as if I was woken up by someone. A Berber put a darbouka in my hands, perhaps he was in my travel! Perhaps he wanted to bring me back!

I started banging my fingers at a rhythm, to go along with their singing and other instruments. I looked around and saw the smiling face of Elizabeth. She had a feather landing on her shoulder. Looking at her, I realized how lucky I was to be with her there. There was no any other person I wanted to be with. An amazing time of our lives. She looked proud of me that I was part of this scene, not knowing where I have just come back from. She looked so happy to be there and do things that were different experiences for her. We watched the fire until its flames gradually died down, and the stars slowly faded away in the sky. It had been a beautiful night. I thought of her, the night she asked me for the advice whether to take that job in Nicosia and my answer was '...live the experience, live life and make something different, make stories.'

We greeted goodbye the last day of the year by making love. I had Lila from Casablanca in my tree house! She wanted to meet a European man and to discover how they were in intimate situations. Just the idea of being in the desert and up there on a tree shelter, it was exhilarating and the adrenaline was high at all expressions! Being in bed with Elizabeth, it felt different. We were not having sex but making love, with all its context. We were looking in the eyes of each other to capture the slow pace to reaching the height of sexual arousal and upon reaching the peak of pleasure in our bodies, we were breaking into laughter. A laughter of happiness and joy!

I felt like dedicating to us, a Greek song by Vasilis Papakonstantinou and a passionate melody. I loved this song from the moment I have listened to it, ' Let's fall asleep in an embrace'-

...'let our dreams get interlaced for all of our
entire life let's share this night in time and space'

'Your sweet kisses on my neck feel like some wonders strange
and queer

They resemble roses opening before the dawn appears
I have thrown my nets into the abysmal depths of your blue eyes
On your solitary beaches I would wish to spend my nights

Let's fall asleep in an embrace – let our dreams get interlaced
To our kisses' melody let our heart provide its pace
Let's fall asleep in an embrace – let our dreams get interlaced
For all of our entire life let's share this night in time and space'

In the morning before dawn, we got dressed and wrapped blankets around us to see the first light of the new year and to be blessed for being there. It was a clear day. You could see as far, as the end of the world and forever. Our thoughts and our existence, our goals and ambitions, our characters and all were sieved through at this moment, making us feel like dust, as the first light changed the from the twinkle of the stars into a pink sky leading to orange flame colour. It was so quiet as the saying 'there is noise in the silence of the desert'. We felt repositioned in life and being together. We held hands and gave each other the kiss of love.

The same year at Easter vacations we traveled to Katmandu in Nepal and saw all the wonderful buildings and many Buddha temples. One of the highlights of this travel was, meeting one of my employees from back at the Guru venue in Ayia Napa twenty years later. Nanda, was just a student and doing some hours work at our venue then days. Now we met him at a coffee shop with his two sons. He brought us two scarfs traditionally to welcome people in Nepal. He talked to us about his own travel agency. Lots of respect was shared, and a wonderful feeling of time and life. A beautiful soul I met on the way. He talked to Elizabeth about his experiences in Cyprus and at Guru and that I was his Guru praising me of being an example of someone doing always the right things. She looked at me showing to be proud of me and searched to hold my hand.

From Katmandu we traveled to Pokhara lake and stayed at a small wooden house by some fields. We took a little boat with a paddler, and crossed the lake to some steep hill where we were to find the biggest Buddha temple on the top. I think we were out of breath for at least an hour climbing the hill but it was fun. I was ahead of Elizabeth and kept leaving traces in the middle of the path, so that she will find the way. Love hearts out of leaves, stones, but my underpants too. From the top of the mountain, we entered the biggest Buddha temple and enjoyed the views of the Himalayas far away surrounded by blue skies. Somewhere, at a distance, there were lots of paragliders in many colours as if they waved at us 'hello, when are you coming to try this?' It was fascinating! Elizabeth said

- ' Wouldn't this be fun?'

A bus full of younger people, I believe all stoned, was taking us up a never-ending mountain to find the right place from where we were going to attempt this sport. As I don't travel well, I had taken a special tablet. Buses, boats and myself do not go together. When we reached the starting point, I was allocated to the main instructor with whom I was to jump the mountains together. He was totally stoned, perhaps we were too from the smoke in the bus! We were striped on to these wings, mine was red and Elizabeth's was yellow. I did not look at the others but, being with the main instructor, we had to go first. He said ' when I call you, run right at the front with me'. At the front there was some mountain slope just about 10 meters and then there was nothing. I put a brave face on, as the younger people were so excited, and I ran with adrenaline, when he called. Suddenly, the Earth left us and we were air born. I had a smile on as he was filming me with his mobile on an extension. He shouted loud

- ' We will circle around until all twenty-four of them are flying too'.

I saw Elizabeth running off like a headless chicken and her jumper became a parachute up to her shoulders and showing her tits to the world from up there, as she wore no bra. There was nothing she could do about it other than smiling to the mobile camera of her guide directed on her!

Being up in the sky, gives you a unique perspective of the

world below. An exhilarating experience that created a feeling of being one with nature as the wind in the endless sky. As I looked out over the horizon, I felt as if I was soaring through the sky like the Avatar in the movie. The wind whistled around me as we soared higher and higher in the sky. I could feel the power of the air as it pushed against me and I was excited being able to float above the world. I looked down and saw the landscape, so far away yet so close at the same time. I could see the rolling hills, the trees, and the rivers snaking their way through the countryside to the lake of Pokhara. I could see some small monopoly blocks which I presume were the houses. It was as if I had been transported to a different world and I was in complete awe of the beauty. The feeling of being one with the air and so quiet, was incredibly powerful. I was part of the wind and the clouds. A connection to the energy of the universe. The experience at first was truly magical.

Up to the twenty circles around I began to compose a different face than the one of a smiler. I got dizzy and begun to feel I was crossed eyes! At that point my guide shouted

- 'Do not be afraid. We are going through two mountains' air stream. It will take us suddenly higher'

And so we did, I could see my legs pointing with my shoes up to the sky and to the sun. It felt as if we were in a highspeed elevator but upside down. My intestines seemed to have reached my mouth, and I thought I was ready to decorate the sky with my puke. I was ready to be sick. The guide was nice and he wanted conversation, but I could not say any words as I realized that there was no engine, and I was not in control. I thought that if the wind drops , we would as well. I could see nothing recognizable under me on planet Earth. He asked me if I wanted to extend our forty minutes flying to sixty to which I quickly answered ' Nye'!

Descending and ready for landing, we flew over the lake and he showed me his expertise, almost touching our feet in the green water and then we ran into the ground and stopped. He untied me and I thanked him, I think! Elizabeth ran to me I could barely hear her saying

- 'Oh my God! You are as white as a ghost! Babes are you alright?'

She confirmed a couple of times that I was white as a ghost!
I lied on the grass with closed eyes and the whole world was turning around. I felt my stomach was brewing some substances to be expelled in the atmosphere through my mouth. Elizabeth sat next to me touching my forehead and holding my hand. Half an hour passed so that all my organs went back in their place and that dizziness withdrew and luckily, did not give way to substances coming out of my mouth. I opened my eyes, Elizabeth looked fine to me and said,

- 'Why on Earth did we do this?'
- 'It was not on Earth!' I replied
- ' Why did we not think how dangerous it would be! I felt we were on an airplane with no engine! Next time I suggest something like that, don't let me go for it!'

After I came back to my full senses, and regained human colour to my face, I was thrilled of the whole adventure and I would do it again. I am sure she would follow me!

SOME COME BACK

Small social circles, gossips and people talk in coffee meetings, when everything else is not as important, I guess we had our turn too. Rumors were spread in social circles that Paris now decided to live with someone or he is living with a woman, or Elizabeth divorced and now living with this eccentric man who had restaurants and he is all over the place with so many interests. At her school, she got to hear from other teachers, many repercussions and stories about myself. People are just curious and as an old saying goes ' it is better that people talk about you because if they don't that means you are dead'

One lunchtime as we were coming out of a restaurant in Nicosia we pumped into Marianna, my first girlfriend, from the old days at school. She was back from France, married with two kids and living in Nicosia. I introduced her to Elizabeth and we were talking standing up, at the exit of the restaurant. I was talking to her husband about his work in property development but one of my ears was following the ladies' conversations. Marianna expressed that

- ' I was shocked to hear that Paris is now living with an Elizabeth. I thought he would always stay a bachelor! Well enjoy it, but he will never marry you, I know him!'

Poor sweetheart, Elizabeth, smiled at her and had not told me about this, until we were well away from them. But how mean that was, or was it jealousy and regrets she was not in Elizabeth's shoes? Elizabeth queried, what was my relation to her and I explained that we were going to the movies as teenagers and we kissed then. Later on, when I was a student, we met in Paris a few times, but it was just a flirt and it did not progress into anything, this was some thirty years ago!

A newly formed jazz bar, where we lived by the sea in Protaras, staged some afternoon sessions either with live music or with vinyl and CDs mixes by anyone who was interested. Since I loved my music, I had my turn one Sunday, where I told many friends that I would be mixing my vinyl and CDs at this place. I was to get back in time to Chicago. It so happened that I had a visit from Ibiza! My old flirt, Valentina from Austria was in Cyprus for a weekend with a friend, and I had of course asked them to come to the jazz bar until I finished my set and to go out for a meal and catch up.

There was a DJ booth and I was well set up, with a bottle of Scotch next to me. I started mixing Dave Brubeck and Miles Davies and played Cheek to Cheek by Sarah Vaughan and songs by Ella of course, bringing memories of Ebony and all my other pals, like John Coltrane, Stan and Louis...

Elizabeth was supporting me as she came with a few of her girlfriends and she was visiting me at the booth and sipping down my whiskey. This happened for a while and I felt we were both tipsy. Valentina came in with a colourful outfit and feathers, fuchsia pink feathers on her hair, her trademark, and lots of makeup. She looked, of course, much older now, twenty-five years later, but still the craziness was there, you could see it from her smiles and appearance. She sat with her girlfriend and I sent them drinks and went to talk to them while music was securely played. Elizabeth had seen me talking to these two ladies and she got interested. On another visit of her to refuel from my whiskey, she asked me who they were. I replied, friends from the past, many years ago. She was over her drinking limit as she went and sat on Valentina and introduced herself as Elizabeth, Paris' girlfriend and straight away asked them if they were lesbians! Needless to say, they reacted with laughter, they got talking and liked each other, with the promise to make an effort and meet somewhere later on, as there was so much to talk about their interests.

A few months later, Valentina came again to visit another friend and Elizabeth insisted we go to meet her as she found her interesting. They were talking about clothes and colors and positive attitude to life, as if they knew each other many years back. Of course, by then, I was truthful and explained to Elizabeth that years back, we had a flirt and some bed experiences and she did not mind that at all. I was happy with this in her.

On a Summer weekday, in Nicosia, I received a message from Mina, Delta of Venus! She was in Cyprus with Byron, her French husband, a chef and her ten-year daughter Shine. She wanted to meet up and get to know Elizabeth. Tricky and suspicious, as I know her well. She was intrigued to see who was this woman was that received so much attention from me and I ended up sharing my life with her. She wanted to know where her Cinnamon Peeler was spreading his cinnamon on. We arranged a meeting at a café and it was a pleasure to meet them all. I got on well with Byron and we had much to talk about, cooking and our careers. Shine, was full of life, she was so much like her mother when she smiled. Mina was beautiful, as if time did not touch her at all. She still had that seductive expression in her eyes, but it did not work for me anymore. I was devoted to another person and I was exploring and discovering other atmospheres. Elizabeth was pleasant and funny as always cracking jokes and commenting on me, and the two ladies got on so well talking about their lives and the new fashion trends, favourite books and films. They both love Ryan Gosling and Tom Hardy, but Elizabeth likes Antony Hopkins too as she is attracted to old charm, she said! Elizabeth was a winner again, sparkling, welcoming and sociable, more beautiful than ever. She made me proud to be standing next to me.

I had a chat with Mina and again, after all that course from when I met her with the Lebanese and other men, Klimt, the Basketball player and so many others I did not know, Byron was not enough for her. She needed more passion, more adventure and excitement from him. I suggested she stays with him and to give it another go, perhaps to talk to him and make him understand what she really needed in romance. I knew very well!

I asked her, if she wanted me to talk to him, but she refused, as she had previously confessed to him, I was a love of her life and had a vast effect on her life. So, he would have been offended if I was to talk to him. I said to her that I wanted her to be happy and I wished her to find happiness, as she is so special. She looked at me with her seductive eyes and said,

- 'Only one like you would know what I need to be happy!'

We left it to that! Her statement made me feel cool.

We all met once more as we invited them to dinner at ours where there was dancing and drinking. Shine loved Elizabeth's disco lights and bubble machine. I feel that Mina saw why I was with Elizabeth and what was between us. She was happy for both of us, like that. Perhaps seeing us, made her wanting to find the same. I also felt that all the others were around and curious to see this development.

It was months later that Mina left Byron and gave him Shine to take with him to France. She is now in Bulgaria, where she works. She found a man that loves her and shares passionate moments and makes new stories in her life. She is still exploring. She still calls me her Cinnamon Peeler and we keep sending songs to each other and dances from people that declare devotion and lust, passion and difference. I feel I am still inspiring her to carry on. At some point, I showed Elizabeth on my mobile phone, a happy picture of Mina with her new lover and she asked me what was really my relationship with her. I was truthful and explained that we were quite close in many versions of ourselves, back then. She was content to know and understanding. She was not at all jealous, but instead she credited my character for keeping friends, after so many years, with souls that I shared a relationship. All the credit goes back to Elizabeth.

After so many years, I got to hear from Joy back from the Ayia Napa times. She was now married, living in a massive house in London with a successful businessman. She had found out that I was living with someone and she suggested we meet somewhere as couples. They visited us for a long weekend in Nicosia and stayed with us in our apartment. Her husband, was tall and had a very impressive and athletic body. Adam was into finance business in London and living well by the description of their lush lifestyle. I was very happy to see Joy happy. She was looking older and mature, now having the responsibility role of being next to a successful husband. She did a lot of well-paid work in property too and managed to some units here and there in England. I felt justified, as it was me that pushed her back then to go and do something for herself and become someone other than a party girl in Ayia Napa.

I was not surprised to see Joy and Elizabeth getting on so well together and sharing lots of laughter. We had a super weekend, going to tavernas for some Cypriot food and bars and talking as if we all knew each other long before. Perhaps we did! We had treated them to a Hammam experience, near our apartment, which was different to the modern spas they were used to.

When they were gone back to London, Elizabeth dropped the question

- ' Don't tell me you had an affair with Joy too? '
- ' What makes you think that?' I asked her
- - 'Normal questions between girls would be on how is your man and are you happy in your relationship. When we were in conversation, I had a feeling as if she knew more!' she stated.

I replied with a smile,

- 'It's not possible, as this may have happened twenty-five, or thirty years ago. Everyone was different then' and she wisely said
- 'Yes, Paris... same, same but different!', and she smiled.

The memories flooded my mind; old friends and former lovers, I had lost touch with. It was as if they were being sent back to me as a reminder of life's fragility and the importance of cherishing our relationships. It was also a relief and quite surprising to me. Elizabeth did not mind to meet any of my friends of the past, whether involved in a relationship, or not. I did not mind meeting any of her friends or partners too. To her credit, she would not be jealous at all. Anyway, she had no reason to be. I did not have eyes for anyone else other then that of her beautiful self. She was in contrary, proud of me that I kept a descent level of respect towards these persons, all these years, and became friends with all. They all knew that I would be there for them, should they need my support or help. Now, I think that Elizabeth and myself would be there for them should they need our support or help.

One glorious morning, on our way to Protaras for the Egg and Rock dive, I stopped at the post office for my mail. I had bills and bills and a postcard with the Queens head on the stamps, from Oxford. I started to read it and my face changed colour, I felt goosebumps, my heart rate shot up and I was shocked. It read like that,

' Hello Sir,

I wish that this card finds you well.

We met some thirteen years ago.

Now, I am twenty-four years old and I have received my diploma in civil aviation in Oxford. I am starting a contract with Jet Airways.

I am writing to you as I always remembered you saying to me you were sure I would be a pilot and gave me a pen, I still have but it run out! I am now married and have two children. This is our address...

with respect, Promote.'

I grabbed Elizabeth in excitement and squeezed her with tears in my eyes. I could not believe it was possible after so many years to get such wonderful news. It was so far away in my mind. I could hardly remember the story back then, but this made me think. It is always good to dream and it is always best not to stop anyone from dreaming. I wrote back to Promote and we exchanged a few letters and photographs. Now looking very handsome with a beautiful wife in a saree and two boys with the same black intense eyes, like their dad's back then in the middle of nowhere in Kerala. One day, we will go back to meet him and his family.

MY QUEEN

Through travels and sharing experiences we were making stories together. We were increasingly feeling closer. We enlarged our circles of friends. Mine became hers and vice versa. We both liked each other's friends and we had of course our favourites. At social parties, it was bothering me, as I introduced her as Elizabeth, and there was no status attached. Perhaps later on I started saying Elizabeth is my partner and in Greek there is a perfect word called ' Syntrofos', meaning, my companion.

One long weekend, I booked an arty room in a small boutique hotel in Athens, named 'Alice in Athens'. It was one of these modern adaptions of a house, where space was cleverly made to look like a hotel. We had a small private courtyard and a separate entrance to our bedroom. Lots of clever quotes in frames and objects on the walls and shelves that made us smile. We spent a super time in a few bars for pre- dinner drinks and enjoyed a Greek taverna in Plaka. We started walking to what it felt on our feet, all the streets of Athens, as I could not find the right way to say what was on my mind. I sometimes started to lead our conversation to what I had in mind but it was not happening. She was taking the conversation to another point, insignificant to the occasion.

My brain was disorienting every time she was talking about something else. I was stocking up bravery to talk and I was losing it at any interruption. So, we needed, or more frankly, I needed a scotch.

We sat at a modern bar, ordered some falafel, pitta bread, tahini dip and our old-fashioned cocktails. There was a young bartender with everything well placed on him. He politely looked after us well and he sensed I was in need of a deep conversation and made room for me staying away.

I did not know how to express things and shyness came back. It was like that dinner at the mountains, when I drunk those four carafes of wine, stresing as to what could happen later. So, we drunk more and more and I had thoughts going through my mind. Yes, it is her, beautiful, I enjoy being with her, I love looking after her, she is the only one I want to cuddle and have in my bed, I feel so many unknown things passing through me when I see her happy, I want to be there for her, I want her to stand next to me and she makes me feel like that. All these are important to me. I feel inexplicable things and cannot talk about anything! Ok I can do it. Another sip of the cocktail, and another and I will do it!

I held her hand, kissed her on the lips and said,

- ‘It has been bothering me that there is no status between us.’

I could not look at her in the eyes but I was looking at the whole package of a beautiful woman next to me. I carried on,

- ‘I want, when I introduce you to people, to give you a kind of a concept or title…. and I think the best thing we can do right now…. is to somehow… to marry!’

At that point, the drink did not make her feel what exactly I struggled to suggest, as normally she would have made me say more. As I was not traditionally asking for permission and on my knees, it was not clear to her what I was saying… I could not express in words that I was in love with her! But she knew I was. I never said these words to any other woman in my life. I was feeling inadequate to express my feelings to her. She was in line with me, but I cannot remember what exactly she said! At the merit point, we were, it felt to me the right thing to do was to kiss again. We kissed with excitement that we established communication, positiveness and we both had happy faces. Myself that I got it out there and probably I got her thinking of her wedding dress!

The morning after, as soon as I opened my eyes, she was

already awake and was smiling, looking at me. I was surprised to see her so animated and I loved waking up and she was still there! She spoke first

- 'Good morning sunshine!' and gave me a kiss
  Can you confirm what you exactly meant last night?'
- ' I suggested us to get married. It bothers me to call you companion or girlfriend, and that I want you to feel that you have me, as your husband to share the rest of our lives together. I want us to be together' I repeated

We kissed, and both had happy faces. I went on to describe the scenario that since she went through marriage and divorce, and all that paperwork and since we both did not believe in any government or Church, it would have been best to design our own commitment ceremony how we wanted it. I felt that this would have been more binding between us. If a person wants to leave you these days they can do so anyway. True love is binding two people. If a person falls out of love, it would be worse to stay with one another. So, in any case what is paperwork nowadays? We agreed to this modern scenario which was more us and more real. For me it was closer to my spiritual thinking and I tried to communicate that.

I had never felt such an intense emotion before. I was summing up, debating perhaps again and again, everything inside me. This feeling of love was strong and overwhelming. I did not know how to accommodate it inside me. I knew I could never go back to being a bachelor. She had ruined it for me and it felt wonderful! Every moment I spent with her felt like it was the best moment of my life. It was something new. I was now released from the fear of commitment and I was not afraid to love.

I couldn't help myself but to be drawn to her and wanted to take her places with me. I wanted to show her my world. I could tell her anything and she would understand. I could be myself with her and she accepted me for who I was. I spoke to her about all the other women I met in my life. I spoke to her about all my friends and my various career moves and what experiences I got from everyone and every place. I wanted her to know everything. I asked the same of her in return.

I knew I was a complexed person. She knew it too! She continued giving me stone love hearts she picked up from the sea. She kept doing that! I wanted to be with her for the rest of my life, and I wanted to make her happy every day. My only thought was to protect her by any means, to take care of her and make sure she was happy. I wanted her to smile and talk and share funny moments.

I cooked for her all the time with love and made sure she had everything she needed. That was my destiny from now on. She had the same pleasure when I bought her clothes, or a packet of Haribo sweets or when I gave her a small flower, I picked from a field. I could never express in words all that I felt, but I could show it to her. She was receiving me. This was as good as it gets! I had finally found love, and with it came a happiness, I had never felt before.

All these did not stay there. The feelings of love were growing with time. They were maturing and were growing bigger and stronger. The same but different!

It was the end of May and on her birthday I drove to the area of Polis, in Paphos, with my best friend Gregory from Greece as my best man and she drove with her best friend Ruth from London as her best woman. Loraine another bestie of hers also from London and our Kia who had the role of the master of ceremony. We asked a friend to take pictures. Six people were to witness this next act. We spotted the small pebbled bay that was under a hill and you could access it through a small rough path going down. There were no other people. There were a few rock formations in the sea that nature left for our backdrop. There was no wind and no sound and yet so many souls around, perhaps my mother and father sat on the pebbles on the beach to watch and bless.

I tied on trees white ribbons so that the girls would find the way. They had instructions to be there and meet before sunset at six thirty. We had a small wedding cake on a round white table with my mother's tablecloth on, some old champagne glasses from my collection, cold bottles of Laurent Perrier rose and a bottle of Hibiki whiskey brought in by my best man. We also had a USB on a speaker.

Dressed in white linen with bare feet, we waited for the girls. Laughter and happy screams from the hill, announced their arrival, as they started coming down the steep pathway. At a point, I could see Elizabeth in a light white wedding long dress and a veil walking towards me to receive her bouquet. There was a glow and it felt like two years from the time I saw her walking towards me. While John Legend sang to us– 'All of me', during those two years, all my life passed through my mind in black and white and was put aside for the new beginning. My eyes were full of tears, happy tears and excited to see the beautiful Elizabeth living her dream too, to get married on the beach. She came close to me and I uncovered the vail and handed her the white Calla lilies bouquet. She was so pretty... aye, a stunning lass! We kissed and both of us were in tears. The kissing went on, my best man Gregory, had to stop it with his comments 'you are not married yet!'

We had Gregory on my right side and Ruth was on her left side while Lorraine was on the opposite side with the photographer. They all wore white clothes. The best man and woman, placed on our heads copper garlands that Kalliroi, a jeweler friend designed for us, and connected with a white ribbon at the back of our heads. Kia stood in the middle facing us. She wore a white dress and a necklace made out of white feathers. She read spiritual scripts on journeys of togetherness that we both wanted to hear.

' All of us need and desire to love and to be loved. And the highest form of love between two people is within a committed relationship. This love in your relationship bears all things, beliefs, hopes, endures all things. Love never dies....

The sand, the pebbles, the wind the sky and us here, will help solidify this bond as you two individuals are joined as husband and wife. Today in this spiritual ceremony, you are promising, in front of us that you want to be with each other and only each other for the rest of your lives and that you will do everything in your power to honor the promises you are making here today....'

Then, I have read my vows to her, written one day when I was advised by all those people in our apartment and promised love, protection, support, guidance, togetherness and my vows ended '*finally, I will entertain, in all its meanings, this sweet little girl hiding inside you and love her growing older to catch up with me!'*

Elizabeth read her vows to me that she would always look after me and be present in bad and good times. '*To be eternally grateful for the gift of life that your parents gave to you, and in turn given me the privilege to experience that...the gift of love from the most remarkable person I ever met'* and ended '*if the event of any illness I will nurse you'*

Then we exchangd rings and kissed as husband and wife.

Ruth stepped in and read a dedicated poem

' Love is'

'......more beautiful than anything
As vivid as a dream
Being there for always
Is all I want to do
Holding you forever
Because our love is true.'

At that point I lifted my wife in my arms, and slowly walked into the sea. The water was in symphony with us and it was still and welcoming. We were both baptized and in harmony. We were bonded by all the elements and laws of nature. There was a fine sunlight and a bright blue sky. It was a gift of love. We kissed and exchanged in silence all our emotions overflowing into the water and multiplying. We floated on the water hand in hand, and felt an underlying vibration bringing pure peace and calmness to us. We talked about our times in the sea when we first met. Our weekly swims at the egg and rock. As she was in my hands and floating, she said

- ' Thank you for this! You made my dream come true to

marry on the beach, a perfect beach a perfect day' and we kissed.

The feeling of the water was an overwhelming experience and a milestone! All the others went into the water with us and shared the harmony of nature adding beauty to this marriage.

After we came out of the sea, we attempted to cut of whatever was left of the cake, as the photographer, in her efforts to reach angles had knocked the cake on the sand. There it laid re-decorated with sand all over the icing! I carved an inch of the icing off and we all managed to get a spoonful of the cake, some with a little sandy taste! The photographer looked apologetic, I went close to her and gave her a hug and said thank you for making our day more unique! Champagne for all and Coldplay- 'A sky full of stars', and feeling amazing, all of us singing, dancing and hugging on the pebble beach for having lived all those emotions. Elizabeth looked like a star in the sky and in my heart too. I kissed her and placed her hand on my heart and said ' you have my heart until it stops beating'. She was then my Queen of the Queens that dropped in my arms. I held her firm!

The joy did not end there. Later in the evening we all gathered at a small taverna by the sea to eat fresh fish together and celebrate. We danced and danced and at a point as we used to do in our apartment like the scene from the film 'Crazy, Stupid Love', when she ran and jumped on him and he lifted her up. Well, that night and with the happy drinking I failed to be Ryan Gosling. I fell forward on the ground with her on top of me and knocked my forehead on the corner of a wooden piece of furniture. I remember me still merry but everyone on top of me making disgusted faces from looking at me. I split my head and blood was pouring out making my white shirt and the wedding dress of Elizabeth's bloody.

All drunk we had the restaurant owner driving us, through this small rural area, to a kind of a hospital. My best man had a glass of wine in his hand and was stuffing tobacco in my split head, as he saw this in some red Indian film. At the hospital and in the stitching room, Elizabeth in her bloody wedding dress was holding my hand, while I was receiving stiches and my best man video graphing the whole scene. Even the attending nurse thought it was funny to see us all so happy.

When we returned to the restaurant, I had my whole forehead wrapped in bandages and had another glass before the groom picked up the bride and took her in for the first official wedding night. All about contrast. We laughed with Elizabeth, at her last vow, as she was explaining to the doctor while he was sewing my forehead.

- 'I read to him...just a few hours ago one of my vows was... and in the event of any illness I will nurse you! but never thought so soon!'

On returning back to the restaurant, Ruth, Kia and Loraine talked to Elizabeth to take care of me and my injury and not to let me do anything on the wedding night, as there may be problems with blood in my head and she promised to do so. Outside our little nest at the hotel where everyone was staying the night, I of course picked up my bride and took her in and placed her on the bed. We were so drunk in the happiness of the whole day; the ceremony was as we imagined and nature agreed with it and gave us peace, calmness and respect, as we went in the water to be baptized. Our friends gave us love and all was so perfect. The noise from the old wooden bed gave us in to all our friends. The ceremony had a little longer to last!

The next day back to Nicosia, we hired an incredible place, an old Ottoman Hammam Omerye stone built, with a garden full of jasmin and rose trees. It's grand history since the fifteenth century and mystique atmosphere added to the exoticism of the night. We invited our close friends living in Cyprus to celebrate our wedding. In this old part of the town, in this hammam, my parents had been for treatments when younger. In some days, they allowed only men and other days only women. Behind this hammam, there was the redlight district that my father used to look after as a health inspector, back in the sixties!

Prior to this invitation, before everyone else came, we had a private dinner at a section of the garden for my brother and sister with their spouses, an auntie of mine as well as my mother's last best friend. We lived disconnected with my brother and sister but it was time they shared these moments with us. Elizabeth looked wonderful in a black lacy dress and her long blond hair and I wore some beige shirt and trouser with a summer hat to disguise as much as I could, the bandages on my head. My mum's best friend said

- ' It is a pity your mum never got to meet Elizabeth; she would have liked her a lot!'
- 'Yes, I feel the same' I said with regrets ' but she knew I was seeing someone, perhaps she now knows her!' I said looking at Elizabeth.
- ' I am also sorry I did not get to meet her. You mum knows of me. I talk to her sometimes as I feel she is around and watching over us' Elizabeth added.

Meanwhile, Lorraine at the entrance welcomed everyone giving them a Lola angel that our friend Kaliroi, the jeweler designer, had made for us. It was symbolic of us she said. We were glowing with joy and welcomed beautiful feelings and blessings from all our friends that marked, our special two days of the wedding with so much happiness.

There was a violin and a harp player staged in the middle of the garden. The gentle and elegant sounds of the harp and violin seemed like a call from some distant land. As the music reverberated through the garden, it was as if invisible fairies were weaving a spell of enchantment....Music took me to Elizabeth's lacy dress. It became white and she was glowing. She had a flowery garland with white ribbons attached. The ribbons were held by muses...I could see some of their faces, it was blurred, Nin, Kate, Juanita, Mina, Ebony, Zoe too. I could see my parents in white monastic robes, holding hands and seated on two thrones looking happy. They held Calla lilies in their hands.

There were white candles everywhere. It was raining feathers, white and large ones. They disappeared before making it to the stoned floor. And more were coming from the sky. The muses moved slowly forming a circle around Elizabeth. They waved the ribbons, as if they were trying to convey a message of love and offering their blessings to Elizabeth, a show of affection and admiration. There were many others. An African couple in war attire and spears, in the corner, watched in silence, touched by the beauty of the moment. A black man in a kilt turned to greet….' Babes', Elizabeth whispered in my ear, and I came back to the party,' are you ok? You seemed lost!', she said thinking that I was dizzy from the head injury. I said to her with a hug

- ' Your presence in my life, it's like a never-ending dream come true, I am simply overwhelmed,...and the others too! One day I will tell you more…'

I looked at Elizabeth. I felt I could now say it,' I love you!' I was ready to compose the words, as she went to greet some friends coming in. When she came back, our eyes met and an electric current passed between us, a feeling of connection that was both, familiar and new. Elizabeth's gaze was full of warmth and affection, her lips curled into a gentle smile. I felt an overwhelming sense of joy and contentment, my heart swelling with emotions. The flowers began to smell of euphoria. There was born inspiration and richness of emotions in my heart. We were overflowing with happiness that we wanted to share with the whole world.

August the same year, we planned a small wedding celebration party at a pub in Beaconsfield, Buckinghamshire, for Elizabeth's relatives and friends and for my friends that lived closer. For this party, Elizabeth asked me to invite her father myself, and she was sure that he would not come. They were in a strained relationship. She thought that he would not be interested to join the event.

So, one day whilst in the car, I built up enough courage to

do so. I stopped the car on the side of the road and called this man Mickey, whom I never met. I introduced myself as Paris from Cyprus, which was already confusing. I continued,

- ' I have married your daughter, some two and a half months ago, and we now live together in Nicosia. I want to invite you to join us at a party, we will give in London in August, to meet and celebrate with us.'

He replied in understanding me

- ' Oh yes' with his Irish accent,'... and what do you do for living?'

I explained that I do concepts for the hospitality industry and more complicating words to buy time and to seem sociable and at ease. He has listened to me carefully, I was sure he did not understand my accent but I concluded,

- ' it will make us very happy if you can be there with us' and I gave him the date and place. He then replied

- 'Oh yes, and what is your name again?'

On the day, he was the first to come. I saw an older version of Elizabeth in a man walking in the pub and told Elizabeth,

- 'Give me five, your dad is here' and she did not believe me until she saw him.

I walked towards him and gave him my hand and said,

- ' Welcome, I am Paris, I am happy you are here today'

We had our first whiskey together and chatted to get to know each other! At first, he looked at me debating whether he liked me or not. I could sense that. As the time went on and with everyone arriving, I felt that I got approved and there was a lot more that we talked about.

Elizabeth was glamorous and very pretty, sparkling with happiness and excitement. I bought her the dress and she honored me in wearing it. It was a strapless up to the knee short dress opening to a full flair skirt. I was in a light pink color, with large embroidered blue flowers. I was in a blazer and an English country style bow tie.

It was another day of joy for Elizabeth and myself. My best man Gregory and wife Tina came with their children, grown up now. My Peter and Erica with their sons, flew in from Sweden, Michailo and Jelena flew in from Serbia, with their two girls. Elizabeth's mum and wonderful family were there and our best woman Ruth, Peggy, Elaine, Chrissie, my friends Claire and Steve and an auntie of mine Margaret, cousins and more family and friends from the past. Even old friends I made from the times of the French Bistro in Ayia Napa honored us, Jill and Mike, Alan and other friends. Elizabeths school friend Nuala showed up too, and her Irish uncle Noel all the way from New York.

We received so much love, a gift, an incredible gift, to carry on with us to our course. Behind them all, were so many other people. My gang, I could see them... there was noise and movement. I was lost with them. There were colours and flares, perhaps fireworks, mountains, forests and caravans with horses! I took a glimpse of many Kikuyus with spears , my dad and mum were there too, I think it was them! They were holding hands. There was the sound of a saxophone from a distance, a few Tibetan monks and the man with a gray suit, gelled hair holding a white flower... so many others I could not clearly see their faces. I was trying to remember them. There was dancing, different kind of dancing. Each one was moving happily and free style, and I think I saw also...... Elizabeth's brother Michael, grabbed my hand to go to the bar for shots with everyone.

There was the feeling of joy and positive energy in everyone around us. There was still jazz in my head or in the room, I was not sure. I had a feeling, I was welcomed to the sky, with open arms, and the glowing atmosphere was so infectious, it filled my mind with infinite space. It traveled through my veins, and I was lost in euphoria. I wanted to look at the sky. I was existing in two merged dimensions and smiling. It was new. I went to get Elizabeth and looked straight into her blue eyes. They were sparkling. I could not tell her where she was amongst all the others and looking at her. I could not tell her of my euphoria and the blue sky right above us not of the smells making my heart bigger to take all these feelings inside me. An energy was calling me. I wanted to jump to the sky and reach the universe, the cosmos!

As we stepped close to the bar, she picked up from the floor, a white feather! She looked at me and winked! We both knew!

THE JOURNEY

Life was getting more exciting and fun with Elizabeth and it showed. We both became more creative with our work. She was directing extravagant and ambitious plays at school, and I was producing more out of the ordinary concepts for businesses mixing and matching contradictive designs and operations. I loved spending time at the apartment reminiscing of all the splendid times we had spent there but also feeling that the others were somewhere around and happy. I would be waiting for Elizabeth to come from school so that we would have dinner on the Moroccan balcony and a good chat over a scotch. I was building up my words to one day explain in detail to her about all the others. I wondered if she would be surprised.

One morning, when I was alone in the apartment, or at least I thought I was, I closed the windows and drew the curtains to completely relax in the dark and practice meditation. I closed my eyes and controlled my breathing. I was calm and in control. There was a blissful feeling, I became relaxed... almost sleepy. Suddenly a strong pain in my belly as I felt hungry. I opened my eyes in a fright. I was curious, as it was not long ago that I had eaten breakfast and I was not hungry.

When the pain was gone, I took the right position again and tried to control my breathing to find the darkness...some voices sounded in my head, I got scared and opened my eyes wondering what was happening to me. I was taken over by something inexplicable. The voices left me with a strange feeling... it was a cry for help... I was drawn into it and went back to... .

... a black young child, sitting under a big tree... a big tree and birds were flying around it... voices of a woman, she was black in tribal attire shouting 'aca... a ca....' She was pulled by a rope next to a black man. He looked big and strong. They had a rope around their necks and pulled by a tall man with a hat who was yelling at them

- ' haud yer wheesht, mouuve...'!

The black woman was in pain, upset, scared as she kept looking back at the child. She was very concerned. She had tears in her eyes. The child was so young and innocently looking around, almost smiling not understanding anything.

There was a caravan with horses, guarded by more men with pistols threatening to shoot the black people as they forced them into the caravan. The black woman was shouting... 'please my baby...my love...' as the caravan moved away followed by a cloud of dust... as if... woah! I was suddenly very hot...

It is very hot and the ground was very dry. I am feeling the pain of hunger in my stomach. I am thirsty. I see a big face of a lion coming closer to my face with its amber eyes looking at me. I am not afraid, I feel euphoria and excitement, it came right in front of me, I want to play... I try to touch it..., I extended my hands...and a big noise shaking the ground... I am feeling it... as the lion runs away, scared from the size of an elephant that threatened it. The elephant wiggled its ears to me and stood there looking at me. I laughed, as it brought its tusk close to my face and touched my head before it went away... but still it....
Woah... the stomach pain, a spasm of hunger, brought me back.

It took me a few minutes to realize what had happened there. I was exploring a scene of the past through the eyes of the baby boy threatened by a lion and saved by an elephant! His mother was in pain and troubled..., I was able to travel back!

I closed my eyes again and found my darkness with my breathing under...it was cold, a bitterly cold and greenfields of tall trees. There was a distinctive smell on the ground. I was

outside a tall stone-built house, a very big house surrounded by trees. There were stables with horses, a couple of men were working around the horses. There was a white girl around ten or twelve, with red curls and a pink bow on her head, running around me and I was running around her enjoying the game, who falls down first. Behind some trees as if he was hiding, I took a glimpse of a tall man smiling at me.
A well dressed woman, came out from the main door with a dark blue long dress and called,

- 'Children....Emily, Alexander, come inside, enough playing... I have some cookies for you.'

I gave Emily a kiss on the cheek and looked back at the trees, the man was gone. I brought Emily in by the hand as if she was my princess. There was a lot of activity in the house, dinner was being prepared and many people had jobs to do. The house was grand and lush with a hall in the middle. A long dining table with silver candelabras in one room and a sitting room on the other side. The sitting room had armchairs and sofas, green velvet curtains on the tall windows and a big fireplace. A grand staircase was leading to the upper rooms. The wooden floors were polished and there was a room with many book shelves and a piano. A small table, next to a comfortable blue armchair had some crystal glasses and a decanter of what looked to be whiskey.

Emily started running after me and calling me a duck as she slipped and fell flat on her face crying, I took her in my arms and stroked her head to stop crying.

- 'Please do not cry, nothing will ever happen to you. I will always be here for you' I said.

There was a loud noise of a roaring car engine passing by the road outside the apartment that disrupted my dream, or was it a dream? I was drawn to seeing more through the eyes of the young boy and I lost track of how much time I was in darkness covering my thoughts as if someone pushed me back to the darkness....

... a wedding...it was years after. There were many people in lighter clothes and colourful materials. Lots of children were playing around. Whiskey was being shared in everyone's glass and there was dancing to the sounds of bagpipes...

Alexander stood there wearing a green, blue and gray tartan kilt and a short blue jacket. He was tall, and strong with broad shoulders, lots of black hair, handsome with green eyes. Emily looked stunning and happy with her red hair curls and a blue wedding dress layered with embroidery. Richard, Emily's dad, came to talk to Alexander, there was a strong tap on his back out of excitement, I felt it too!

- ' Alexander, I waited for this day to tell you a story of the past...I am sure you have been wondering... your real parents were from Kenya in Africa. They were from the tribe of Kikuyus. Very proud and hard- working people. No one could ever touch their territory. They were tricked, supposedly recruited to work in a plantation at the coast but ended up being sold as slaves by Richard Holden. One of his Scottish guards apparently returned to where your mother was forced to leave you. He saved you bringing you on a ship to Scotland. No one has seen him even after. They described him as tall with a clean face, rich blond hair and vivid blue eyes. My wife Iona, found out about you and fetched you here with us. We brought you up like our own son, well you are our son and we are so proud of what you have grown up to be.'

There was another tap on the shoulder and Richard continued,

- ' Ever since you began to walk, you were obsessed to be a protector to Emily. You two were inseparable. No one can understand how you grew to love each other so much. After your journey as a baby, it is as if you were meant to meet in life. Someone was looking over you and saved you. Someone sent you

to us! We thank God for that!
Today, I am more than happy to give you our daughter, as no one else would possibly love her more than you. '
- 'Thank you, father. I knew I was not a real son to you; I did not look to be! But never asked out of respect. Strange as it sounds to have two fathers but you brought me up with so much love.... Have you met my real parents then? Are they alive?'
- ' They were sent to the West Indies. There was a fatal disease on the ship... but let's drink some whiskey ... We must leave the past behind and focus on the days to come... and before that... you must know that when Iona and I pass away, all the property will be yours to live well with Emily and your children too. But hurry up and have children as I am getting older by the minute!'

A hand stroked my head...my head...

- Hi, what are you doing alone in the apartment and with the curtains drawn? It's a beautiful afternoon, let's do something' Elizabeth said
- 'I had fallen asleep, babes and had... dreams ' I replied
- 'Have you dreamed of me?', she said laughing
- 'I want to ask you something '... I said getting her attention ' Do you believe you lived another life before?'
- ' Hm... I would like to think so...,' she said,' but I feel that we are not alone here, there are some people or powers around us and looking after us, sometimes there is a scent when they are around!' She replied with a smile.

I remembered the words of the Osho in Tibet and I could not stop thinking of where I have been. It was as if someone was pushing me to go back there. I was impatient to be alone in the apartment again.

It was afternoon, I closed the shutters and drew the curtains to darkness. I controlled my breathing, found the darkness and it was like passing through a tunnel. There was a spinning noise as I was going through to... Emily screaming loud and I was so upset to hear her in pain, I was crying at the bottom of the stairs, she was suffering and I was hurting too... Emily was nonstop crying begging for relief and in a lot of pain... she was pushing and screaming and I was feeling hopeless not being able to help her...there was a baby crying...I ran up the stairs and got in to see her laying on the bed, as the two maids handed me this baby boy who stopped crying when in my hands. I turned to show the baby to Emily but she was not well...not well at all...I gave the baby back to the maids and held her hand, she could barely talk. She had her eyes closed. I touched her forehead, she was cold. I called her name as loud as I could, I was devastated, I was crying for her to give me a sign of life...she was so white, she was not breathing, she left me.... I was in terrific pain, helpless and in tears. No one to understand that she was the most important purpose I had in life, now gone...forever!

Emily gave me a gift of love, and left me alone to bring him up, wrapped up with the memories of her. I named him Arran, like she wanted. A mountain of strength and power, our son.

Since, Emily died more and more workers started to leave, as they did not want to work for a black estate owner. Alexander fought and kept the house as good as possible. After a lot of hard work and with Arran's help the crops were selling for our survival until it was time for Arran to decide for its future.

- 'Father, people talk about America. So many Irish people went there. They were promised land and developed trading. Perhaps we should go too. There is no future here for us. The estate is ready to fall apart we will spend everything we have on it and then what? Arran said.
- 'I think you should go and leave me here; I am now too old to travel. I have lived my time and I belong to Scotland' Alexander said.
- 'No way father, I will not leave you here. You have no one to look after you. I know it was your choice, back then, not to marry again...but no way you will stay here alone. I will not leave without you. We only have each other, father. You must

do this once more for me ' Arran insisted.

- 'I loved your Mum, no one in the world was ever good enough like her! I have not ever stop thinking of her and feeling she is somewhere around us all the time. I even smell her sometimes!' Alexander spoke with nostalgia,

'Arran, it's time for you to find yourself the love of your life and have a family! You are a good man, you are my son and you will live well'

Within this atmosphere and recording all the feelings of everyone, my brain pushed further through the tunnel again as I was thirsty for more... There was that spinning noise going through the tunnel a headache and voices and the clinging of glasses of people drinking and piano sounding jazzy. It was a scene in a jazz bar, there were four musicians, Arran was holding a saxophone. He gelled his hair and wore a gray suit. At the bar I had a glass of Irish whiskey in my hand and was proud of my son blowing the saxophone. He looked so tall and smart, I admired him, my son!

The bar was buzzing with people and was smoky from cigarettes. There was a red hair lady at one table looking at me in a different way. She had the eyes of seduction. A black singer with a flower on her hair and a big smile stood in front of the microphone and sung with passion like I have never heard before... such a melody!

' If I give my heart to you
Will you handle it with care?
Will you always treat me tenderly and in every way be fair?
If I give my heart to you, will you give me all your love?
Will you swear that you'll be true to me by the light that shines above?
And will you sign with me when I'm sad
Smile with me when I'm glad
And always be as you are with me tonight...'

The red hair lady looked at me as if she was provoking my attention. I smiled back as I turned to look at Arran blowing that saxophone. She walked to the bar and sat next to me.

- 'Hey... handsome', she said proposing to light a cigarette and looking at me with provocative eyes.

I stroke a match and offered the flame to her as she grabbed my hand and brought it close to her cigarette. She looked attractive and sexy, I thought of my Emily, I was missing her!

- ' I like your looks, a real man, perhaps we can get to know each other?' she said looking like she was undressing me.
- 'Sweetheart... I am too old for romance and my heart is given away a long time ago' I replied.
- 'Is that your son with the saxophone? He is handsome too, but way too young for me, I want the father with all his experience', she insisted
- ' You are a bonnie lass but you are wasting your time with me' I said
- 'One night of your life?' she said touching and stroking my leg.

It felt sensational, I was tempted to grab her and kiss her. She was smelling of a scent, I have not touched a woman since my wife died more than thirty years. I could not leave behind my memories of the love of my life. I tried to look at her in the eyes but could not and said,

- 'I have found what is important in life for me, the love for my wife! I am not looking for anything else any more'
- 'Well that's a pity...I admire your self-control. It is strength... I am longing for a strong man in my life' She replied
- 'I am sorry myself too, not to know of what it is like to explore love with other women. I would have liked to do so if my heart allowed me and was not given to my wife. This is my destiny. Perhaps in anotrher life I may experience the love of many women!' I confirmed to her.
- 'Again that's a pity! Perhaps we may meet later...or in another life then!' She said disappointed and made her way back to her table.

Arran, had a break and came to the bar next to me. He asked for a whiskey from the bartender. We clinked our glasses with a toast for Arran's success.

- 'Arran my son, I am very proud of you... your mum may be watching us from somewhere and I am sure she is proud of you too. You did not get to know her but I am sure she has been watching you all the time! You are so much like her full of joy and love, kind with the biggest heart.

Here in America, it looks like you will find your way to success, you will find a woman to build your dreams together. Find real love. I did! Perhaps one day you may go back to Scotland. Perhaps, I would, if I was you. there is so much there!!' I said feeling content and nostalgic.

- ' Father... I feel that you did so much for me, thank you..thank you. You deserve to... How are you feeling? You look pale! Dad.. dad.... look at me! Look at me! Some water please... some... help please... please call the ambulance! Oh no...Dad! Dad!

There was noise, in the tunnel and it was dark..., I have a strong, pounding heart beat and pain in my chest, my heartbeat is increasing, I feel it... I am dizzy, I cannot breathe... Emily is calling me... ' Alexander!' Arran, is holding my hand, I feel his warmth. I am torn between their love.

The tunnel is long and I cannot see the end of it, there was a scent, one that swept the air around me, one that made you feel there was someone next to you or more...or many... The pain is increasing as the heart beat is faster, it stopped... it is very dark, I cannot breathe, I am uncomfortable... I am suffocating...I am fading away in the dark. I cannot see in the dark. I am wet and my whole-body aches... the noise of the tunnel is stronger.

I can see some light. I push to reach it and more pushing to get out of this tunnel to breathe again. My heart beat started... it is weak. I opened my eyes, the noise was gone, no pain, I was breathing... all was gray in a room full of people... they were covered in white feathers and smiling as they looked at me... the scent was stronger bringing out a feeling of euphoria in the

room. I smiled back and stretched my legs and hands to them out of excitement. A big person, a nurse was holding me tight in her arms... and happily said,
- ' Here you are... Mrs. Ero... congratulations..., you have a big and healthy baby boy!'

ABOUT THE AUTHOR

Paris Christofides

Paris Cristofides is a world traveler, a high-spirited individual, never happy to only live experiences but unfailingly see through them and feel the romance, the spirituality and more. He has channeled these experiences to his creative world of hospitality concepts where he coached and inspired many who came to his path of life. As an author, he has written many articles in lifestyle magazines and books of gastronomical interest and humored the psychology of all personalities involved around him but himself too. Paris lives on the Mediterranean island of Cyprus with his wife, from where he branches out to the world for those unique mere moments and making more stories...

Printed in Poland
by Amazon Fulfillment
Poland Sp. z o.o., Wrocław